Management
of Retail Buying

Management
of Retail Buying

R. PATRICK CASH

CHRIS THOMAS

JOHN W. WINGATE

JOSEPH S. FRIEDLANDER

WILEY

JOHN WILEY & SONS, INC.

For general information on our other products and services or for technical support, please contact our Customer Care Department within the United States at (800) 762-2974, outside the United States at (317) 572-3993 or fax (317) 572-4002.

Wiley also publishes its books in a variety of electronic formats. Some content that appears in print may not be available in electronic books. For more information about Wiley products, visit our web site at www.wiley.com.

Library of Congress Cataloging-in-Publication Data:

ISBN-13: 978-0-471-72325-7
ISBN-10: 0-471-72325-8

Printed in the United States of America

10 9 8 7 6 5 4 3 2 1

Contents

Preface

In 1920, the Wanamaker Department Store in New York City billed itself as "one Grand Palatial Bazaar where from every corner of the whole world are gathered the products of the field, the loom, the mills, the factories . . ." You have to wonder what the same flowery copywriter would say today about Wal-Mart!

From the turn of the last century—that is, 1900—department store retailing had been under fire for restricting competition and reducing opportunities for small-business owners. The idea of sharing savings by centralizing store functions and getting discounts from manufacturers for buying in bulk was shrewd and admirable, but controversial—and wildly successful.

However, by the 1930s, sales had slowed and the criticism was different: that the stores were too conservative to be fashion trendsetters, and too big to really care about their customers. The charge, as stated in a 1937 political science journal: "Like all behemoths, many department stores have become so elephantine in structure as to lose much of their capacity for adjustment to changing conditions."

Responding to the charges, some stores made their basements into bargain-priced outlets. Others opened suburban locations, taking their first steps in becoming national chains. Still others started mail-order catalog divisions. Retailers adapted—and thrived.

The same can be said today. There is still plenty of criticism about retailing. (Just type "Wal-Mart" into any Internet search engine and you'll get an eyeful!) But you can't argue with success, and the global retailing giant now leads the Fortune 500's list of the United States' largest companies, based on income. In fact, 11 of the top 50 companies on the list are retail chains, from Home Depot to Target, and Costco to Albertsons.

The global economy has opened up huge new opportunities for growth and product availability. That's where the retail buyer comes in. In this text, you will learn what buyers go through to make their decisions, from thousands of possibilities, about what to put on store racks and shelves. The process includes:

- Researching customer demographics
- Determining customer wants and needs
- Planning the inventory for the sections or departments of the store
- Finding the items that best fit the customers' wants and needs
- Negotiating with vendors—manufacturers, wholesale distributors, importing companies, and so on—to purchase the items
- Getting the goods through U.S. Customs, if necessary
- Transporting the items from source to store at the least cost
- Pricing the items in ways that are both fair for the customer and profitable for the store
- Helping to train and motivate the sales force
- Working with the sales and advertising departments to jointly promote the goods and attract customers
- Deciding when to reduce the prices to move slow-selling items or highlight new ones

If that sounds like a lot to do, you're right. And even when much of it can be done with the help of sophisticated computer programs, digital imagery, and Internet research, the retail buyer will always be needed to add what customers still fully expect from their shopping experience, whether it's online or in a department store—someone who understands what they want and is capable of procuring it.

It's an exciting field, and the goal of this text is to launch you into it. Good luck!

An Overview of Retail Buying

Whether you work for the controversial retail giant Wal-Mart or a tiny specialty boutique in your hometown, and whether you are selling banking services, pet food, or lingerie, there are basic similarities in the retail world that stretch to cover each of these situations and everything in between. In this chapter, you will learn more about just a few of these retail basics, which include the following:

- The responsibilities of buyers and merchandise managers
- Skills and personality traits for success in this field
- How different types of stores are organized to meet their buying needs
- The pros and cons of centralized merchandising
- Opportunities for women in this field

1

Buying is the business of choosing, and the person who embarks on a career as a retail buyer focuses on choosing those products he or she thinks will satisfy the demands of a particular group of consumers, who were also carefully chosen. The longer term goal is, of course, to make those consumers into loyal customers, since it is easier (and costs much less) to get additional sales from an existing customer than it is to find and impress a new one.

The buying process can be subdivided into four separate activities:

1. Estimating the needs of the prospective customer
2. Procuring the goods to meet those needs
3. Making them available, when and where they are wanted
4. Motivating the consumers to buy them

These four are probably most accurately depicted as a large circle, as one activity flows into the next, since customers' needs are constantly being researched, procurement goes on throughout the business year, and so on.

It is a common complaint that, as consumers, we don't have much "freedom of choice"—that the giant retail chains and dominant manufacturers throw their weight around, using their enormous advertising budgets to dictate what we buy, as well as why and when we buy it and how much we pay for it. Whether or not you agree with that premise, even the largest corporations need buyers who use a combination of market research, experience, and gut-level intuition to shape, and then meet, customer demand. Successful retail buyers most definitely combine art and science in their careers.

ESTIMATING CONSUMER NEEDS

One of the biggest differences between modern and traditional retailing—let's say, in this century versus the last one—is that in the "olden days," the merchant went to market, checked out the products of a variety of vendors or manufacturers, decided which ones were the best quality and value for that merchant's prospective customers, and made selections to bring back home and sell at retail.

Today's merchant can contact a variety of vendors and manufacturers and negotiate with them to custom-make and deliver exactly what is needed—and often, it can be done by phone or Internet, without leaving the office. The largest retailers can take it a step further, negotiating better wholesale prices and faster delivery times, and even demanding that the suppliers pay the bulk of the advertising costs. This global marketplace is diverse and flexible, and offers incredible variety. Greater quantities ordered in advance mean greater cost savings for the merchant; however, they also mean a greater loss if the product turns out to be a failure in the marketplace.

What's the similarity between yesteryear and today? No matter how large or small the merchant company, it still needs to hire people who can make those big decisions about what the customers will want. These professionals are called *retail buyers*.

Anticipating customer demand is a tightly integrated set of skills, so let's break it down into steps. As a retail buyer, you must do the following:

- Study consumers, both as individuals and as members of families, and highly mobile groups, to learn what drives their purchase decisions.
- Use the research to determine which consumers you want your merchandise and image to appeal to in the first place.
- Determine the exact types of products these consumers will buy, and decide the quantity and timing of your purchases.
- Find and become familiar with the vendors that can supply the items you need—their prices, business reputations, willingness to negotiate, capability of filling your order, credit terms, and more.
- Determine the logistical factors of the purchase. Think of this step as mapping out every point between the original order and final sale, how it will be accomplished, and whose responsibility it is. The map includes packaging, shipping, storing, deciding how to price the item (and who marks it with that price), delivery to store inventory, entry into the store's database, and so on.
- Work with other pertinent departments in your company to determine display and advertising parameters for the products.
- Maintain and interpret the database and other records to see if the purchasing decisions you've made are actually resulting in profit at retail.
- And don't forget to watch the competitors' strategies and tactics as they, too, try to buy and sell profitably.

With those steps in mind, the process for buying high-fashion women's apparel would be more complex than, say, buying bread and milk for a rural supermarket. Or would it? Bread and milk are perishable items; what if unexpected icy weather prevents the regular, reliable deliveries from the closest larger suppliers, for a full week? There are closer local vendors who might be able to fill in, but their prices are higher. That's why you didn't choose them in the first place, and they might still be upset about it. How will your emergency decision impact prices? Will it change your advertising plans for the month? And did we mention . . . there are at least 15,000 items in the average conventional grocery store?[1] As its manager, you're juggling these kinds of day-to-day decisions about hundreds of them.

From a retail buyer's standpoint, consumer demand has not truly been anticipated until the requirements are translated into specific assortments of merchandise from which the customers can select; and this inventory of merchandise must be managed—planned, ordered, coordinated, organized, and priced. Buying for retail includes the additional responsibility of helping others in the company to decide what will be promoted, as well as when, where, and how it will be offered to customers.

The whole retail buying cycle is sometimes referred to as **merchandising**, so it is easy to get the two terms confused. Generally, merchandising means managing the first two phases of the cycle (estimating consumer needs and procuring goods), which entail the process of anticipating demand. Using the term as a verb, in a retail store, both the buyer and the merchandise manager **merchandise.** The merchandise manager anticipates the customer demand in many product lines, each with its own buyer. The buyer manages these functions within a particular product line and, to varying degrees, actually performs the work involved. Together, their end objectives are the same: to achieve sales and gross margin objectives by effectively managing the merchandise decisions in a department, or group of departments, of a retail outlet.

A Buyer's Responsibilities

The list you're about to read was compiled from the job descriptions used in several major department store companies. You'll notice it contains references to presentations, advertising, and other areas, but we are focusing primarily on the buying and merchandising functions. Also remember, the smaller the store, the fewer individual support staff members there will be to assist with some of these responsibilities.

Buying and Merchandising

1. Under the guidance of a divisional merchandise manager (DMM), and within the framework of company policy and quality/image positioning, develop a merchandising strategy for the departments. Take into consideration the target customer, classifications, resource structure, major vendors, fashion trends, numbers of items, and price points.
2. Develop and achieve planned goals in sales, mark-ons (i.e., markups), markdowns, shortage, turnover, gross profit, and controllable elements of net profit.
3. Analyze the company's (or department's) daily or periodic reports (sales, stocks, styles, classification activity, vendor performance, etc.) and take action if needed.
4. Prepare detailed buying plans for DMM approval before any buying trip.
5. Make regular buying trips, working closely with the buying office to submit the preliminary buying plans and to follow up afterward.
6. Negotiate with vendors for favorable terms, discounts, and transportation allowances. Conduct ongoing performance ratings of vendors, and take action on the results if necessary.
7. Participate in product development for private labeling, importing programs, and group buying.

8. Stay current on new trends by reading trade publications and exploring new merchandise trends and the wares of new vendors. Test new items in the market and feature them early in the stores.
9. Conduct informative meetings with department managers, salespeople, and other store personnel to share trend and sales information.
10. Identify and maximize fast-selling items; find timely ways to dispose of the slow sellers.
11. Maintain well-balanced stocks and assortments in each store location, with an effective basic stock program that is reviewed and revised regularly.
12. Regularly review unfilled purchase orders and take appropriate action.
13. Make regular visits to store locations to check displays, assortment, stocks, and so on. Give appropriate feedback to store and department managers. Gain customer exposure by spending time on the sales floor.
14. Shop and analyze competitive stores with price, assortments, and display in mind.

Merchandising Presentation

1. Define a point of view toward merchandise presentation (displays) in a department, and convey it clearly to managers.
2. Work with the assistant buyer to maximize the excitement of the displays, and coordinate different departments' displays.
3. Work closely with display department staff members on future merchandising themes. Create a calendar of ideas and deadlines for them.

Advertising

1. Prepare advertising and promotion plans, budgets, and schedules.
2. Inform branch stores of advertised promotions well in advance, so they can plan ahead for them. Schedule deliveries to make sufficient stock available for all advertised goods.
3. Track and analyze the results of any advertising, for use in future planning.
4. Conform to the requirements of the Robinson-Patman Act, and all other applicable laws and regulations.

Shortage Control

1. Ensure that all purchase orders, requests for price revisions, transfers of goods, and vendor returns are processed promptly and according to company procedures.
2. Review purchase journals regularly and take appropriate action.
3. Maintain good working relationships with operating divisions (receiving, marking, etc.) to promptly resolve problems in those areas as they arise.
4. Participate fully in all shortage control audits and loss prevention programs.

Staff Development and Training

1. Train your assistant, associate buyer, and other staff members in merchandising and management skills. If they are capable of helping with routine tasks and orders, you can concentrate on trends and troubleshooting.
2. Maintain regular communication with department managers, area sales managers, and sales teams to convey information and strategies for each department with which you work.

As you can see, the retail buyer's job deals partly with product selection, identifying and monitoring trends, and keeping up relationships with vendors; but equally important is the frequent contact with other, internal departments to let them know what they'll be receiving and what will be on sale, as well as to provide feedback about how they're doing. In this way, the buyer is very much a supervisor, trainer, and motivator within the sales organization and is usually considered an executive-level position.

A Merchandise Manager's Responsibilities

This executive is the direct supervisor of the buyer and therefore is typically less involved in performing actual buying functions. Instead, the merchandise manager devotes more attention to administrative functions, like planning, control, and human resources. The motivational aspects of the job are much like those just described for buyers—training, coaching, counseling, appraising people's performance, and helping to develop them as employees. It is the merchandise manager who most often hires, promotes, transfers, decides on pay rates, and discharges employees. In broad terms, the merchandise manager is a conduit between buyers and top management, who interprets the company policy and objectives and achieves implementation through ongoing interaction and control.

In terms of inventory, the buyer for a particular department is accountable to the merchandise manager for every item in stock in that department. In turn, the merchandise manager is accountable for the assortments of items in each department they manage—even if they delegate the selection of those assortments to the buyers.

It follows, then, that the nature and amount of supervision provided by a merchandise manager depends mostly on the strengths and weaknesses of each buyer. Strong merchandise managers trust their buyers. They are careful not to usurp the buyers' authority by second-guessing all the buying decisions, and not to relegate the buyer to the de facto role of an assistant who simply carries out orders. Instead, a manager may offer a valuable second opinion in decisions that can help counteract the impulses of an overenthusiastic buyer who would otherwise buy too much, or the manager can prompt a buyer who is generally a good selector and promoter into doing the necessary paperwork to organize his or her department and sell at a profit.

Of course, merchandise managers are also expected to keep up with the styles and trends in their industry. They go along on (at least some) major sales trips to trade shows and season openings. They investigate new resources and forge contracts with suppliers. They have input about the orders to be placed, the purchasing negotiations, and pricing or repricing decisions.

Back at the home office, the merchandising manager keeps an eye on which items are "moving" and which items are not. The job involves more than learning to read the sales and stock reports; it includes teaching (and prodding) the buyers to do the same, so that the data is analyzed to benefit the bottom line. In many retail operations, this position also includes periodic briefings of the sales force.

Are You Cut Out for This Field?

Many of the personal qualifications necessary for success in the highly competitive field of retail buying and merchandising management are common to other managerial professions, but here are a combination of qualities, aptitudes, and cultivated skills that are especially pertinent to these positions:

- **Decision-making skills.** Probably no business executive of any kind makes as many decisions as the retail buyer. Every inspection of a new item, every price of that item, every markup and markdown, every order and reorder, every negotiation or return of merchandise to vendors requires a decision. Many of these are made on the basis of company policy or established procedure, but some are also the result of knowledge and experience. This type of know-how is unique because it must not be based on one's personal preference.

  Most of the decisions are, frankly, not earth-shattering . . . but they often seem endless and must be made quickly, in the face of uncertainty about the results. To make constant decisions and choices can be difficult and frustrating. The mature buyer learns how to consider advantages and disadvantages, take some action, and learn from the experience either way.

- **Drive.** Successful buyers exhibit an ability to thrive under pressure. Some are called "aggressive" or "dominant," and in this field, these are *not* negative traits. The stamina is partly physical, but also mental. This is the "sales" part of the job, requiring perseverance and the ability to focus even when things aren't going well or in tough negotiating situations.

  In addition, much of the work is done outside the reach of direct supervision. Much of it is also complicated, and the effectiveness of the outcome won't be judged immediately. Less capable people might be tempted to postpone unpleasant tasks—but in these careers, that only means self-created emergencies later on.

- **Creativity.** Buyers for chains and larger retailers commonly work with manufacturers to design exclusive items or lines to achieve product differentiation. It may be as simple as suggesting a minor modification in a sample line, an existing product, or a competitor's product; or as complex as mapping out the strategy for a major line of private-label merchandise. Either way, the push for product exclusivity has created the need for buying and merchandising professionals with design sense, a knowledge of raw materials and manufacturing processes, and an understanding of both wholesale and consumer markets.

- **Critical, analytical, and conceptual skills.** The buyer or merchandiser has a formidable arsenal of skills that, together, make up the thought process for the buying decisions. You might say they are this person's "business sense." They include the following:

  1. The ability to be a tough judge of any item's value, appeal, color, texture, and so on. Critical thinking takes the person's own tastes and preferences out of the equation and allows him or her to "think for the business" about the ultimate success of a product.
  2. Analytical thinking, which permits the person to weigh factors like the seasonality or trendiness of the merchandise, the reputation of the manufacturer, and how much of a "stretch" this item will be for the target consumer to accept.
  3. Conceptual skills, which are necessary to view the item in broader terms. Does it really fit the store's image? Is it compatible with existing assortments; suitable for advertisement or promotion? Will it enhance the sales of other merchandise, or steal volume from key lines or other brands? Does it achieve the goals that have been set for the department?

- **Financial savvy.** Another important filter is the merchandiser's or buyer's money sense. How good is this person at assessing risk and reward? Does the person understand the financial implications of his or her decisions? Can the person accurately see how each item will fit into the budget, gauge its relative profitability, suggest how to price it, and note the probability and percentage of markdown for stock that doesn't sell quickly?

  These positions also require a certain capacity to write and/or decipher budgets and sales reports.

- **Organizational skills.** Buying demands keen observation and, at least, a short-term memory for detail. Hundreds of items may be inspected before a dozen are chosen, and the variations can be mind-boggling. It is important to be well organized and detail-oriented, and to be able to marry the details with knowledge of trends and customers' interests. Orders must be prompt and accurate for deadlines to be met. If a manufacturer or supplier promises something, the buyer must also be able to second-guess them when necessary, with timely follow-up and details about what was promised and when.

- **Communication skills.** Both written and verbal communication are vital to buying and merchandising functions, with tasks as varied as business correspondence, lengthy meetings and telephone follow-ups, and presentations to coworkers (both up and down the chain of command) that motivate them to sell. Often, people in these positions write, edit, and approve catalog copy and signage, or, at least, have to explain the features of the merchandise to copywriters or ad agency representatives.

In today's business environment, communication also includes a high degree of computer literacy. The ability to do Internet research about competitors, to keep in touch and place orders by e-mail, to create and interpret spreadsheets, and to illustrate presentations with graphics—all of these will make one job candidate indispensable compared to competitors with less technological experience.

- **Managerial and/or "specialist" capabilities.** There is room in all retail organizations for each of these two types of employees. The management candidate learns to work with people as human resources: to nurture, motivate, and evaluate them, while challenging them to consistently do their best.

  The specialist concentrates on accumulating knowledge about the goods and the marketplace, developing the aesthetic skills and value judgments that will eventually result in expertise in their field. Specialists would rather work in their own niche—although some retail businesses have merchandise managers who are "super-buyers," specialists in several related departments. Specialists do have to master at least some of the management functions, especially organization and coordination, both of which are discussed in the section, "Organizing the Buying Process."

- **Trading acumen.** Much of the purchasing arena today is governed by a specific company policy, industry practice, or law. There are federal safety standards for some products and advertising restrictions for others. There are also plenty of laws about price-fixing and what makes a business deal illegal or unethical. Companies of all types have had to adjust to these regulations without limiting the effectiveness of their buyers.

  Where pricing alternatives exist, a buyer must be fair but shrewd in negotiating the best possible deals for the company, to get the quantity, quality, and service the company expects. A smart businessperson knows when to make demands, when to make concessions, and when to make friends—all within legal and ethical boundaries.

Now that you know the traits for success, are you still interested in a retail buying or merchandising management career?

THE SUPPORT STAFF

There are plenty of other retail behind-the-scenes jobs, since merchandise managers and buyers are supported by staffs of specialists. In the organizational chart (see Figure 1-2), these are the "staff bureaus" at the far left side of the chart. Using a retail department store as an example, some of the staff functions would include:

- **Seasonal fashion programs.** Develop, implement, and monitor companywide fashion programs for each season, well in advance of the buyers' visits to market. Give direction on styles, fabrics, colors, and other trends that will be useful to the buyer, and ensure that all departments storewide present an integrated fashion message. Often, there are separate fashion offices and personnel for apparel and home furnishings. This group is also responsible for keeping the buyers, merchandise managers, and publicity people informed about styles and trends, and for making sure the seasonal programs are being correctly executed by the merchandising staff.

- **Merchandise selection and control.** This staff uses sales and inventory data to suggest to the buyers the types of merchandise most likely to be best-sellers, as well as those that haven't worked well in-store and should be flushed out of the system. These people may even accompany the buyers to market, or assist a manufacturer in styling certain items in their lines. The selection and control team also sees the "big picture" and can make suggestions about what items will work well (i.e., sell well) with others.

- **Sales promotion.** This team decides which merchandise sparks the best ideas for advertising and promotion. Depending on the size of the store, the sales team may write the ad copy or, at least, list and describe the product benefits for an advertising agency to do the writing. Sketches, photos, and graphic design are created or obtained from the manufacturers—again, based on the size of the store or chain—to go with the copy. The promotion staff approves all ad and display materials, and arranges for fashion shows, charitable tie-ins, and other special events that favorably showcase the company as well as its merchandise.

- **Research and product development.** This group does research in a wide range of areas. Some of it is related to product safety, but most of it centers around exploring the challenges and benefits of new products, new markets, and new techniques that the company is considering to boost business. "R&D" prevents a company from pouring lots of money and energy into a new venture or product line before analyzing the consequences. The research staff works closely with all other departments on a project basis.

- **Training.** This department also works closely with other departments to communicate the company's procedures and policies, the "rules" for everyday business and for improving individual job skills. Its responsibilities include employee orientation and mentoring programs, sales training, safety training, and preparation of handbooks, videos, operations manuals, and so on.

ORGANIZING THE BUYING PROCESS

To organize a buying function, a manager must first identify all the work in his or her area of responsibility, then group the tasks into related areas and place an executive in charge of each area. The executives, in turn, are given sufficient authority to exercise their responsibilities. Delegating authority in retail happens in two ways—through line organization and staff organization.

Line Organization

The word "line" connotes purposefulness. It indicates a direct chain of responsibility that leads to the achievement of the main objective of profitable sales. The two ultimate functions of the line are buying and selling. All other functions (personnel, financing, acquisition of store sites, etc.) are ancillary to these two. It's a little bit like a military chain of command—other functions are important, but only insofar as their usefulness as support services to reach the ultimate goal, victory!

The term "line" in a retail management organization refers to the chain of command itself. An executive "in-line" receives his or her responsibilities from their direct superior, along with the authority to carry them out by directing the performance of other employees "down-line." Thus, the general merchandise manager (who is accountable for the complete buying performance in all departments) delegates a large share of the work to the divisional merchandise managers. Each of them supervises a group of departments; in the departments, there are merchandise buyers "down-line." The merchandise buyers each delegate various duties to assistants and/or the floor sales staff that sells directly to customers. In this hierarchy, each person along the line is accountable directly to their "up-line" supervisor, and looks to the supervisor to assign tasks and assess performance.

Staff Organization

In an ideal business relationship, each member of the line may give information and advice to superiors and, in so doing, can participate in making policy and objectives for the business. However, in real-world organizations, some employees are assigned (or take on) more of this responsibility than others. These are the staff members of the organization, and they include the support teams we've already discussed.

As an example, a merchandise controller may monitor sales and stock data in order to help plan the business needs, and to determine that the operation is running reasonably close to its current plan. A fashion coordinator assists a general merchandise manager in carrying out the store's policies that directly relate to its fashion image. These staff members are both specialists, and in their roles, they may suggest, counsel, and offer critiques—but they cannot command. This makes them staff members. The ability to make decisions, and the responsibility that goes with it, rests with the line managers.

Of course, just because a staff member lacks the power to command does not mean he or she lacks "power," per se. A capable specialist can get and keep the ear of his or her superior, who will heed their counsel and pass it down the line in the form of a directive. It is simply impractical for everyone in a retail buying organization to be endowed with decision-making authority.

It should be noted that certain staff functions, like the financial division of a large business, are set up as their own line organizations. The managers of the division are the line executives; the workforce they command is the staff organization.

Coordination

This management function includes the work of balancing, timing, matching, and integrating work. Some examples of coordination are:

- Pricing different types of merchandise in ways that are compatible with the store's policy and image. If the best-selling skirt price is about $60, most of the blouses and sweaters should not be priced at $15 to $20.
- Pricing between different departments should be coordinated such that no one department has unfair profit-making advantage over others.
- Using the same standards for each department or division—for quality, branding (private label, designer, etc.), service, expense control, display, advertising, and so on.

In short, coordination is the work of making a multifaceted store look like a cohesive business instead of a jumble of different buyers' whims that more closely resembles a flea market.

Planning and Control

Although planning is the first stage of a management cycle and control is the last stage, they are directly related. New planning grows out of the control exercised over the former plans. As results are evaluated, new plans are made.

Planning involves the activities of forecasting, setting objectives, formulating policies, and setting standards for merchandise and overall operations. Planning also includes creating programs and procedures, scheduling, and making cost and sales estimates into budgets.

Controlling is the process of measuring the performance of these plans, budgets, policies, and forecasts. It includes projecting what might happen if there is deviation from the plan; reviewing and authorizing performance of many jobs that make up the plan; and taking corrective action when the results don't happen as planned. This may mean adjusting the work, or adjusting the objectives.

Buyers do participate in planning and control, but they are primarily job functions of the merchandising manager, as you'll see in this list of typical responsibilities:

- They participate actively in making long-range merchandise plans that cover sales, stock levels, purchases, initial margins, advertising, and selling costs.
- They check results (daily, weekly, monthly, seasonally) against the long-range plans.
- They control the purchases with some form of "open-to-buy" plan that shows how much more a buyer may order for delivery within a specific time period without exceeding the purchase allotment.
- The merchandise manager is usually required to countersign any order over a certain number or cost amount, and can set these limits depending on the size of the store and/or how confident they are in the buyer's ability.

- When merchandise has to be returned to a vendor, the merchandise manager approves it and makes sure the return meets both companies' policies.
- Price changes must be explained, not just made, and it's the merchandising manager who hears the explanation and approves or challenges it. Markups and markdowns are compared with long-range plans to see if they are accomplishing the longer-term goals of the department or company.
- Sales events and sales promotions are scripted out a few months at a time, with budgets and anticipated sales results. The merchandising manager is one of the executives who must approve these plans and usually helps to create them as well.

Control functions may seem like a lot of number-crunching, but they are *not* boring! From surveys of business conditions and consumer research to profit-and-loss statements and sales reports, the merchandising manager is in the unique position of intelligently shepherding individual departments to success—with the authority and knowledge to step into tough situations and turn them around, if necessary.

EVALUATING AND MOTIVATING THE BUYER

Now let's look briefly at how the company's executive management team judges the effectiveness of a buyer's work. There are three basic criteria—and all, or some, may be used:

- **Sales results** may be measured in dollars, in units of merchandise sold (or numbers of sales transactions), or in sales per square foot of selling space. The *sales increase*, rather than actual volume, is commonly the major consideration. The buyer is expected to achieve a certain sales goal based on a reasonable appraisal of circumstances both inside and outside the store . . . so if he or she *exceeds* that expectation, the increase is measured accordingly. Different stores use different databases for comparing their buyers' results with their competitors' or, at least, with buyers of comparable types of merchandise.
- **Inventory results** are revealed by stockturn (how often the merchandise "turns over" and must be reordered—there's a formula for it that you'll learn later in this text), by the proportion of "old" stock that must be carried over into a new season or year, or the merchandise shortage and its percentage to sales. Trade associations can provide standards of comparison.
- **Margin results** is the term for the way profit is analyzed in the business. There are several ways in which profit margins are measured:

  1. **Initial markup.** The total of all the original retail prices, less the total of all the related invoice costs.

2. **Gross margin realized.** The actual sales price of an item, less the retailer's full cost of the item, is the gross margin. It is expressed as a percentage of the sales dollar.
3. **Gross margin per dollar of cost inventory.** This is obtained by dividing the gross margin realized by the average amount of inventory at cost. The resulting figure is the return on the investment the store made to buy the merchandise in the first place.
4. **Controllable margin realized.** This is the gross margin, less all direct department expenses.
5. **Operating profit realized.** The gross margin, less all expenses that are chargeable to the selling department.

Which of the five margin criteria is used depends on the degree to which senior management holds the buyer responsible for price changes and for expenses. If things like advertising and payroll are largely controlled by other departments, the buyer's responsibility does not usually extend beyond the "gross margin" level. But if the buyer has a lot of responsibility for a department's direct expenses (particularly sales force, advertising, and display) he or she is judged at the "controllable margin" level.

The buyer can be evaluated on an "operating profit" level only if the store has set up an expense plan, in which every kind of store expense is given a "unit of service cost"—a unit cost for each employee trained, for each check processed, for utilities per cubic foot of store space, and so on. In this scenario, the buyer "buys" the specific services necessary to run his or her department from the store—and becomes responsible for controlling the expenses attributed to the department.

With all that, you may wonder whatever happened to someone saying "Great job!" and giving the buyer a raise when things are going well. In the world of retail, analyzing performance is far more complex than that, and you'll learn more about it in upcoming chapters.

ORGANIZATIONAL MODELS OF STORES

Now that we've discussed the skills and responsibilities of buyers and merchandising managers, let's look at the retail environments in which they work. We'll start small and work our way up to the larger store model.

The Independent Store

In the shadows of the retail department store giants, many smaller retailers continue to thrive. About 80 percent of all general merchandise retailers have annual sales volume of less than $1 million, so it is useful to look at smaller store organization as well. The term "mom-and-pop" retailer comes

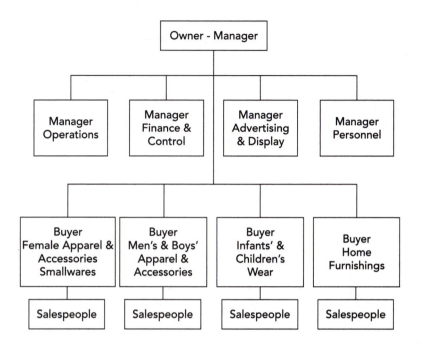

Figure 1-1 Example of organization: Small-to-intermediate size, single-unit company.

from the fact that many of these businesses are run by husband-wife teams, and the division of responsibility is commonly based on the two individuals' backgrounds, talents, and interests. Generally, one handles the buying, selling, and management of a small number of employees; the other is responsible for nuts-and-bolts store operation, with duties like inventory and accounting.

In this type of operation, the owner *is* the store—at least, until the business grows and it becomes necessary to hire people to assume the nonmerchandising functions. Typically, the buying and merchandising tasks are retained by the owner/manager as long as possible, and are the last to be delegated. When the demands on the owner's time become excessive, when a need for some type of specialization becomes clear, or when an opportunity arises to open additional locations, the introduction of new people is mandated. At this point of development, the store becomes a small- to intermediate-sized company, still small but fully capable of supporting substantial sales volume with the right people in place. Figure 1-1 shows the organizational chart of a typical company of this size, still a single business unit but poised for continued growth.

The Department Store

As a store grows in size and in the variety of merchandise it carries, the assortment is typically split into departments, with separate buyers and separate accounting (or both) for sales, purchases, inventory, profit margins, and related expenses. Thus, even a so-called specialty store may establish separate departments for different types of merchandise. Each department may have a separate buyer; but in some stores, a number of departments are assigned to a single buyer. There are pros and cons to the latter system—a danger exists for energies to be spread too sparsely over a number of departments. However, some stores decide that it is more cost-effective to have one experienced buyer and a number of assistants in departments than it is to hire multiple single-department buyers. The organizational chart of a large, traditional department store is shown in Figure 1-2.

In Figure 1-2, you see that some stores go on to separate the department management function from the buying function. Others split a single department into two as soon as they show promise of being able to support the salaries of two buyers, each of whom is then expected to bring sales up to the level of the original department.

As the store becomes still larger, it may set up a "budget" department for lower-priced or closeout garments, or add separate sections to appeal to lifestyles or age groups: juniors, maternity, plus sizes, and so on. This standardized classification of merchandise by department has been the norm since the 1970s. It seems simple enough, but Figure 1-3 shows just how complex a single item of apparel ("Dresses") can be subclassified into dozens of groups.

The Grocery Store

The organizational chart of a small grocer mirrors the small retailer; for a larger supermarket, it resembles the large department store hierarchy. Supermarkets (that is, grocery stores with annual sales volume of over $2 million) also departmentalize, and they are learning how to do it in fascinating new ways in order to compete with the giant supercenter stores. For example, it is common knowledge that traditional supermarkets place their "highest traffic" items—milk, eggs, produce, bread, beer—along the walls of the store, which is supposed to prompt customers to wander all the way around the store to get to them, ostensibly picking up other, impulse purchases along the way. But today's frantically busy shopper has learned to duck in and duck out, leaving the entire area known as "center store" relatively unexplored. The shopper then visits the (often less convenient) supercenters less frequently to stock up on bargain-priced staples.

Bad for sales? You bet. Center-store sales have declined at the rate of about 3 percent per year. The slump is partly because warehouse-style competitors offer lower prices, but also because—other than introducing new products frequently—supermarket departments have looked pretty much the same for years.

In an article in *Store Equipment and Design* magazine (April 2000), space planners discussed ways to beat this trend. They agreed that the center store ought to be made up of convenient, "interior departments." One mentioned making shorter, double-wide aisles and creating "power centers" for items like snacks

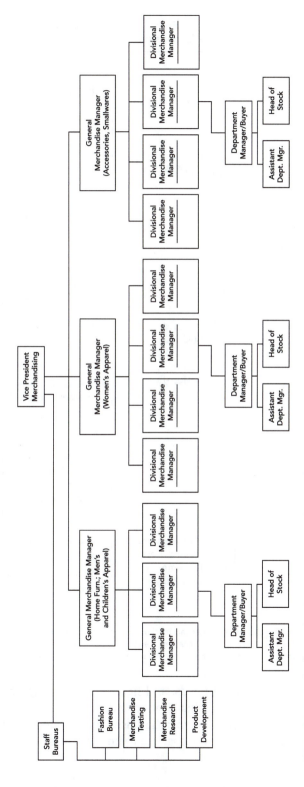

Figure 1-2 Example of a merchandising organization of a large department store company.

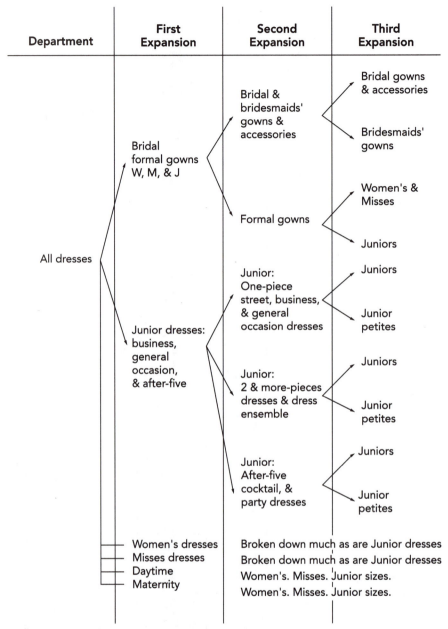

	First Expansion	**Second Expansion**	**Third Expansion**

Department

All dresses

Bridal formal gowns W, M, & J

Bridal & bridesmaids' gowns & accessories

Bridal gowns & accessories

Bridesmaids' gowns

Formal gowns

Women's & Misses

Juniors

Junior dresses: business, general occasion, & after-five

Junior: One-piece street, business, & general occasion dresses

Juniors

Junior petites

Junior: 2 & more-pieces dresses & dress ensemble

Juniors

Junior petites

Junior: After-five cocktail, & party dresses

Juniors

Junior petites

Women's dresses — Broken down much as are Junior dresses
Misses dresses — Broken down much as are Junior dresses
Daytime — Women's. Misses. Junior sizes.
Maternity — Women's. Misses. Junior sizes.

Figure 1-3 The expansion of a department, based on merchandise classifications.

Note: A further expansion may be included that segregates long and short gowns, and woven and knit, and pants suit dresses, etc. Classifications may be refined further by price groups, styling, vendor, or other factors based on the individual retailer's merchandise mix and control requirements.

and beverages, infant needs, and household cleaning products. The trade-off for stores, of course, is that shorter, wider aisles limits shelf space compared to the long, parallel rows of merchandise. This is true for any type of retailer, not just grocery stores—more space to roam means less space in which to showcase merchandise.[2]

We mention the supermarket example for two reasons: (1) the workings of other store specialists, like designers and space planners, can certainly have major impact on the jobs of buyers and department managers; and (2) although the "org charts" seem stodgy, the departments they represent are not. For consistent success, even the most venerable department-style organization must adapt itself to meet new trends and market conditions.

The Branch Store

When department stores and large specialty stores began to become chain stores, they attempted to treat their new **branches** or locations simply as offshoots of the main or **flagship** store. They held buyers responsible for the total merchandising of their departments, even when those departments were located in different geographic locations. They were expected to visit each branch once or twice a week, and to carry out their continuing responsibilities with an assistant in each branch—a practice that still fits some of the smaller chains.

In other stores, however, other solutions became necessary as the number of branches multiplied and their size began to rival, or even exceed, that of the flagship store. Depending on geographic and demographic diversity, it was no longer smart to put the same merchandise assortment in every store. The largest branches could support their own senior management staffs, and were given more and more autonomy to develop their own product mixes and merchandise and to promote their stores.

In this model, the purchase of new merchandise is still a central buyer's responsibility. This buyer has a copy of the merchandising plan for each store that indicates how much merchandise (in dollars and in units) should be received each month in each department. The buyer determines the timing of orders to meet these targets.

Vendors ship their new merchandise to a consolidator, who acts as a central distribution point (rather than directly to the branches), which saves on transportation costs. The vendors usually have their shipments packed and labeled by branch, however, so the consolidator doesn't have to repackage the merchandise when it arrives, just keep track of it and warehouse it until needed. Each branch carries a minimum amount of **floor stock**, and has a record of what is available in the warehouse. Deliveries to customers generally are made right from the warehouse, not from the branches.

Some buying may be done at the branch-store level for some departments, but advances in computer technology have allowed increased centralization of the buying function. With all merchandise labeled with **stock keeping unit (SKU)** numbers, it is extremely easy to track merchandise, no matter where it is stored. More about that when we discuss the impact of technology in Chapter 6.

All this does not imply that today's branch store managers have declining influence on the product mix in their stores. If anything, they likely have more influence than before! The actual buying function, however, is increasingly centralized.

CENTRALIZED BUYING AND MERCHANDISING

Among the most profound trends in modern merchandising has been for two or more stores to unite in order to combine their buying activities. This is why **centralized buying** is not to be confused with chain operation, per se. Centralized buying means performing all (or most) buying activities from a single office, and this is the way most chains organize their buying. It may mean a group of independent stores working together as members of a cooperative, or a single buying headquarters that serves different store concepts all owned by the same company. The following characteristics distinguish the buying-selling work of multi-unit merchandisers from those with a comparable job at a single-location store:

- **Successful central buying needs continuous input from the selling locations.** The single-unit retailer has the advantage of customer contact, but the centralized buyer depends almost entirely on an ongoing flow of sales data from its stores, primarily by networked computer systems.
- **The demand patterns of individual outlets are not completely uniform.** Although consumer demand has some surprisingly common themes, variations exist by region, and by neighborhood within a region. Stores of the same supermarket chain will sell larger sizes in one part of a city, and smaller sizes in another. The same groupings, trends, and colors may not sell as well in one store as in another. Timing of seasonal goods will vary between different parts of the country, and so on.
- **The buying organization's involvement in the selling function diminishes greatly.** The buyer just can't keep a supervisory eye on floor sales and must rely on the department managers of what may be numerous and far-flung outlets. However, a buyer's duty to report (to the stores) the selling features of the goods they have bought, and a certain amount of enthusiasm to motivate sales, remains constant. Ideally, the buying organization still has the last word on what will be promoted, when, and to what extent.
- **Planning and control functions are more vital to multi-outlet retailers.** Not only are these systems apt to be more sophisticated than with single-unit stores, but the functions are probably performed by staff specialists. Buyers have their hands full with the buying duties, leaving the other details to other departments.

As you might assume, these differences require that tasks, facilities, and people be organized differently than in independent, single-unit stores—and of course, they would be organized differently for a cooperative than for a chain. Figure 1-4 is an example of such an organization, with the merchandise manager as the senior executive at a chain store's headquarters. Dissecting the chart:

- The merchandise planners who report to the manager lay out budgets for their particular divisions on the basis of past performance of the chain as a whole, on current figures, and by anticipating upcoming needs.

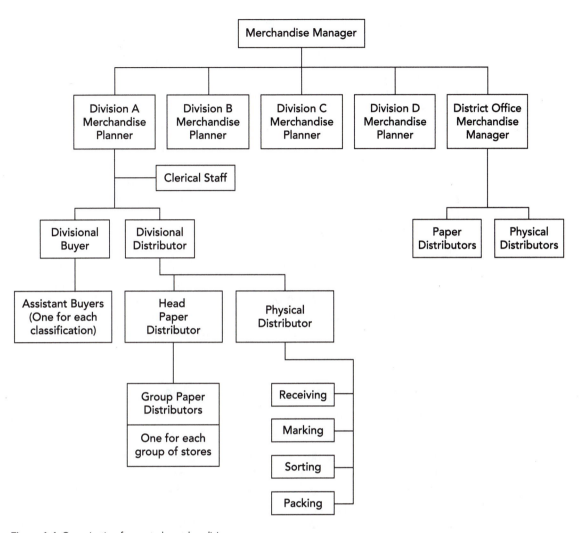

Figure 1-4 Organization for central merchandising.

- Next are the buyers for each division, who select merchandise in the quantities determined by the merchandise manager. The buyer has some input in the selection of items and does participate in the planning, but most of the planning duties belong to the specialized merchandising planning staff.
- Then there is the distribution division, which is responsible for keeping each unit properly stocked. This division operates a holding facility at which shipments from manufacturers are received, inspected, priced, sorted by store, and shipped to the various locations. It's not like a warehouse, which stores goods indefinitely, but a delivery point that accepts merchandise, "checks it in" (so to speak), and ships it out, usually within 48 hours or less.
- Within the distribution division, there are **paper distributors** and **physical distributors**. As their names suggest, the paper distributors generate the

paperwork to get the incoming items sorted and shipped to each store within a district. They are guided by the sales/stock position of each category in each store, which is developed from daily sales data, transmitted electronically from the stores.

- The physical distributors actually handle the goods when they arrive from the manufacturers. These distributors may report to the merchandise manager, or to a warehouse manager in the store's operations division.

Whatever the variations in the "org chart," the buyer is typically responsible for procurement, pricing, and sales information. The buyer also maintains a strong voice in determining what, when, and how much to promote. The buyer is responsible for quality inspection for the merchandise received, either by visiting the distribution facility or the stores regularly. And finally, the buyer is the person who authorizes invoices and protects the department against being charged for goods incorrectly.

All other stock keeping work is performed by the storage facility personnel or in the stores. Together with the sales promotion team, the stores do all the work of selling. Stores have limited merchandising functions, but they maintain liberal communication with merchandisers, buyers, and distributors in order to impart information about customer demand, and advice about how to meet it.

The Advantages of Centralized Merchandising

First let's look at the advantages of using a central merchandising plan—in this case, for the clothing sold in a department store.

1. It provides a steady flow of merchandise from markets to stores, because buyers can spend more time in the markets making their selections, and because central warehouses are able to make the frequent, small shipments needed to keep a store's inventory filled and balanced.

2. "Safety in numbers" means forecasts of demand for all units, as a group, are more reliable than forecasts for each unit separately, simply because they are a mathematical average of highs and lows. There's no way to ensure perfect forecasting—but by doing it centrally, the peaks and valleys tend to smooth out on paper.

3. Centralized data allows better control of styles—a clearer "big picture" of how they are moving—than individual stores can possibly accomplish. Today's technology allows a centralized buyer to receive sales data for an entire chain within 24 hours or less. The small number of sales of any particular item in one store cannot possibly give a basis for quick and accurate judgment of the overall success of that item, and as a result, many potentially successful items probably are not given the real chance they need to "take off." Being able to see the big picture remedies that.

4. Centralized records also provide a better basis for markdowns when things must be put on sale. A single store decline may be caused by any number of chance factors, from bad weather to out-of-stock merchandise. But

when the sales of a particular item in many stores are combined, it is easy to see when it's just not moving—and to take appropriate action, chainwide or in individual stores.

5. Central buying provides a high-grade specialist in merchandise selection. This usually leads to:

- **More salable styles.** Because of the volume that central buyers represent, they can often pick and choose from a large line of merchandise, selecting only those items they know are going to be top sellers. Smaller buyers may have to agree to take a manufacturer's entire line of items to get what they need.

- **Faster turnaround time from order to store.** Not only are styles chosen more wisely, but central buyers can have orders processed very quickly because of the volume they represent. Small buyers, on the other hand, often have to wait until a manufacturer can accumulate enough orders for a sample item to get it made economically. As a result, central buyers sometimes receive the latest merchandise a month before smaller retail outlets! In terms of fashion and seasonal trends, that is a huge advantage.

- **Higher standards of quality.** Central buyers' sheer volume works for them once again, because manufacturers will allow them to custom-order in bulk. The buyer can literally create his or her "own" merchandise, from the fabric and color to the standards of construction.

- **Exclusivity.** Custom ordering, in turn, leads to greater opportunities for "exclusive" merchandise—or exclusive distribution agreements—for part, or all, of a manufacturer's line. These trends are seen most often in apparel and housewares. Another term for an exclusive line is *confined merchandise*.

- **Lower prices.** The other enormous benefit of volume buying is that the buyer can negotiate lower prices that can then be passed on to consumers at retail. In the case of clothing production, which requires a great deal of manual labor, the savings aren't as great as with other, machine-produced goods—but the sheer economic clout of volume buying cannot be ignored.

6. Central buying provides quality control. The buyers may inspect and test goods at the prototype stage, and again before they are shipped to stores. Faults are promptly detected and the merchandise can be returned immediately, rather than being shuttled back and forth between locations. There's just a bit more assurance built into the system that the stores will receive only the merchandise that is in good condition. This has two beneficial results: increased sales volume and fewer customer complaints.

7. Central buying is less expensive. In terms of labor costs for the business, fewer people make the buying decisions, instead of a team from each store that must all visit the same markets. In terms of advertising, one set of ads can be created instead of multiple ads for multiple stores. Display plans, layouts, and fixtures can be determined by specialists and then used by all

the stores, which not only saves money but ensures uniform quality standards that create the "look" of the chain as a whole.

8. Centralized buying leads to better stock control. Since all stores in the group enjoy careful merchandise planning, no store can shirk its responsibilities to maintain adequate assortments of goods—and there's a uniform system to keep track of these goods. Individual stores may introduce a good control system but not make the best use of the data it reveals. Central buying organizations absolutely require uniform systems and good records in order to keep the stores correctly stocked.

9. And, finally, concentrating the buying duties leaves the stores free to do what they're supposed to do best—that is, sell! Department managers with leadership ability and promotion skills can use them in-store, without having to also be expert buyers and sharp traders at wholesale.

The Disadvantages of Centralized Merchandising

In spite of its many benefits, there are also some distinct downsides to buying and merchandising from a central, "headquarters" location. Luckily, most of them can be remedied—which we'll discuss in a moment. But first, the list of disadvantages:

1. Central distributors have difficulty adjusting their shipments to local conditions. For them, a store too often is just a number on a page. The distributor may not have visited the stores or studied the history or business climate of the cities where the stores are located. The result is attention to numbers, not the reality of actual merchandise and live customers.

2. Centralized buying requires quite a bit of cooperation, and when items hang on the store racks without selling, the blame starts to fly. Is it an apathetic store manager . . . one who disregards the suggestions of the promotions and merchandising teams . . . perhaps one who just is not happy with what the buyers are sending? Is it a buyer who's out of touch with the local stores' needs . . . or a distributor who is overworked and getting sloppy about the shipping details? When personal friction leads to poor sales results, central management has a difficult time deciding what's really going on, and what to do about it.

3. Central merchandising comes with inherent difficulties in maintaining an informed and enthusiastic selling organization. Store managers and salespeople may, as mentioned previously, be critical of merchandise sent to them by people whom (they feel) are too distant to comprehend what really goes on at the store level. Psychologically, there is nothing that can fully replace the personal supervision of a local buyer for a single store who comes back from the wholesale markets with terrific new items, excited about the "finds" and anxious to share them with the floor sales staff.

These, of course, are compelling reasons why mom-and-pop retailers *can succeed,* despite their odds against the so-called superstores. Now, let's take a look at what major retailers can do to minimize the problems.

Overcoming Potential Problems

Learning to treat each store in a chain or cooperative as an individual business entity can be tough. The truth is, except for climate variations, consumer demand in the United States is remarkably uniform. Whether you think of this as good or bad, it is the result of the popularity of television, movies, and other forms of mass media, as well as the fact that today's American travels a lot more than in past generations.

Of course, there may be regional, ethnic, and other differences that develop because the demographics of an area have changed since the original store was opened or purchased. Both buyers and distributors should visit the stores periodically to keep up on the special requirements and concerns of the unit. A brief history and fact sheet, in writing, should be prepared for each unit so that when a visit isn't possible, the buyer and distributor can read it. The history can contain information not only about the store but about its neighborhood, region, and demographics.

One good suggestion we've heard is that headquarters personnel should treat each new store as a "baby." Every buyer, merchandise manager, and distributor should make an effort to learn that store's particular needs, and to merchandise it separately from all other stores as, like any infant, it grows and develops its own "personality." As soon as it becomes apparent that the baby has developed all the characteristics of the other stores in the group, it is then made a full part of the group and receives the same assortments as those allotted to the other stores in the group. Care must be taken, however, to watch for changes in the community that may point to the need for regrouping.

For things like housewares and apparel, a sales analysis should also be made of styles, to determine whether there is a geographic progression of demand. For example, a central buying organization may report that in women's fashion, new styles are accepted first in California and the Southern United States, next in the East, then in the Midwest, and finally in the Western and far Northeastern states. The "map" will be different for different types of products. The point is, if a time frame can be mapped out, orders can be staggered to meet the demands of stores in different areas.

In terms of employees' lack of cooperation, this problem may be partially solved with a clear-cut division of responsibility for persons in each type of job. The human resources department should write job descriptions that make clear the role and authority of each position in both line and staff organizations. Store managers must not be frustrated buyers who constantly try to second-guess the up-line buyers; the buyers and distributors must not regard themselves as selling experts, coming across as know-it-alls to the store managers when anything goes awry. Some chains find it works well to give department managers bonuses based on their store's profit, even though they have no control over merchandise selection at that store. The message? Do your best to sell what we give you, and you'll be rewarded.

The final keyword that can ward off many prospective centralized business headaches is communication. If you're a headquarters-based person whose decisions impact life at the individual store level, go out of your way to ensure that these decisions are communicated to the troops in the field. Technology has made this so much easier in recent years, with e-mail, CDs, digital cameras, phone-in or video meetings for folks who can't be there in person, and the like. There is no reason not to keep store personnel informed—and enthused—about what's coming up for them to sell. Up-line executives should also make use of this technology to thank staff members for individual reasons as they come up—the month's top floor salesperson at a store, the manager who has held a successful charitable event, the buyer who negotiated an exclusive deal with an exciting new supplier, and so on.

Store-Level Buying Systems

We just mentioned technology, which is critical to the whole process of centralized buying and merchandising. Computerization has made it much easier for stores to replenish their stocks of basic goods, using what is called a **buying system**—although, more accurately, it is more like an "ordering system" because they are mostly reordering. We'll list the most common buying systems and describe (in very basic terms) how they work:

- **The Warehouse Requisition Plan.** In this centralized buying system, the store manager has little control over the assortment of merchandise received, but a lot of control over quantity. Grocery and drug chains are good examples of this plan, since they carry a lot of staples and must carry wide varieties of some goods. The store is provided with a checklist and is required to compare its stock against the list at certain intervals. The store is required to stock "enough of" each item to carry through to the next period and can "requisition" (request in writing) fill-in items from a warehouse location, usually located in the same town as the store. The store manager can also opt *not* to stock certain items if they don't happen to sell well in that location.
- **Approved Resource List.** This system, also called a **price agreement plan**, has been used by smaller chains for staples. Central buyers provide the store managers with a list or catalog of approved goods and the vendors that make or market them. The stores then order in quantity, directly from these vendors. The buyers have already negotiated the prices on behalf of the chain, so there's no haggling, and the store department managers have more control over what they choose to stock.
- **Opening Stock Distribution Plan.** In this plan, which is typical of clothing and department stores, brand-new items are treated differently than staples and reorders. Department managers within a store control the beginning ("opening") stocks for the staples and reorders, which they have authority to order directly from vendors. The central buyers select and handle the opening stocks for new items, augmenting the staples with the most up-to-date styles.
- **Automatic Open-to-Buy (OTB).** This system is sometimes used in conjunction with the opening stock distribution plan. Store management allocates a

dollar amount for each department (after its opening stock has been decided on) that the central buyer uses for purchasing new, seasonal merchandise. This is the most problematic system, because the store's dollar amount and the buyer's wants may not mesh, resulting in unbalanced stocks and conflict about what, and how much, new merchandise to buy.

THE DISTRIBUTION POINT

Under any one of the central buying plans listed previously, goods may be shipped by the vendors either directly to the stores or to a central distribution point (that may or may not be a warehouse) maintained by the group. So which is the best alternative—direct from vendor to store or with a distribution facility in the middle? There are advantages to each.

The ideal roles of a distribution facility are to inspect incoming merchandise and immediately return things that are damaged or do not meet specifications, to price and ticket the goods (less expensively than doing it at the individual stores), and to package and consolidate items going to the same store. Partial shipments are held until there's a full truck, saving on transportation costs. A good distribution point provides a steady flow of merchandise to each store in its region.

So why is it that many central buying offices do not have them? First, maintaining a separate facility can be more expensive than having the vendors ship directly to the stores. Inspection of outgoing merchandise can be done at the vendor's location. Arrangements can be made for the merchandise to be shipped when it's actually needed, instead of when it is first ordered. Store managers and their staffs can be trained to mark the goods properly and enter them into the store's inventory database. The vendor may also agree, especially for large customers, to keep a certain amount of backup stock ready for quick shipment to stores as needed.

The need for warehouse-type facilities will always exist for some types of products—home furnishings, for instance, and advance-of-season purchases. But the use of central distribution points is diminishing in retail largely because computerization makes all the ordering and distribution tasks so much easier. How automated can the system get? We'll examine some of the technological advances throughout the rest of this book.

EDUCATION AND TRAINING

That brings us to the final portion of this chapter. Increasingly, as is the case with many careers, the important buying and merchandising jobs are being filled by college-educated, technologically savvy people. This does not imply that academic preparation alone can produce savvy buyers or assistants. However, as others have aptly put it, one of the benefits of higher education is that you are proving you *can* be taught. Retail is big business today, and it requires a better grasp of global marketing, economics, financial forecasting, demographics, research, design trends, and computer skills than ever before. These are topics of many college-level courses, much like the ones in which you are now enrolled.

Nevertheless, it is important to realize that much of your specific training in this field will take place on the job. Experience in direct sales to the customer—"floor sales," in department store terminology—will be invaluable if this is your career of choice.

Many large companies have training programs geared toward the buying position. Work assignments may vary, such that you are able to spend time on the sales floor, in warehouses and stockrooms, in marketing or display departments, and in a merchandising manager's office. If you have the opportunity to take one of these intensive training programs, we highly recommend it. A few of the largest retailers even offer so-called intrapreneur training for managers, granting them varying degrees of entrepreneurial freedom to achieve profit objectives in their areas of responsibility.

Although the order of advancement varies after a formal training program, a common plan for a newcomer to the system is to make them a buyer's assistant in the central office of the chain. If that works out, the trainee becomes a department manager in one of the company's branches (individual stores); then perhaps later, the trainee returns to the buying office as an associate, and eventually assumes the position of buyer—first for a smaller department, then for larger or more complex areas as he or she advances in skill and confidence. Along the way, superiors will take notice of things like these: Is this person better suited to supervising salespeople . . . dealing with customers . . . selecting merchandise . . . researching competitors and market conditions? Remember, this field is competitive. A bright, well-organized buyer's assistant in a top apparel chain may never become a buyer if he or she doesn't show the negotiating skills and fashion sense to eventually be responsible for millions of dollars worth of purchases each year. And, of course, the assistant will need the guts to ask for the chance to try it!

Being an Assistant

There are two distinct types of assistants in a departmentalized store hierarchy: the assistant manager or buyer, and the assistant *to* a manager or buyer. Understanding the difference is important. An assistant manager or assistant buyer is a line executive who has specific responsibilities, some authority to carry them out, and the authority to direct others and make decisions as approved by the manager or buyer.

A manager's assistant, or buyer's assistant, is typically a young person in training for an eventual manager's or buyer's position, or a specialist in some technique (ordering, fashion coordination, and the like). This type of assistant may help his or her superior with scheduling, correspondence, checking on orders, and so on. It is a staff position, not a line position.

Women in Retail Careers

At this writing, the president of the International Mass Retail Association is a woman, Sandra Kennedy, who jumped to the IMRA after seven years as a senior vice president of the National Retail Federation. However, the last half of the twentieth century was difficult for women in retail. They were relegated largely to floor sales positions and passed over for upper management.

This is particularly ironic because in the marketplace, women are responsible for the majority of retail purchases; and yet for decades, most designers and manufacturers of women's apparel, and most retail chain executives, have been men.

Back in the 1990s, Catalyst—a national nonprofit group representing women in business—surveyed chief executive officers and women in senior management positions in Fortune 1000 companies and reported three factors that, according to the women surveyed, were "holding them back" from achieving executive status:

- Male stereotyping and preconceived perceptions of women
- Exclusion from informal networks of communication
- Lack of significant general management and line experience

Interestingly, the CEOs in the same survey agreed with women's lack of management and line experience but did not mention elements of their corporate cultures that might exclude them from advancement. Some added that women just "haven't been in the pipeline long enough" to qualify for promotion.[3]

Perceptive major retailers have set out to remedy that problem. Today, *Working Mother* magazine's annual survey of the "100 Best Companies for Working Mothers" includes two national retail chains:

- Sears, Roebuck and Company, where women make up 45 percent of the 219,000 employees, 43 percent of managers, and 30 percent of executives. Many belong to a career development program called the "Sears Women's Network."
- At Target Corporation, women compose 63 percent of the workforce and half of all managers and executives. In 2004, Target hired a director of diversity to oversee all women- and minority-related programs and strategies.[4]

Networking and mentoring programs, along with diversity and gender sensitivity training, have been hallmarks of these companies' progress. In 2003, the National Association for Female Executives counted six retail chains among its "Top 30," in terms of advancement opportunity for women: Sears and Target, plus Federated Department Stores (owners of Bloomingdale's and the Macy's chains), Nordstrom, Office Depot, and Charming Shoppes (owners of Catherine's, Fashion Bug, and Lane Bryant stores). Wal-Mart, the world's largest retailer, recruits at women's colleges as well as historically black colleges and has won numerous awards for its employee diversity as well as its outreach programs to buy from diverse suppliers.[5]

A "BIG BOX" GETS BIGGER

In November 2004, the formerly ailing Kmart Holding Corporation—which had dropped from thirty-ninth on the Fortune 500 list of the nation's largest companies in 2002 to sixty-seventh in 2003—acquired Sears Roebuck and Company, number 32 on the Fortune 500 list.

The $11 billion buyout surprised almost everyone in the retail industry. Although it was considered an ailing company, Sears' annual sales had been $15 billion more than Kmart's; and Kmart had filed for bankruptcy just two years earlier, closing about 600 stores and laying off 57,000 workers. Some of Kmart's store properties had been sold to Sears and Home Depot to help pay off debts.

The comeback (or "gamble," as some retail experts put it) has suddenly created the third largest U.S. retailer, behind Wal-Mart and Home Depot. The new Sears Holdings Corporation is expected to have 3,500 store locations and annual revenue of $55 billion, with headquarters at the former Sears headquarters located in Hoffman Estates, Illinois.

At this writing, both Kmart and Sears stores will continue to exist, although long-range plans are to convert some stand-alone Kmarts to Sears locations. The company's chairman, Ed Lampert (who is also a major Sears shareholder) also promised "up to $500 million a year in savings" from store closings and conversions, job cuts, and more efficient buying practices. The impact of the merger on either company's previous training, mentoring, and diversity programs remains to be seen.

Source: The Associated Press, New York, November 18, 2004.

CHAPTER SUMMARY

Filling a retail store with the goods for consumers to purchase is an ongoing process that can be broken down into several major steps, and further into smaller tasks. The buying process begins with research into lifestyle trends that pinpoint consumers' needs. Then these requirements are taken by the retail buyer, who goes to vendors and looks for specific assortments of merchandise, then negotiates a purchase on behalf of the retailer.

The buyer may work for an individual store, a group of separately owned stores, or a chain of multiple stores. His or her direct supervisor is usually a merchandising manager, who trains and develops buyers and has a hand in merchandise selection. (The experience level of the buyer is a major factor in determining exactly how involved the merchandising manager must be in the buying process, or whether the manager can maintain a hands-off supervisory role.)

The incoming merchandise must be managed—planned, ordered, received, distributed, organized, priced, displayed, and so on. Eventually, it must also be promoted (advertised) and salespeople must be trained and motivated to sell it. Depending on the type and size of the store, or the number of stores in a larger chain, there may be several people, several dozen, or several hundred who divide up these tasks. This chapter details several of the most common organizational charts for retail stores.

Most large retail chains today use a centralized buying and merchandising system, in which products are bought in bulk and distributed to individual stores, rather than each store doing its own buying. There are advantages and disadvantages to this system, but today's technology has made it easier for large chain headquarters and buyers to communicate with their individual outlets and, therefore, centralized buying is a fact of life in retail.

DISCUSSION QUESTIONS

1. Let's say a store manager wanted to improve her store's merchandise offerings. In a *centralized merchandising* system, how would the manager go about doing this? Briefly describe the process.
2. What is the difference between a *retail buyer* and a *merchandising manager*? Could one person do both jobs?
3. Of the skills listed on page 3, rank them in order of importance. Write a sentence or two about why you ranked them the way you did.
4. Have technological developments in retailing made the buyer's job easier, or more difficult? Why do you think so?
5. Who is able to delegate less work to others: (a) a buyer, (b) a store manager, (c) a department manager, (d) a fashion specialist? Which of these are line executives, and which are staff members?
6. Of all the ways a buyer's sales and profit results might be evaluated by senior management, which do you think is the most fair? The least fair? Why?
7. Why would a giant retail organization choose to have decentralized buying (done by local stores or regional offices) rather than fully centralized buying?
8. A merchandising manager in a chain feels that a large seasonal commitment should be made to a fashionable new product line, and that it will result in a much-needed sales boost. The buyer is dead set against it, and the merchandising manager has been unable to convince the buyer to place the order. What action, if any, should the merchandising manager take next?
9. In retail management, what is the difference between *planning* and *control*?
10. It's your retail chain, and you're the boss. Would you choose to have distribution facilities, or not? Explain your decision.

ENDNOTES

1. *Supermarket Facts: Industry Overview 2003*, Food Marketing Institute, Washington, D.C. (www.fmi.org).
2. Monica Buckley, "Center-Store Profit Zones," *Store Equipment & Design* magazine, April 2000.
3. Gale Duff-Bloom, "Women in Retailing: Is There a Glass Ceiling?" Arthur Andersen Retailing Issues Letter, copublished by the Center for Retailing Studies, Texas A&M University, College Station, Texas, May 1996 issue.
4. "100 Best Companies for Working Mothers—2004," Working Mother Media, Inc., New York (www.workingmother.com).
5. "Top 30 Companies for Executive Women—2003," National Association for Female Executives, New York (www.nafe.com).

C H A P T E R

2

The Roles of Buying Groups

Retailers cooperate with others in a variety of ways to obtain goods more easily and less expensively, and they use one or more specialized organizations to direct their efforts—that is, to give them advice and help them choose from among thousands of suppliers and manufacturers. This chapter introduces the following topics:

- The different types of buying groups
- The functions, services, and programs typical of these buying groups
- The role of centralized buying in group purchases
- The detailed activities involved in the buying-selling cycle

Any retail store (or chain of stores) uses a number of buying groups, which differ in size, ownership, breadth of market coverage, and so on. They are   **33** commonly known as **buying offices**—a term that is not truly accurate but is so widely used in the retail business that, yes, we will refer to them as "buying offices," or sometimes just "offices."

This link in the retail chain was created back in the 1920s, a decade in which the first retail multi-unit chain stores began. Some things never change—independent, single-unit stores wanted a way to counter the new "retail giants," and so buying offices sprang up in large cities to be the communication conduit between stores and manufacturers. This was also the era in which mass production of clothing began, which created a need for continuous representation in that brand-new and fast-growing industry.

During this time, when travel from distant store locations to wholesale markets was far more difficult, buying offices did indeed buy merchandise for their clients. Today, however, they are engaged in a wide range of services that are just as handy, including product development, merchandising consultants, and import programs.

A buying office is an organization located in a major market that represents retailers who have their own buying staffs. It is not to be confused with centralized buying, which we learned about in Chapter 1. These buyers are not buying and merchandising for the stores. Instead, a buying office is a source of information and expertise for store buyers, to help them make their *own* smarter buying decisions. Both small and large stores depend heavily on the flow of information from buying offices. This is where they learn about best-selling items, interesting trends, and emerging new resources, from people who follow the industry for a living.

The buying office and the retail company are organized similarly. For the most part, each executive position in a client or member store has a counterpart in the buying office. The store chain has a buyer; the counterpart in the buying office is the market representative. The store chain has a merchandising manager; in the buying office, it's the head of a division.

The dramatic changes in retailing and general merchandise markets since the 1990s have changed the needs of retail companies, so buying offices have changed (and expanded) their roles in the buying process accordingly. We discuss these functions, and how they developed, later in this chapter.

SPECIAL SERVICES OF BUYING OFFICES

Information exchange is the chief activity of the buying office. In the smallest office, it may mean reporting on best-selling styles and the types of merchandise submitted by clients. In larger corporate offices, the process may be far more sophisticated, with detailed merchandising results (suggested price points, gross margins, estimated turnover, and so forth) and other vital operating data that can be used to monitor the performance of various merchandise lines, stores, departments, and divisions.

Product development has become the most critical modern-day function of the buying office. It is the process of identifying items or lines of merchandise that have some type of advantage over a comparable national brand, in terms of quality, price, exclusivity, and so on. It also involves actually designing the product and/or its packaging, developing specifications so that it can be manufactured, and arranging for its manufacture as a **private-label brand**, exclusive to that particular store or chain (at least, in that region of the country). This is a specialty of the larger buying offices, as they seek ways for their clients to counteract discount retailers and manufacturer-owned stores, as well as allowing the clients to achieve product differentiation and added **mark-on** (suggested prices necessary to increase profit). The areas most active in product development are grocery and drugstore items, family apparel, accessories, and home furnishings.

Most giant retailers shop for and import goods from other countries to offer in-store, but for the smaller retailers, the large independent buying offices have their own **import programs**. They may or may not have foreign offices, but they do have buying connections in different countries. Imported goods may become private-label exclusives, or simply a group purchase divided among stores. The buying office is helpful here in having the technical knowledge of importing laws—duties, quotas, taxes, and so forth. We talk more about both private-label and import programs later in this book, but for now, it's sufficient to note that retailers depend heavily on buying offices to handle the details of product development, and working with international vendors.

Buying offices may also offer promotion services like catalog production. The vendors and manufacturers pay the cost of preparing the catalogs, which can be branded with the company name and shipped to stores and on to consumers. Advertising calendars, promotion and sale ideas, and suggestions for window and interior displays may all be part of the services offered.

There are several types of buying offices, so let's take a closer look at each type.

THE INDEPENDENT BUYING OFFICE

The independent buying offices were the original buying offices—service organizations that provided helpful links between distant retailers and manufacturers. They were all located in New York City, until regional markets in Chicago, Dallas, and Los Angeles were developed. Their staff began as market representatives, advising clients on trends, best-sellers, and special offers, helping and guiding store buyers who came to the "big city" for a market or event, and following up on delivery details after an order was placed.

Buying offices still provide these basic services, but the independents have dwindled in numbers over the years. This does not mean their impact has diminished. Several thousand of the smaller merchants still use independent buying offices; they are mostly either discount department stores or specialty clothing stores.

The independent buying office also plays greater (and multiple) roles for its clients than in the past. Market coverage and expert advice is especially critical to the survival of a small retailer, and an insider's knowledge of what other retailers are doing is considered by some to be the single most important benefit of a buying office affiliation. Once almost entirely production-focused, the offices now are as sophisticated as the fashion industry itself. They can "land" exclusives, create private-label brands, and/or arrange for imported products for their clients.

The consulting function of the buying office is at the core of its usefulness to the retail buyer, who depends heavily on its expertise, both with competitors and manufacturers. Buyers can do the following:

- Ask for research in a certain market for a particular item or need, or request market reports on just about any topic.
- Call ahead and have the office schedule appointments for the buyers' visits to manufacturers' and importers' showrooms.
- Ask for guidance about opening inventory amounts by merchandise classification.
- Attend meetings hosted by the office at the start of each season, to preview new products or styles and get recommendations before they even visit the vendors' showrooms.
- Depend on the buying office to make airline and hotel reservations, reserve meeting space when they're in town, and so on.

One reason there are fewer independent buying offices today is that there are fewer independent retailers. Just as the smaller chains are being bought out by larger ones, buying offices have been merging as well. The trend has been to create "niche" offices, in which larger offices absorb a number of smaller ones, each with its own specialty market expertise. One office, for instance, consists of eight formerly independent smaller firms. Together, the group now serves more than 500 retail companies! What has emerged from this trend is buying office organizations with strong, complementary resources capable of meeting the needs of many different types of retailers. Some have invested huge amounts in technology upgrades to ensure their communication and information is up-to-the-minute, which experts believe is a trend that will keep the buying offices in business in the fast-paced future, along with the addition of even more services, like recruiting and placement of retail executives, and store site selection assistance.

Before this consolidation, numerous small offices served perhaps 50 clients or less, which meant close ties between office and client. Of course, some of this was lost when high-tech replaced "high-touch." A small store owner/buyer can easily come to resent being one of a crowd of 500 to 700 clients, and receiving less personal attention as a result. The surviving buying offices have tried to mitigate this by splitting themselves into divisions for different types of merchandise—the largest apparel buying office, for example, has 11 divisions, each with its own director and personnel. The store buyer may come into contact with only one or two of the divisions, making personal relationships still possible.

An example of a major independent buying office is The Doneger Group, headquartered in New York City and focused on apparel and accessories. The company is made up of five different merchandising divisions, including specialty divisions for plus sizes, high-fashion (designer and couture) apparel, off-price deals, and even a division that negotiates the import of United States-made goods to foreign markets. Doneger also has a consulting division for individual clients' custom projects, as well as an online division that maintains three Web sites so clients can view research, download style photos, and so on.

Buying offices make their profit in a couple of different ways. Most are paid by the retailers they represent. The arrangement is usually an annual contract with a set monthly fee for service (called a **fixed fee**, it is usually one-half or 1 percent of the store's annual sales volume), but the terms depend somewhat on the types of services required. The buying office agrees not to work for direct competitors of its clients, or at least, no other direct competitors in a certain geographic area. This is especially important to maintain the clients' trust—and to ensure that the special services of the office are, indeed, "special."

Some buying offices are paid not by retailers, but by the manufacturers they represent. These are called **commission offices** or **merchandise-broker offices**. The manufacturer pays the buying office based on a percentage (usually 2 to 4 percent) of what the retail store has purchased from that manufacturer, through the broker.

CORPORATE BUYING OFFICES

When a department store chain is large enough, it opens its own buying offices—in major United States cities and/or foreign markets—for the exclusive use of its subsidiary companies. The **corporate buying office** is similar to the independent in function, but its emphasis is on corporate merchandise programs, including private brands and imported goods based on that chain's profit goals and consumer research. A corporate buying office is also called a **syndicated office** (if it works for a large ownership group with several different store names) or a **private buying office** (if it works for a single store). These buying offices exert considerable influence on the companies they serve. The buyers and merchandise managers in these offices are responsible for choosing vendors and setting overall buying policies for the store or chain of stores. They are also the headquarters for the company's product development programs.

Corporate offices can afford highly expert and specialized buying staffs to closely monitor their respective markets, and they have large support staffs for the buyers and merchandising managers. This ensures that their stores have the most current access to research about market trends. And because of their constant and powerful presence in the marketplace, they are able to closely watch manufacturers' production schedules and even monitor the manufacturers' of the raw goods that make up the product—fabric, for example, in the world of apparel. They can set quality standards and double-check that shipments to stores are made as ordered. They know when price changes will take effect, and how much they're likely to be. The sheer size of the office is indicative of its ability to buy in bulk for savings, on behalf of several store chains owned by a single corporation.

Group buying (or bulk purchasing) is a significant part of the corporate buying office duties. Vendors are usually happy to comply, and to offer discounts, because such large purchases allow them to better plan their production. Group buying—even if the items are split up and sold in half a dozen different stores under common ownership—is used frequently for seasonal items, like Christmas and back-to-school goods.

In addition to strong, solid relationships with long-time vendors, the best corporate buying offices are always on the lookout for interesting new products and vendors—emerging designers with unique ideas that they might develop for mutual benefit.

In the corporate buying office, private-label programs are key. It is not uncommon for the largest store chains of all types to have 100 or more people working on product development activity. Depending on the type of retail store, from 30 to 80 percent of its sales may be private, store-branded merchandise.

The private-label trend shows no sign of diminishing, so the corporate buying office function has changed accordingly—from buyers who select or "shop for" products to buyers who actually supervise the creation of custom-made and/or custom-labeled products for the company. A number of huge manufacturers specialize in producing *only* private-label products, for a wide variety of customers, both in the United States and overseas.

ASSOCIATED BUYING OFFICES

An **associated buying office** (also called a **cooperative buying office**) is owned jointly by a group of independent companies, most often full-line department store retailers. The costs of operation are split between the retailers based on their sales volume and the level of service they require. The member stores must be willing to trust each other enough to exchange confidential data and assist one another in all phases of buying and merchandising, publicity, store management, and control.

There are only a few associated buying offices, but the multibillion dollar sales volume of the stores they represent make them major players in the retail industry. The largest is Associated Merchandising Corporation (AMC), which is owned by Target Corporation and has more than 50 offices worldwide. AMC also does the product development and importing for Marshall Field's and Mervyn's stores, among others.

For stores that carry general merchandise—particularly with a fashion component, like housewares and apparel—this joint buying office is the major device for cooperation between independent stores. The offerings include certain wholesaling functions: scouting for new products, assembly, packaging, storage, and delivery in appropriately sized lots. Remember, the office takes the place of an actual wholesaler and therefore eliminates the wholesaler's "middleman" profit from the cost of goods. The theory is that the functions will be more effective if they are directed entirely for the benefit of retailers.

Centralized buying is just one function of the cooperative, and it generally takes two forms:

- The **joint retailer-owned wholesale establishment** was first developed in the drug and grocery arenas, and is now an important conduit for general merchandise-type stores. The supermarket chain creates a wholesaling subsidiary. This is especially useful for purchasing staples that all retailers carry (but in limited quantities in each store), and for the development of private brands (which may be either warehoused or drop-shipped to the stores). The service charge to participating retailers is considerably less than using a third-party (unaffiliated) wholesaler. The extra selling costs are eliminated, and only items in active demand in all stores are stocked. (Remember, the "extra selling costs" are only the wholesaler's *profit*. The wholesaler still makes money, by charging for performing the functions listed previously.)
- A voluntary chain is created when a wholesaler, distributor, corporate chain, or even a manufacturer decides to "sponsor" a buying group for retailers. The retailers don't have to make the financial investment of setting up individual buying offices themselves.

    The wholesaler that undertakes this function is known as a **contract wholesaler**, because they are entering into buying and servicing contracts with several different (usually independent) firms. The wholesaler gets a certain amount of guaranteed business, because the retailers naturally concentrate much of their buying there. The retailer often pays a fee for the service and gets special deals, assistance in merchandising and promotion, and other management services from the wholesaler.

    Today's contract wholesaler has expanded services to include things like accounting and recordkeeping, joint advertising, and suggestions about signage, store fronts, and merchandising policies. (Sometimes, these "suggestions" are mandatory, spelled out in the contract). Hardware retailing is one area that makes extensive use of the contract wholesaler system.

Finally, there are a couple of alternatives for busy stores that just don't want to be involved with a buying office for every purchase in every department. They prefer the autonomy of hiring subcontractors to utilize some of their floor space:

- The **leased department** has become common in supercenters, those large combination food and mass merchandise stores. Have you noticed that at least part of their space is contracted out to other businesses—a jeweler, bank, hair salon? This is another way for the retailer to relinquish some, or almost all, of the responsibilities for buying those items and furnishing a full store department. Instead, the supercenter's parent company offers the space on-site, in return for a percentage of sales volume of the lessee.
- In some categories, buying authority happens through a working relationship between the retailer and either a manufacturer or wholesale distributor. In this arrangement, the retail buyer (not a buying office) primarily selects the brands or lines to be carried and allocates selling space for them. It is up to the manufacturer's salespeople ("detail people") to visit the store regularly, keep the displays full and looking good, count the inventory, and write up reorders. This **vendor control** practice (i.e., "Let the *vendor control* the space") is standard in the grocery industry, for everything from soft drinks to greeting cards.

    The retailer doesn't ignore these brands or lines—they track the volume of sales and profit returned from that space—but the vendor accepts the overall responsibility for the space. It works well, because both parties keep an eye on the space, and the vendor may be able to keep it up more efficiently than the retailer.

A FINAL WORD ABOUT BUYING GROUPS

No matter what the buying method, it is equally important that it be efficiently administered. We've covered a number of ways retailers organize the task of market coverage. Interestingly, none of them has demonstrated a clear and substantial cost advantage over the others—except, that is, when inefficient individual operations are replaced or improved by being part of a group that benefits from volume purchases or discounts. You will also notice that the different buying group methods do not eliminate any of the tasks required in the buying-selling process, nor those connected with wholesaling. The burdens may be shifted, but they still exist. The costs of performing the tasks also remain—whether they are absorbed by the individual retailer, a buying office, a chain headquarters, a wholesaler, or a manufacturer—and these costs must somehow be passed on when the goods are priced.

If a retail buyer is able to select the buying offices he or she wants to work with, it is important that the buyer assesses honestly whether he or she will actually use the many services the retail company will be paying for, and whether the buyer feels the alliance is a good fit for both parties. This decision will be partly based on the compatibility of the retail and buying office employees, but also on the types of merchandise represented, the other merchants in the buying office "stable," and the overall quality of service.

Remember, there are other types of businesses that provide research and advice to the fashion industry and other retail businesses. *Reporting services* do what their name suggests: report on trends and analyze market changes, sending the results to clients regularly by mail or e-mail for a subscription fee. *Fashion forecasters* work even farther ahead, predicting style trends for their clients months in advance to assist in the planning process. *Trade associations*, like the National Retail Federation and the U.S. Association of Importers of Textiles and Apparel, research market conditions and product trends. Trade associations often publish magazines and newsletters, produce training materials, and sponsor conferences for industry members.

A CLOSER LOOK AT THE BUYING-SELLING CYCLE

Now we can expand on the retail buyer's job description first mentioned in Chapter 1. For purposes of more detailed analysis, the three phases of the buying-selling cycle may be expanded into five to more specifically describe the work being performed. The five activities are buying, stock keeping, pricing, selling, and planning/control. Although they are the chief responsibilities of the buyer, in most retail companies, they are split among a number of people.

1. *Buying* is only briefly detailed here because the topic is greatly expanded in the following chapters. The work of buying includes:

   a. Deciding specifically what to buy, and how much to buy
   b. Deciding when to buy, and when to bring the items into stock
   c. Deciding where to buy, how much to pay, how to pay, and how to ship the merchandise
   d. Doing the actual work of selection, negotiation, and placement of the order, or delegating these tasks
   e. Training assistants in all of these activities

   No hard-and-fast rules define the scope of tasks involved in any specific buying function, or in how much time "should be" devoted to each.

2. *Stock keeping* is the process of handling, checking, and protecting the goods between the time they are received and the time they are sold. The term is also used to describe some of the ordering and sales-expediting tasks in

order to maintain a store or chain's preplanned inventory assortments. There are a few subcategories that make up the stock keeping function:

a. Receiving, assembling, and distributing. This task list includes the following:

(1) Checking incoming orders for correct quantities, general condition, and obvious conformance to the purchase order—are these the right colors, style numbers, sizes, and so on? Except for small stores, this job is done by receiving department staff, who usually report to an operations manager.

(2) Checking less obvious elements of material and workmanship. This is a quality control function—how does the finished product compare to the specifications or samples we saw months ago? It is nearly always the buyer's responsibility.

(3) Furnishing the information to mark or ticket the items for sale is the responsibility of the buyer. If not marked automatically by the vendor at the point of production, the buyer must give information about the price, classification, SKU numbers, UPC codes, and so on to . . .

(4) The people who will do the marking or ticketing. Again, many manufacturers do it themselves; but it may be receiving room personnel, or marking may be done centrally at a warehouse or the buying center of a chain.

(5) Determining where to store the incoming goods.

(6) Moving and storing the goods. Where stores have stockrooms, the function of seeing that they are filled with the right amounts of merchandise is the responsibility of the selling department manager (who may or may not be the buyer). Storage and handling of goods in bulk is a specialized function of the Operations Division of a store or chain of stores.

(7) Distributing the goods, in the case of multi-unit operations. **Distribution orders** are the written documents (from the Merchandising Division) that instruct Operations about what is to be delivered where, and in what quantities. A distribution order cues the Operations Division warehouse or distribution center to store, assemble, and ship orders.

(8) Notification of the shipment's arrival. The buyer's duty is to inform everyone concerned with the new shipment that it is on the way from the manufacturer, so they can schedule their own work around it.

(9) Checking and authorizing invoice for payment. The buyer checks the invoice to be sure it reflects the original agreement with the manufacturer, and that everything promised was delivered in good order. In central buying operations, where the buyer may not be the only person involved in the pricing agreement, the buyer still needs to double-check the invoice but may not have to "approve" it.

(10) Authorizing return to vendors and transfers. This is the responsibility of either the buyer or the manager who is accountable for merchandise received in a department.

b. *Protection* includes all the functions of keeping the merchandise in good, salable condition until the consumer buys it and takes it home:

(1) Safeguards against theft, including loss prevention and regular physical inventories.

(2) Cleaning, folding or hanging, packaging, and other means by which the store protects against items getting soiled, broken, or (in the case of foods) spoiled.

(3) Repairing or reconditioning goods that have been damaged. Often, this includes returning the goods to the manufacturer; if it can be done in-house, it is a function of the Operations Division.

Protection is the responsibility of the manager in whose charge the goods may be at any point. The buyer (who is not a department manager) is responsible for approving any type of packaging, and for authorizing recondition and repair.

c. *Inventory control* refers to the specific tasks of maintaining the planned assortment of inventory. We discuss major planning and control functions in Section 5 of this list, but here's an outline of the major tasks with some planning functions included for convenience and clarity:

(1) Checking the unit composition of the assortment as a whole. Quite a bit of analysis goes into this seemingly simple task. Sales and stock data is collected, organized, coordinated, and interpreted as a basis for whether items are reordered or not in the future. Decisions must be made about how to group items, not only for best sales, but for control of them in inventory. These plans, programs, and schedules must be made and followed.

(2) Monitoring of staples to make sure they are always in stock in sufficient supply and creating "never-out" stock plans to that end.

(3) Making special checks on fast-selling items—should they be reclassified? Should they be ordered or promoted more often? Should the current plans be changed to do this?

(4) Distribution is also a stock keeping function in centrally merchandised, multi-unit operations. Its primary function is to maintain the unit composition of inventory assortments in individual stores, by checking their stocks and ordering appropriate replenishments (not from the manufacturer, but from the chain's warehouse), as well as correcting over- or under-shipments by transfers from one store to another.

3. Pricing is not only highly integrated with the buying activities but also with selling activities to ensure the final profit objective is met. The idea is that a combination of price and rate of sale should produce an optimum dollar profit. So pricing involves the following tasks:

a. Setting markup and margin goals
b. Setting price lines and ranges or "zones"
c. Pricing individual items
d. Repricing, to move slow sellers or anticipate changing costs for replacements

This is where the buyer's financial savvy is much needed, in ways that are as creative as the initial buying process. Most buyers have either the authority to price, or the obligation to suggest prices. To do this well, the buyer must have a probable selling price in mind for every item he or she chooses, closely observing the company plans and controls, as well as the competition.

4. *Selling,* as mentioned previously, is the twin main-line function along with buying. For the buyer, it means taking responsibility for passing on information about how and why to sell everything they have bought! All buyers have input, whether it's a recommendation or the final decision, about what will be promoted, when, and to what extent. It is usually the case that the more experienced and knowledgeable a buyer is, the greater role he or she will have in selling activities. These include the following:

a. Management of the work and personnel required to operate a sales force, including some of the actual selling (especially in closing difficult sales) and arranging for special orders.
b. Deciding (or at least, helping to decide) what to promote and when.
c. Giving information to (and of course, motivating) the store personnel that will be selling the products. This may include requesting or writing memos, bulletins, e-mail correspondence, and display pages, as well as making presentations to senior management, store management, and floor salespeople.
d. Sharing similar information with advertising and display staffers, and requesting appropriate media and space for advertising. (The final decisions here usually rest with the Advertising Department or an outside advertising agency, but the buyer's recommendations are very important).
e. Requesting and/or outlining window and interior store displays, including signage, as well as arranging for display materials directly from vendors (or negotiating allowances with which to purchase them).
f. Making decisions about floor or fixture position and display space to be given to specific products.

5. *Planning and control* are interactive skills. Both involve the coordination of all the tasks just listed, in order to best cater to customer demands and make a profit. This may be handled by the buyer's superior in the line organization, or by a number of staff specialists. Sometimes, the buyer does it personally, although it always involves other divisions of the business.

Planning and control tasks include the following:

a. Actively helping to determine the company policies and objectives about the following:

(1) The consumers whose patronage is desired.

(2) How to serve the consumers with respect to pricing policies, quality, selection, brands, fashion position (in the case of apparel and accessories), the depth and breadth of assortments, and ancillary services (How will the stores' image be reflected in design and decor? Will they offer charge accounts? Layaway? Delivery services?)

(3) Promotions: How will they be handled and emphasized? How often will they be scheduled? How will displays, store decor, and advertising be impacted?

(4) Sales: margins, expense, profit, and turnover of merchandise.

b. Analyzing and forecasting demands and requirements of the target customers.

(1) Watching economic trends, generally and in the market areas of the vendors and the stores, as well as the competitors.

(2) Learning the characteristics (**demographics**) of customers as individuals and groups, including their shopping habits and motivations.

(3) Determining trends in merchandise and service preferences.

c. Budgeting sales and stocks.

(1) Formulating estimated dollar sales by category and by time period.

(2) Estimating the value of the merchandise in stock at certain points, and checking it against the turnover goals.

(3) Estimating unit sales and reconciling them with the financial plans.

(4) Building "model stocks" by unit, to get an overview of the assortment and decide the depth (how much of each item) of stock that is necessary; then reconciling this with the "dollar stock" (value of the merchandise) according to the plan.

(5) Determining the required purchases by certain time periods.

(6) Allocating the funds for purchases at the start of each selling season, with enough in reserve to "fill in" the planned assortment or take advantage of a special promotion if it comes up mid-season.

(7) Estimating and setting objectives for markon, markdown, and other elements of margin, as well as certain expenses and profit levels.

d. Control involves creating systems to track all of these goals and plans:

(1) Checking on the performance of inventory control systems, which were mentioned in Section 2.

(2) Setting up checkpoints, standards, and guidelines for all operations from the previously mentioned forecasts and budgets.

(3) Setting up systems (often by computer) and procedures for measuring performance against plan, and checking the condition of any aspect of the business.

(4) Measuring and projecting deviations from the plan, and recommending (or making) the required adjustments—in the operation, the methodology, or the plan itself.

In later chapters, we discuss the control functions at work. In the next chapter, however, we turn our attention to retail customers—how to determine what they're thinking, and how to perform buying functions accordingly.

CHAPTER SUMMARY

Retailers count on the work of buying offices to keep them current on trends in their industry and help them make intelligent buying decisions. There are several types of buying offices, which are organized much like the retail store hierarchy, into divisions with executives, specialists, and staff members. Most divisions specialize in a particular type of merchandise. They research every aspect of the business and can pass this "insider's knowledge" on to their retail clients. Most buying offices have the skills on staff to develop private-label products and import goods from international markets.

Retail buyers (and, to a lesser extent, merchandising managers) will work extensively in partnership with their buying offices, so the buyer and buying office counterpart should be compatible; and the retail store itself should "fit" well with the specialties and services of the buying office. Buyers should also avail themselves of the other market research available to them, also on a fee-for-service or membership fee basis, from fashion forecasters, trade associations, and reporting services.

The detailed outline that ends this chapter covers many of the buying-selling duties, and mentions in most cases whose responsibility they are—or, at least, to what extent the buyer or buying office is involved in them.

DISCUSSION QUESTIONS

1. Does the major emphasis on private labeling and group buying today diminish the importance of the retail store buyer? Of the market reps who work in the buying office? Why or why not? If you feel it has, how would you work to maintain your influence?

2. What job skills might be necessary to be good at product development?

3. What is the difference between an independent buying office and a syndicated buying office?

4. Why would a retailer want to be a member of a voluntary chain? Name and briefly describe two of the advantages, then two of the disadvantages.

5. Do you think the buying office does too much of the work of the retail buyer? Shouldn't buyers have to do their own research to realistically stay current on trends?

6. Are there any situations in which you think a retailer would *not need* a relationship with a buying office? If so, how would they obtain some of the comparable services?

7. Look at the list of buyers' responsibilities in Section 4, and decide which of these could safely be handled by the buyer's assistant. Which could not, and why not?

8. Why would retailers prefer domestic manufacturers as sources of private-label merchandise, even if they are more expensive than foreign sources?

9. In which type of buying office do you think the retail buyer for a large chain has the most autonomy to make decisions? In which does the buyer have the least autonomy?

10. What do you think the future of buying offices will be as technology continues to improve? Will they become more influential, or less? Will there be more of them, or fewer?

C H A P T E R

3

Understanding the Consumer

Why do *you* buy the brands and items that you do? What makes you enter one department store and pass up another in a busy mall, even when their offerings seem somewhat similar? Exactly what do you expect from a retail experience—can you describe it? Most of us probably don't think much about our inner motivations as shoppers, but the retailers think plenty about them! In fact, in today's dynamic society, retailers will tell you that consumers are the least manageable and least predictable of the many variables they face. Think about it—society is more homogenized than ever, and yet we all strive to be thought of as individuals, and we want others to respect our diversity.

The retailer has a business to run, and that means setting short- and long-term objectives and creating plans to meet them. So a retail store's capacity to identify and understand its customers is key to planning every other facet of the buying-selling equation. In this chapter, you will learn:

- How retailers and their research teams decide what motivates consumers
- How economic and social trends impact consumer preferences (and therefore, retail buying)
- Where to find both internal and external data that can help forecast demand for products

As you will see, gathering this data involves tapping many sources and interpreting it is a combination of math, science, psychology, and gut-level intuition.

ANTICIPATING DEMAND

The prime objective of the buying function is to anticipate the needs and wants of customers. This means being ready to either shepherd or gratify a customer's desire for a product. Stringent limits on the size of the inventory that can be gathered for this purpose means that these desires must be forecast with some accuracy, and that the goods must be ordered quickly enough to meet the demand for them. This intense focus by makers and sellers on what consumers will want and how soon they'll want it is known as a **marketing concept**. It includes the following three elements:

1. Both producer and distributor of the goods must be consumer-oriented, ready to do their own research and help the buyer make decisions.
2. Marketing activities (promotion, advertising, floor sales) must be closely coordinated with the procurement of the goods.
3. The effort must be aimed at a profit that will enable the business to make back the capital it has invested, and attract new capital for growth.

At its simplest, consumers will accept or reject what is laid before them. Their needs do not even have to be expressed specifically, because not all of these needs are conscious. Some are gut level, latent, or subconscious. Here's an example: When the first electric refrigerators were put on the market, the need had to be inferred. Nobody knew they "needed" a refrigerator—they'd had no personal experience using them. The predecessor in the appliance world (the icebox) was a hassle, requiring frequent replenishment of the ice supply and drainage of water for what amounted to poor and uneven cooling of foods. But the need was there—that is, the need for a machine that would reduce household labor and allow a homemaker to more closely lead the life she wanted to lead. She wanted freedom from drudgery, a better storage option to keep food fresh and safe longer, and easier meal preparation. Whether this woman could actually state her desires in those particular terms, they were the latent or underlying lifestyle needs that prompted the invention of the refrigerator—and, when Frigidaire marketed the first one, those were the points they used to make it an enormous success. The first refrigerator was soon copied and improved, and production accelerated. As the incredible demand was met and consumers' initial needs were satisfied, they became more selective (about features, colors, brand names) and the product lines progressed to meet these shifts in demand. Each new and successful product tends to follow this pattern.

An apt quote comes from Lee Iacocca (of Ford and Chrysler fame) in an autobiography more than 20 years ago: "There's a widespread myth that those of us who run the car industry somehow manipulate the public, that we tell people what kind of cars they should buy and that they listen . . . if only it were true! The truth is that we can only sell what people are willing to buy. In fact, we follow the public far more than we lead it."[1]

In the days before mass production of goods, there was a scarcity of products, and so great a demand that consumers were not very picky about them. Manufacturers focused on what could be made the most cheaply and in the largest quantities. They didn't need to analyze how well a product would be accepted, and it was largely assumed that if you made a big enough promotional effort, whatever you were marketing would sell. If the producers of apparel, for instance, decided what the style was going to be in a season, that was what they made and advertised, and the public fell in line with it.

Then in the mid-1980s, criticism rippled through the retail world with the release of the book *Marketing Warfare* by marketing consultants Jack Trout and Al Ries.[2] It makes for fascinating reading even today, as these two likened marketing to actual combat over the centuries, with the same jargon, tactics, basic battles, and characteristics of heroes. "The true nature of marketing today," they said, "involves the conflict between corporations, not the satisfying of human needs and wants." (Incidentally, both men are still in business as marketing experts, in their own very successful firms—Jack Trout in Greenwich, Connecticut, and Al Ries in Atlanta, Georgia.)

The truth is probably somewhere in between. There have been big promotional campaigns that failed simply because they ran counter to customer demand in some way. Then again, other products have become sensational hits even with little promotion, because they met a particular need and people learned about them by word-of-mouth.

Most new product successes grown from a concept of consumer want that is based on a perceived central idea—Domino's Pizza, Liquid Tide, Macintosh computers, and Softsoap, to name just a few. Launching a new product is an expensive undertaking because it usually demands huge investments in research and development, perhaps years of market testing, and costly promotion when it finally hits the marketplace. Hundreds of millions of dollars may be required to introduce this new idea; hundreds of millions of dollars are lost if it fails. And yet, manufacturers must generate new products to ensure their long-term growth. The 3M Company, for instance, is reported to have a long-term goal of generating at least one-quarter of its sales from products less than five years old. Retailers are receptive to these offerings, because they are also eager to present fresh new ideas to their own customers.

Finding out what makes consumers tick is a whole interdisciplinary study of motivation and behavior that uses math, economics, psychology, sociology, and cultural anthropology. Let's take a closer look at it.

CONSUMER MOTIVATION

In research, our motives are often classified as primary and secondary. (Some researchers refer to them as "rational" and "emotional.") A **primary motivation** stems from physical needs that are part of most humans' survival instincts (hunger, thirst, procreation, sleep). **Secondary motivations** are a learned or psychogenic set of characteristics for social interaction (recognition, inquisitiveness, empathy, ego, greed, and many more). These could be summarized as traits that aren't necessary for survival, but that somehow make people feel good or improve their own self-perception when exercised.

Interestingly, primary motivations may be postponed or even renounced in the name of strongly felt secondary motives. That's why you'll hear of hunger strikes, for example, by political prisoners with passionate beliefs. Individual customers are just that—individuals. Each has a unique set of drives, with a set of priorities for meeting and satisfying those drives. Neither the drives nor the priorities are stable, or even necessarily logical or rational.

An example of these changing priorities is food selection. Yes, there is a primary motivation to eat. But what you want to eat is based on fads and cravings, personal taste, convenience of purchase, ease of preparation, class conformity, and so on. Nutritional value is *not* usually one of the big motivators. Then again, market researchers look for countertrends—if enough people decide they've had enough junk, and go for nutritionally sound foods, for instance, this indicates a separate market segment and a whole new trend that may be just as faddish as the trend it was created to counter. The group that represents a large enough market to be profitable becomes the market to pursue. A current example in the 2000s is the major soft drink companies, all turning product development cartwheels to develop "better-for-you" (or at least, less sugar-, calorie-, and caffeine-packed) carbonated beverages in the wake of headlines about the "obesity epidemic," and some schools banning soft drink vending machines.

Predisposition + Perception = Patronage

Predisposition has a powerful influence on purchasing decisions. It is an attitude toward the product and/or seller that has built up over time, partly a sense of loyalty but also familiarity. Think about the times you go to the nearest supermarket for groceries when you know there are lower prices elsewhere, just because you're more familiar with the store that's closer. Familiarity is a comfort factor that prompts you to save time rather than money—not exactly true-blue loyalty, but, hey, the store will accept your money nonetheless!

Predisposition can be equally powerful when it's negative. To use the same neighborhood store example, you might go out of your way *not* to shop there if you were embarrassed by the way they handled an accidentally bounced check or because they didn't allow your daughter's Girl Scout troop to sell cookies in front of the store last spring. And yes, you may drive to another store simply because the prices *are* less expensive elsewhere. "It's a matter of principle," you tell yourself.

So, whether it's positive or negative, predisposition is a built-up set of beliefs, opinions, and attitudes, and each of these involves perception. *Perception* is the process people use to select, organize, and interpret what their senses tell them—making it into what is, for them, a meaningful and coherent picture. A designer dress in a store window may be perceived as beautiful by two different women who stop to look. One instantly dismisses it as inappropriate for her budget or her lifestyle (without even looking at the price tag, incidentally); the other woman imagines herself as looking stylish in the dress, confers a certain amount of status to that designer's (or that store's) label, and hurries into the store to see if they have it in her size.

Can you see how perception is determined, at least in part, by each woman's motivation, needs, and values? We can conclude, then, that:

- Perception is selective and can be so to the point of rejection.
- Perception is interpretative and can be so to the point of distortion.

This is why we often hear it said that people "see what they want to see," "hear only what they want to hear," and so on. If two individuals get a whiff of the same perfume, one will say it's "enchanting," and the other will wince and call it "disgusting." In fact, it probably is neither.

The customer's self-perception is a major buying motive. With the disposable income of many of today's consumers, self-perception is expressed by what you wear, how you decorate your home, what kind of vehicle you drive, and how you spend your leisure time. Hundreds of product categories now have lifestyle implications in their marketing, from health clubs to personal computers to prescription drugs.

Selection Factors

The elements that go into making a selection or rejection of an item in a retail setting are complex and often subtle. In product development, they are called **selection factors**. Each factor contributes to making a certain product especially suitable for a certain use—a purpose, occasion, customer, or group of customers. A sample list of selection factors (there are probably hundreds) might include the following:

- The style of an item (basic or generic—a good, all-purpose wineglass, or an etched crystal Venetian wineglass; a single-breasted suit versus a double-breasted suit, etc.)
- The way an item is packaged for aesthetics (a designer logo on the box, a colorful exterior to catch attention, or a design that prevents tampering)
- The "pack" for customer convenience (single-serve sizes, easy-to-open cans, six-packs, cases, family packs, etc.)
- The size of an item (a compact car, a midsized car, a minivan, a truck)
- Ease and cost of maintenance (no-stick surfaces, crease retention, ability to machine-wash instead of dry cleaning)
- Health and safety factors (diet and nutritional benefits, natural versus synthetic ingredients, antiallergen properties)
- The ability to save or conserve energy (meaning either gas or electricity; or the human energy expended to perform a task that will be easier with this gadget or device)
- Quality of workmanship (the perception and/or labeling of top-quality or "firsts" versus "seconds" or "irregulars")

As you can see, the list could go on and on. Most products cannot possibly be made in every possible permutation that represents every possible desire, of every potential consumer. The solution is a never-ending compromise—products are made in combinations of selection factors, designed to appeal to the core preferences of a group of (we hope) carefully researched consumers. The members of each group weigh the pros and cons, and settle for those products that come closest to satisfying their own individual combinations of desires. ("I wish it came in black, but I do like this blue one . . .")

These are the ideas behind the processes known as **market segmentation** and **benefit segmentation,** the targeting of products to meet specific trends or needs. The growing proliferation of products—in more styles, patterns, colors, sizes, and so on—are attempts to hit on the best combinations of selection factors. Unfortunately, they also make a nightmare of inventory management.

What does all this mean for the retail buyer? Well, when standing in a designer's showroom staring at a cushy, bright red velvet couch shaped like Marilyn Monroe's lips (and yes, this *is* an actual product) the buyer has to put his or her own tastes and preferences aside and think about the customers. True, many of them would reject it immediately as garish—but if a sufficient percentage of the store's clientele would "absolutely love it," then it should be bought and displayed. The buyer must learn to see all products and all promotions through the eyes of the customers, and must also remember that what the customer perceives as the total benefit of a proposed purchase may far transcend the actual physical attributes or obvious characteristics of a product. Now you know why—because everyone's perception is different, placing them into different target markets.

TREND EXTENSION

In today's dynamic consumer marketplace, it is often easy to gloss over the importance of **trend extension**, which, briefly, is the practice of using ("extending") past experience to help predict the future. Yet it plays a major role in forecasting demand. We're not suggesting that customer demand does not change. Clearly it does, as fashion affects all of the most basic merchandise categories, from appliances to apparel. But no matter what the product, there is at least some continuity from season to season and from year to year. Despite the hundreds of new toys released annually, for instance, there will always be teddy bears.

Trend extension data can be seen in action in two different types of buying. **Replenishment buying** is most common with items like food, liquor, and hardware. It is making repeat purchases of items to replace the ones that have sold, in order to bring planned assortments up to a predetermined level and keep a store fully stocked. There will be seasonal fluctuations, but the liquor retailer knows when these will occur, and how much more rum to purchase. For multi-unit chains, the buyer may or may not actually make the replenishment purchases—in a price agreement plan or warehouse requisition plan, it is the store manager (or each department manager) who does the reordering, and the system is computerized or even automated.

For the retail buyer, though, the replenishment data is important because it provides a reliable basis for creating a **staple stock system**, or **staple assortment**—a list of items (and quantities) the store should carry because there will always be a need for them. Items in very active demand will be categorized further, onto a special **never-out list**, so they may be slightly overordered to ensure they're always in stock. The other good reason to have a staple stock system is for opening new stores in the chain, which can then automatically be stocked with the basics.

In department and specialty stores, much of the merchandise is purchased using **anticipatory buying**. Using trend extension data allows the buyer to predict how customers will react to new merchandise, and to place orders well in advance so the goods will be manufactured and delivered promptly. The Christmas season is a perfect example of a time of year for which the best-organized buyers plan many months in advance, based at least partly on what sold well the previous year.

Don't be shy about asking manufacturers and wholesalers for information and advice. They also must anticipate trends. They are active in product development, always scouting for better technology and materials, and in close touch with the designers of new styles. They know your business, and your overall industry. They also know the sales results from other stores to which they sell, and within reason and the bounds of confidentiality, they are happy to share this information if it will prompt an order . . . from you. Information from vendors comes in several ways:

1. Directly from them, or their sales representatives
2. From their Web site, catalogs, and price lists
3. From their market showrooms

As with so many other statistics, however, it is not enough to simply gather trend extension data. It must be analyzed with logic and creativity, and its impact on future buying habits must be measured to the best extent possible.

DOING CONSUMER RESEARCH

It's a big and diverse nation, and although national trends definitely matter in retailing, most merchants want data that more closely mirrors each store's local market. A neighborhood store can use the U.S. Census Bureau figures or check with their chamber of commerce or mayor's office for details about their immediate trading area. For larger areas, the U.S. government uses three geographic designations based on population density. From smallest to largest, they are as follows:

- A Metropolitan Statistical Area (MSA) is (1) a city with a population of at least 50,000, or (2) an urbanized area with a population of more than 50,000 and a total metropolitan population of at least 100,000.
- A Primary Metropolitan Statistical Area (PMSA) has a total population of 1 million or more and contains counties that each have (1) a county population of at least 100,000, (2) a population that is at least 60 percent urban, and (3) fewer than half of the workers who reside there commute to jobs outside the county.
- A Consolidated Metropolitan Statistical Area (CMSA) is the largest designation and is made up of component PMSAs that total at least 1 million people.

Before locating a store in a particular area, or making a decision to close or remodel an existing store, there's plenty of research to be done about the traffic patterns, other merchants, and lifestyles of the population of that area. Are people aging? Just starting families? Moving away? Losing their jobs?

For retail buying and marketing personnel, additional studies must be done about what motivates their potential customers. **Demographics** are statistical analyses, the various ways people are counted and grouped by gender, age, nationality, income, and so on. **Psychographics** are lifestyle details about their priorities and values, and how these things are reflected in their behavior. A retail research team will want to find out the following:

- How many people live within a certain number of miles from the store?
- What are their genders and ages?
- How many different ethnic groups are represented?
- What are their occupations and average incomes?

- What is their marital status? If married, do both spouses work? What are the typical household and family formations in the area (Single parents? How many kids, and how old? Empty nesters? College students?)
- What is their education level?
- Are there political or religious affiliations that might impact shopping habits?
- Are the neighborhoods stable, or are the residents highly mobile? Are they homeowners, or renters?
- What kind of purchasing power do they have? What is important to them, and what do they spend their money on—both necessities and nonessential items?

Lifestyle Trends

You may hear the terms **lifestyle marketing** or **lifestyle retailing**. A person's lifestyle is how his or her pattern of living is exemplified in the way the person buys and uses merchandise. So lifestyle retailing is selling goods to people who may have similar demographic characteristics, but tuning it more finely to acknowledge and meet their different expectations, behaviors, and motivations. Briefly, here are some examples of trends that are impacting today's major U.S. retailers, from *New York Times* editor Sam Roberts' analysis of the 2000 U.S. Census. *Who We Are Now* makes for fascinating reading for anyone in marketing or retailing.[3]

Growing Ethnic Populations

In the United States, nonwhites account for only 16 percent of the population over age 65, but fully 39 percent of those younger than 25. Black and Hispanic Americans each compose more than 12 percent of the population, and their numbers are growing at a faster rate than whites. In the 1990s, for example, the number of U.S. residents of Mexican ancestry grew by 53 percent. Asian immigrants account for 3.7 percent of the population; one in three of them live in California.

In terms of buying power, the University of Georgia estimated in 2004 that African-Americans represent $688 billion, Hispanic consumers $653 billion, Asian consumers $344 billion, and Native American consumers $45 billion, annually.

The Aging Population

The nation's total population tripled in the last century; but during that time, the number of people over age 65 increased tenfold as our life expectancy improved with medical advances. A little over half of our senior citizens are between 65 and 74 years of age, another 35 percent are 75 to 84, and 12 percent are considered "elderly," age 85 or over. (The 2000 census also counted more than 50,000 centenarians—folks who've celebrated their 100th birthdays!)

For retailers, perhaps the most important trend in this area is the glut of "baby boomers" who are just starting to hit their retirement years in 2008 to

2111. In 2000, senior citizens made up 12 percent of the U.S. population. By 2030, that will grow to 30 percent.

Marriage and Family Shifts

Census findings show that what we know as "the nuclear family" has been on the decline since the 1960s. Of the 35 million families with kids under age 18, almost 10 million are single-parent households. Only about 60 percent of today's kids live in one home, with both of their parents.

There are about 105 million U.S. households, which is an increase over past years and the result of more, smaller households. Today, one in three Americans lives in a two-person household; and more than one in four people in the United States live alone.[4]

Gender Orientation

This category includes two different facets. First, about 27 million Americans describe themselves as gay or lesbian, with an estimated buying power of $500 billion annually—a larger share of the retail pie than the Asian and Native American markets combined.[5]

Retailers are also becoming well aware of the increase in *crossover purchasing*—that is, men and women who are buying items in categories that have for years been considered gender-specific. Handy single mom Barbara Kavovit is making her Internet fortune selling toolkits and basic home repair advice to women, at barbarak.com. It makes sense in a world where single women are purchasing homes at twice the rate of single men, and women shop for and buy at least one-third of the home improvement tools.[6]

When you look at this type of lifestyle data, other trends in the marketplace begin to make sense—like America's preoccupation with health and fitness, and the obesity epidemic, as the baby boomers "fight back" to stay younger, longer. What others can you think of?

There are magazines and scholarly journals about demographics and research, probably too specialized to subscribe to for the average retail industry employee, but available in many campus and public libraries. They include *American Demographics* and *Consumer Behavior*.

TYPES AND SOURCES OF INFORMATION

How does a store possibly find out all of the details discussed previously, about every customer or potential customer? There are several basic types and sources of information:

- **Primary information** is collected by a retailer (or on a retailer's behalf) for a specific purpose. It is data that has not been collected anywhere else (or at least, not that the retailer has been able to locate), and it is potentially valuable enough info for them to spend the money to obtain it. Primary information is typically a survey or report, either to find something out, or to support or modify existing data.

- **Secondary information** is existing data. It includes a wide range of data, in many forms, that might have originally been published by a trade association, government agency, or research firm. It may not fit the exact requirements of a company, but it can often be modified to be more useful.
- **Internal information** is gathered on an ongoing basis from within the - company—reports of sales, markdowns, turnover, department overviews, employee surveys, and so forth—or reports prepared internally to analyze this data.
- **External information** is data gleaned from sources outside the company—secondary data, from vendors, customers, competitors, government agencies, trade associations, and the like.

Using Internal Sources

For the established retailer, perhaps no sources of information are more insightful than "the basics": sales made and lost, returned merchandise, customer complaints, and the impact of advertising on sales. To get the data required, the proper records must be kept. For an advertised promotion, this would include:

- The dates of the promotion/sale period
- The exact description of the merchandise, including SKU number, size, price, markup, and so on
- The types of advertising, with quantity and cost of each
- Clips of any supplementary publicity that was done (a feature story in a newspaper food section, for instance, about the product)
- The weather conditions during the promotional period
- Actual sales (in dollars and units) for the week before and the week after the advertisements ran
- The ratio of advertising costs to direct sales of the item
- A brief analysis of whether the promotion was a success or failure, and suggestions for making it better next time

With a comprehensive record, the buyer has an excellent guide for future promotions that includes tried-and-true details about what worked and what didn't.

Computerization has made data compilation and storage simpler—but not if no one keeps up with entering, summarizing, and interpreting the data. Customers supply a store with a wealth of information, even things that are not reflected in their purchases. Many stores with their own credit cards can "mine" the information on the credit applications to their benefit—for age and marital status and income levels of their customers. Some stores include

CLARITAS DATA PROVES: "YOU ARE WHERE YOU LIVE"

With the zip code serving as its lynchpin, the term **geodemographics** was coined in the mid-1970s to describe demographic and consumer data that are gathered based on where a person lives. Today, some 30 years later, the same company that pioneered geodemographics has developed the fourth incarnation of a lifestyle segmentation system that harnesses geodemographic research through a combination of census and survey data, segmenting consumers into 66 unique groups based on where they live, work, and shop.

Claritas (Latin for "radiance") uses this segmentation system, called PRIZM NE®, to divide areas into "clusters" with catchy names that reflect their inhabitants' socioeconomic standing and consumer behavior. A few examples include:

- **"Young Digerati."** They are the ethnically mixed, well-educated residents of fashionable, urban neighborhoods. They are technologically hip—more likely to get their news online than from newsprint—hence the Digerati (for "digital") moniker. With median incomes of almost $80,000, they frequent health clubs, boutiques, and trendy dining spots.

- **"Brite Lites, Li'l City."** These residents are double-income, childless couples who choose to live just outside urban areas to avail themselves of both suburban convenience and big-city amenities. With professional-level jobs and median incomes of almost $68,000, they also enjoy the latest technology at home.

- **"Shotguns & Pickups."** They are, literally, the folks most likely to own those two items—hunting rifles and trucks. Most are young, working couples, half of whom have at least two children. Nearly one-third live in mobile homes, more than any other group. Their incomes (of just under $40,000 a year) are earned in agriculture and other blue-collar jobs.

- **"Mobility Blues."** This population is comprised of transient, working-class singles (and single parents) under age 35 who will pull up stakes if necessary for better wages. Their occupations are service-industry and other blue-collar jobs; with incomes of about $28,000, their lifestyles are modest and they're more likely to be renters than homeowners.

From major newspapers to automakers to hardware stores, companies partner with Claritas to hone in on exactly the right market clusters for their products. What does your zip code say about you? To learn more about your own cluster, enter your zip code on this website: www.yawyl.claritas.com. (Click on the tab "You Are Where You Live.")

Source: 2004 PRIZM NE segmentation system data used with the permission of Claritas Inc., San Diego, California.

optional lifestyle questions with the applications, to more closely pinpoint customers' wants and needs.

Every failure to buy is almost as important in determining demand as every purchase. Some customers will come in, describe what they're looking for to the salesperson, and leave because it's not in stock. A color, size, or price of a garment may not sell simply because it is inadequately represented in the stock. This is why it is critical to listen to the floor sales staff. The salespeople are typical customers themselves, and their reactions to new goods presented by vendors may be a true index of sales possibilities.

Some stores have a **want slip** system in place. This is a daily form, filled out in a department, that lists every request for merchandise not in stock, and whether a substitute item was sold in its place. Most stores also have some sort of "rain-check" form, so a customer can fill out a request for an out-of-stock item and be contacted when it is available again. The value of these records is questionable, though, because most people instinctively resist doing the paperwork and/or are often too busy to bother with it. A better method for the buyer is to maintain close contact with the floor staff (or in large chains where this is impossible, with the sales managers). The buyer can attend some of their meetings, or call his or her own meeting to discuss upcoming events and shipments. Ask questions about what customers request, and what is out of stock most often. Bring in clothing samples and ask their opinions, about price as well as quality and style. If it's a new food product, let them taste it.

Nearly every major purchase of a new style or product line may be viewed as a test of its preliminary sales. Mail-order and multiple-unit companies wisely start with a relatively small order from the vendor, to see how it goes—just enough goods to back up a limited mailing, or to distribute to a few key stores. Of course, arrangements are made with the vendor to be able to back up that initial order with larger quantities if the item takes off. As soon as the winners are perceived, a reordering program begins. Again, computerization allows a buyer to check the figures daily.

Catalog Retailing

Another reliable forecaster of demand is customer response to a catalog mailing. We include this as an "internal" data source because the retailer develops the catalog "internally" (although there are consulting firms that specialize in catalog production) and mails it out, hoping to generate both sales and trend data from those sales.

Catalog retailing, once the almost-exclusive domain of Sears, Roebuck and Company and Montgomery Ward, is bigger business than online sales at this writing. A 2004 study by the global business consulting firm Bain & Company noted that the top four catalog companies have 20 times more transactions per day than the top four online-only retailers, which apparently underscores the need to do both well. The venerable JCPenney catalog, for instance, takes 35 million orders by telephone annually and handles 457,000 mail-order transactions per day, compared to just over 25,000 per day at e-retailing giant Amazon.com.[7]

In a never-ending cycle, retail chains find out about their customers and then target-market catalogs to those customers. In addition to their "big book" catalogs, Spiegel Catalog, Inc. distributes 72 different catalogs; JCPenney has 94 catalog titles. Both have been in the mail-order business since the early 1900s. Lest you assume that people are sick of junk mail and throw away catalogs, this type of shopping has grown double-digit rates since the 1990s. Catalog retailers may spend a fortune on postage, but they offset this with lower-cost orders filled from warehouses, saving on labor costs. The after-tax profits average twice that of profits on normal sales in a "bricks-and-mortar" store location.

Using External Sources

Retail intelligence is the term for collecting secondary information, and the more you look, the more you'll find. The Internet has become absolutely invaluable as a research tool, provided the person doing the research is savvy about what sources are reliable. The trouble is that, as with internally gathered information, what you collect may not be useful in its current form. After determining that the data is legitimate, someone has to analyze and interpret it, adapting it for the company's buying needs or (just as important) discarding it if the information just doesn't fit the situation.

Federal and state government sources are handiest for two types of information: economic data and basic demographics. The U.S. Commerce Department releases regular reports on retail sales and durable goods shipments. The U.S. Department of Labor's Bureau of Labor Statistics releases two key monthly economic indicators, which generally make front-page business news:

- The Consumer Price Index (CPI) is considered the best indicator of inflation. The CPI is a report on price fluctuations in these basic spending categories: housing, food, transportation, apparel, medical care, communication, education, recreation, and so-called "other goods and services" that don't quite fit the categories.
- The Current Employment Statistics, a survey of 300,000 businesses to track employment (and unemployment), hours, and wages by market sector.

The Federal Deposit Insurance Corporation (FDIC) publishes regional economic conditions, taking employment, income, housing, and real estate data into account. In addition to the U.S. Census Bureau consumer household data discussed earlier in this chapter, the agency also polls a random sample of 5,000 retail and foodservice companies each month, and extrapolates the figures to represent more than 3 million businesses in order to chart sales trends. This report is released monthly, at mid-month.

There is even an indicator . . . of all the other economic indicators! It is called the Composite Index of Leading Indicators, a snapshot of 10 major market reports that helps economic analysts to predict short-term trends.[8]

State and local information may be gleaned from sources like the Secretary of State's office (new business openings) and the state's Department of Commerce (business and demographic data about a state as a whole, or specific counties and cities). The Web site EconData.Net offers free links to an enormous list of government Web sites and specializes in regional economic data.

Trade associations are amazingly fruitful as information conduits. In their respective industries, these membership organizations gather and disseminate data on trends, developments, legal battles and concerns, technological improvements, and more. They keep their members informed with Web sites, and most publish newsletters or magazines. Many hold annual conferences or periodic workshops, attracting expert presenters on a wide range of topics. As a member, it can be a major networking bonus (and obvious career boost) to become more involved in the association—writing for its publications, presenting at conferences, being an elected officeholder.

There are hundreds of *trade publications*—also known by the catchy and more modern terms business-to-business or B2B publications—and not all of them are published by trade associations. Pick any industry and there are multiple magazines that represent the retail facet of it. Imagine curling up with a nice glass of wine or a hot mug of tea and the latest edition of *Chain Store Age* . . . or *Floor Covering Weekly* . . . or maybe *Progressive Grocer*. Some of the larger publications (like *Chain Store Age* and *Progressive Grocer*) also have Web sites that are updated daily with industry news. In the fashion industry, Fairchild Publications dominates the magazine business, with *Women's Wear Daily*, *DNR* (formerly the *Daily News Record*, for men's fashion), and the weekly publication *Footwear News*, to name a few. Fairchild publishes 16 magazines—10 trade pubs, and 6 newsstand magazines for consumers (three fashion and three bridal). Fairchild also does extensive market research that can be purchased.

In addition to the articles in these publications, buyers should be studying the advertising. In fact, advertising in all forms is important to notice. Newspapers in a market area should be combed daily, to see what the competitors are advertising. In large cities, there are **clipping services** that can be hired to keep track of ads or news items about particular topics, in area newspapers and on radio and television. These services make copies and deliver them to clients on request. Online, services like LookSmart (www.looksmart.com) and FindArticles (www.findarticles.com) archive thousands of magazine articles by magazine and by topic. Many are available free of charge; others require an online subscription to the service.

Reporting and research agencies publish market reports of various kinds, usually on a subscription basis. Among the best-known U.S. research firms are ACNielsen, Retail Forward, and the Market Research Corporation of America (MRCA). With a combination of retailer surveys, sales results, and consumer opinion data, these reports are available on national, regional, and sometimes city-specific basis and can be extremely useful. A recent perusal of current retail buying reports available on Internet sites (like marketresearch.com) found some of them for as little as $500.

There are also specialized companies, like Frank About Women (the North Carolina-based consultants who help businesses build loyalty among female customers), and well-known research firms, like Perception Research Services (PRS), that can be hired to perform a custom study of consumer attitudes about a product line or company. In business since 1972, PRS claims to have performed more than 8,000 custom studies for 700 clients. The benefit of a custom study is, of course, the expert analysis of the data as part of the package. However, custom study projects by a national firm can be quite costly, so their use is reserved in most companies only for decisions of highest financial significance.

Do-It-Yourself Research Options

Some retailers choose to do their own outside research instead of relying on external sources or buying groups to provide it. Who says you can't organize your own focus group? A buyer or division merchandising manager, senior store management, and the company's advertising agency are all capable of gathering a representative group of customers—or vendors, for that matter—to express opinions. If you give them enough advance notice, and are prepared to lead the discussion with specific questions or topics, make them comfortable, feed them well, and not take too much of their time, you will find these get-togethers can provide a wealth of information. There are several types of groups to consider:

- The *customer advisory panel* is organized to make suggestions about store policies, services, merchandise assortments, advertising, and more. Some groups are asked to give input on what types of charitable and community-related involvement a particular store might be considering. Some of these groups meet regularly, with the same members; others choose a different group of people for each meeting.
- The *consumer experience group* reports on the performance of products in use, shopping habits, and brand preference.
- Customers who agree to participate in a *home inventory group* report to the store about the goods they have on hand, by brand and amount; or they fill out a *continuous purchase record*, a monthly itemization of their family purchases by commodity class.

Arranging for customer participation in the research process can be a bit more labor-intensive, but it creates a core group of consumers who truly feel they are important to the retailer—so they'll shop there, and they'll tell their friends. It also offers an interesting way to glean common sense and new perspectives at very little cost.

Interviews, either in person or by telephone, also glean information but require a skilled specialist to make the consumer instantly comfortable, then ask the right questions and be, shall we say, gently persistent. The decision to hire a telephone research firm is a tough one, because of the "telemarketing" label with its intrusive connotations—but a survey is a survey, not a sales call, and some people are glad to share their opinions. Daily newspapers in many areas conduct surveys that are often available to area retailers (their advertisers) at no charge.

Observation and customer counts may sound like the simplest, most low-tech research options, but think about it. Buyers should train themselves to notice what the influential members of a community are doing and wearing, not only in their own city of residence but when they travel to attend markets. Floor salespeople should be trained to notice what people *do* when they shop—how they act, what they pick up and put back, their facial expressions. Department managers should be required to comparison-shop at their competitors' stores, with a keen eye for more than styles or price tags, but for breadth of assortment and new or best-selling lines. In sales meetings, employees should come in expecting to share their observations, no matter how small, and a sharp buyer or merchandising manager will recognize and reward the gems.

CHAPTER SUMMARY

The retail buyer or merchandise manager seeks to discover who the store's target customers are, what makes them loyal to that store, and what they want to purchase there. Conversely, negative data—who *does not* shop there, or why someone looks but leaves without purchasing—may be equally insightful. A combination of *predisposition* and *perception* creates a repeat customer, but it also creates one who swears they'll never reenter a certain store *if they perceive* they were treated badly there.

In terms of individual products, consumers make their purchase decisions based on wide-ranging *selection factors*, which are sometimes obvious (package size or color), but sometimes less apparent (like whether the manufacturer is perceived as environmentally conscious). Product development is an attempt to satisfy the selection factors that matter most to a target segment of potential customers.

Would-be buyers are urged to look beyond the obvious internal sources, like sales reports and trend extensions, to gauge the success of a product. These factors are important, but they probably don't tell the whole story. To fill in the details, never overlook the opinions of the floor salespeople, the customer service team that handles complaints in the store, and the input of consumer focus groups that are asked specifically to brainstorm about products and service.

Business partners—vendors, manufacturers, and buying offices—have plenty of specialized information to share. Trade associations and business-to-business trade publications cover almost every facet of retailing in great depth. For bigger-picture economic and population statistics, federal and state governments do extensive research that is almost always available to the public.

American consumers are a tough group to categorize. But there is an oversupply of demographic and psychographic information that can assist retail buyers, and much of it is free for the asking on Internet Web sites. In fact, retailers may have a bigger problem interpreting the data than actually finding it. However, analysis is key to applying the data to make informed buying decisions.

DISCUSSION QUESTIONS

1. Is there a role for intuition in making retail buying decisions? If so, how does it fit?
2. Who do you think does a better buying job in the long run: the retailer who minimizes losses from error by buying cautiously and consistently, or the one who risks failure in order not to miss a big sales winner?
3. Why would a written record of a sales promotion include a note about weather conditions?
4. What kind of focus group would you use to determine consumers' perceptions about the reliability of a certain brand of home appliances?
5. What is the difference between *predisposition* and *perception* in determining a *selection factor*?
6. Some consumer groups say Americans today are being manipulated into most of the buying decisions they make. Do you agree or disagree, and why? Can you cite evidence for your belief?
7. How might a buyer use data from the following:

   a. The Consumer Price Index figures for the previous six months
   b. The mail-order catalogs of two direct competitors and one well-respected merchant in a completely different field
   c. Two different trade associations, with conflicting views on the upcoming Christmas season's sales

8. For each of the lifestyle trends mentioned in this chapter, list one retailer that might benefit from the trend, and one that it might be bad for. Briefly explain your answers.
9. How can a buyer who has a great sense of style be objective in selecting the goods they buy for their company?
10. Answer the three questions in the first paragraph of this chapter.

ENDNOTES

1. Lee Iacocca with William Novak, *Iacocca: An Autobiography* (New York: Bantam Books, 1984).
2. Jack Trout and Al Ries, *Marketing Warfare* (New York: McGraw-Hill, 1997).
3. Sam Roberts, *Who We Are Now: The Changing Face of America in the Twenty-First Century* (New York: Henry Holt and Company/Times Books, 2004).

4. Ibid.
5. Economic impact figures of minority groups from Witek-Combs Communications, Washington, D.C.; and Selig Center, Terry College of Business, University of Georgia, Atlanta, Georgia.
6. Jennifer Ganshirt, cofounder, *Frank About Women*, Winston-Salem, North Carolina, on PRNewswire, May 8, 2004.
7. Melody Treece Vargas, "Catalog Companies Set the Multi-Channel Standard," *Retail Industry* column, October 2004, www.about.com.
8. "Shedding Light on Economic Indicators," *American Funds Investor*, Los Angeles, Fall/Winter 2004 issue.

CHAPTER
4

Merchandise Assortments

In this chapter, we examine the various means by which both manufacturers and retailers strive to distinguish their goods from those of competitors. For the retailer, this involves not only visual identification of the product (its styling, packaging, and so forth) but also a number of policies that influence the assortment of merchandise. You've seen the term **assortment** in this text already—it refers to the selection or range of choices available to consumers within a particular product line. We'll also discuss how buyers "balance" an assortment. This involves deciding the depth and breadth of an assortment or, in consumer terminology, "how many of which sizes, colors, and styles to buy."

The major topics of this chapter provide a basic overview of what to consider as you plan an assortment. They include:

- The different types of brand identification, their potential benefits and challenges
- The importance of private-label merchandise in today's marketplace
- Theories about the optimum breadth and depth of assortment
- How demand and selection factors, seasons, and (in apparel) size, fashion, and fit all work to influence assortment and buying patterns
- Setting policies about assortments for buyers to work from

DIFFERENTIATION THROUGH BRANDING

If you ever feel overwhelmed when you enter a grocery store without a shopping list in hand, you're not alone. There's so much to choose from in stores today! Most of us gravitate toward the products we like and are familiar with, and we made our choices using a variety of selection factors we've already learned about in previous chapters. When we recognize an item by its brand name, we are *differentiating* it from other, similar products—acknowledging that it has a personality, of sorts, that we are choosing over the rest. Manufacturers spend big bucks to prompt this differentiation by packaging and advertising the product in appealing ways. The U.S. Department of Agriculture's Economic Research Service estimates that for each dollar a customer pays for food, 8 cents of it goes to packaging and 4 cents goes to advertising.[1]

The retail buyer's role is to outfit the store with a product selection from which the customer can choose. In most stores (with the exception of manufacturer-owned retailers that sell only their brand name, like Pendleton or The Gap) this means providing a mix of different brands at different price points and quality standards. The buyer does have a target market in mind—a certain type of customer—but uses the product mix to offer a wider range of items to appeal to other consumers as well.

What's in a Name?

National brands are nationally advertised, so they are well known to consumers and have held a dominant place in the retailing of most product categories. They are often referred to as *name brands*. Retailers want (and expect) national manufacturers to maintain fresh, clever, and creative advertising to keep their products "top-of-mind" with the consumer.

However, the growing popularity of **private label** (also called *private brands, store brands,* and *house brands*) has changed the role of national brands, and has made the highly competitive retailing industry even more so. Private labeling is a product development process, in which retailers create their *own* "name-branded" products to be sold exclusively at their stores. Rather than sell the same designer's towels as several other department stores, for instance, you develop your own private label, and sell it at a slightly lower price point than other towels in the department.

The private-label revolution is impressive. In U.S. supermarkets, about one out of every five products purchased is a private label, with dollar sales of almost $43 billion, or 16.3 percent of dollar sales. Sales of store brands grew faster than sales of national brands in supermarket and drugstore chains in 2003. Private-label sales in the grocery industry were up 2.2 percent, compared to only 1.4 percent for name-brand products.[2]

On a store brand, the store's name is evident on the package. But under the private-label banner, there are other major opportunities to build customer loyalty:

- **Co-branding** is the hottest new private-label category, often called **product licensing**. This is when a retailer and a brand-name manufacturer team up to create more "perceived value" than an unknown or generic product. Almost all major drug chains, for example, co-brand diapers and other baby products with major manufacturers, or license the use of celebrities and/or cartoon characters. (Then again, most retailers don't count on their prime co-branded celebrity having to serve a prison term—something Kmart had to deal with, with its still-popular "Martha Stewart" housewares and linens.) For the buyer, picking a hot property, like a new movie, instead of one that ends up being a dud makes all the difference here in the success of the product line.
- **Umbrella branding** is the term for different products in different categories that all are part of a line sold exclusively at a particular store. Most recently, the major supermarket chains have gone head-to-head to develop their own upscale house brands. The Albertsons "Essencia" name is on everything from coffee to cookies to frozen chicken. Kroger has "Private Selection"; Safeway's upscale line is known as the "Safeway Select Gourmet Club."
- **Ethnic branding** may be used to court the diverse U.S. consumer. Kroger has "Buena Comida," and Ahold has the "Mi Casa" brand, to name just two, but specialty Asian brand lines are popping up in grocery chains as well as Latino brands.
- **Price branding** is just what its name implies, a name that indicates a bargain price for the consumer. Kroger's "FMV" (which means "For Maximum Value") and Topco's "ValuTime" brands are examples of this.

There is very little difference between a price-branded product line and a generic product line, except that a particular retail chain has "adopted" the price-branded line as its own. Generics have not disappeared, and there will always be a market for them among price-conscious shoppers. The problem with generics is that marketers have done such a great job over the years, giving shoppers the impression that "generic" means "lower quality."

Private-Label Pros and Cons

That brings us to the benefits and challenges of private-label programs, which vary depending on the group being addressed. For the consumer, private-label goods mean the following:

- More variety, more products to choose from
- Major price reductions (an average of 25 percent less compared to name brands)
- The availability of specialized items, like diet foods or ethnic foods

However, private labels also mean the following:

- Less trust of overall product quality than with national brands.
- One bad experience with one product in a line, and the consumer is likely to decide that the entire line is second-rate.
- In some product categories (apparel, accessories, housewares), the private label may lack the style or prestige of a popular name brand.

For retailers, the pluses and minuses are as follows—first, the positives:

- Increased customer loyalty, as they depend on the store for more products
- More (and more profitable) sales, especially in a tight economy when people are looking for bargains
- A positive image, as the store is perceived as caring about its customers enough to offer them "custom-made" or "specially selected" items
- Freedom to price strategically, without regard to minimums required by name-brand manufacturers

The negatives for retailers often involve the national manufacturers. After all, a private label competes directly with them!

- Less financial support from manufacturers whose products compete directly with the private brands (called "cannibalization" in the industry). The retailer is deprived not only of advertising opportunities but markdown and advertising allowances and other vendor services as well.
- A negative image with consumers, who may resent the store focusing on "off-brands" instead of name brands.
- More difficulty standardizing (and ensuring the quality of) a line of diverse items that come from different manufacturers.

And finally, the retailer must look at the vendors or suppliers and what's in it for them to develop private-label plans and products. The benefits for manufacturers are as follows:

- Smaller vendors, not big enough for national ad campaigns for their products, can thrive doing private label.
- Manufacturers doing business under several brand names get more shelf space in stores and, therefore, the opportunity for more sales.
- Vendors who agree to make private-label products are keeping their competitors from doing it instead.

- The arrangement offers solid partnership opportunities, to grow sales jointly with a committed retailer.

The disadvantages to the suppliers are as follows:

- The relationship with the retailer is jeopardized if the products don't do well.
- Relationships with other retailers are strained when the vendor gives the lion's share of attention to one or two.
- Profit margins on private labels are lower—sales must be much higher to make up the difference, and there also may be higher inventory cost.
- Cannibalization of the vendor's other brands may occur.
- There's always the threat of even cheaper private brands made by others, to drive profit margins down further.

The king of private-brand retailing appears to be the king of retail corporations. Reliable estimates are that between 40 and 50 percent of Wal-Mart's sales are private brands. Its "Great Value" product line debuted in 1992 with 350 items, and has grown annually since then. In both 1997 and 2004, Wal-Mart was given the "Store Brand Retailer of the Year" award by the editors of *Private Label* magazine. But in a variety of well-respected business publications, former vendors and others sworn to anonymity say the company is incredibly tough on its vendors. The demands include allowing Wal-Mart access to suppliers' financial records, and that suppliers' prices and margins be cut, in order to do business with Wal-Mart.

ASSORTMENT PLANNING

Brand names aside, let's look now at planning an overall assortment of products. A store must have policies for the retail buyers and merchandising managers, so they can understand what's expected of them and can do their jobs effectively. Ideally, they have major input in creating the policies. The areas prime for policy making will result in the buyer going to market fully prepared, knowing the following:

- The product lines for which they are responsible, and the price ranges in which they must buy
- The budget they must stick to, and any inventory limitations that requires
- The standards of quality and style that will govern their selections
- The degree to which they must buy, or avoid, standardized goods and seek exclusivity or uniqueness
- The company's ideas about timing of product introductions and seasonal merchandise
- The requirements for meeting (and, ideally, beating) the competition

The following paragraphs offer a brief discussion of a few of these topics—all important, but some less tangible than others.

Quality

Quality means different things to different people, which makes it especially important to define it for a particular retailer's buying staff. The policy can be as simple as, "We always look for the best materials and workmanship available," but specifics are better in our litigious society. These should include definitions of what is an "irregular" or a "second"; when they can be sold and/or returned to the manufacturer.

Some of the larger retailers have a set of written product quality specifications and controls, and little wonder—under most state laws and some federal laws, every product carries an implied (if not expressed) warranty, and the seller may be sued right along with the manufacturer. Product liability cases can result in multimillion dollar settlements and devastating negative publicity.

Price Ranges

To be an important part of the purchasing decision, a selection factor must be significant and observable—and price is among the *most* observable. When all else is equal, most consumers will choose the lower-priced product or, at least, try to find what they want at a lower-priced retailer before going to a higher-priced one. Retailers have used this fact for decades as a simple, direct sales device—mark it down and they'll snap it up—but it is probably too simplistic. It is also true that price is *not* the dominant factor for large segments of the market: customers who are firm in their demands for certain product qualities and services and who are quite willing to pay for them.

From the retail buyer's standpoint, it is important to note that there are trade-off points in most customers' minds when it comes to price. The person who asks about or vaguely intends to buy a $40 shirt may willingly pay $45 for one with an especially appealing color, pattern, fabric, collar design, or combination of these selection factors. If the shirt is marked down to $25 this week, this person may buy two of them. In short, price lines within a broader range may be permissible.

Standardized versus Exclusive Merchandise

In this area, the store policy may be to sell only highly standardized goods—excellent quality, well-known brands that may also be found at other competitor stores—or to specialize in exclusive lines. Exclusivity in retail is a relative term. It typically means the manufacturer will agree to sell to only one store in a market area while, in another market area, it's selling to your competitor. Whatever the policy, it should be in writing and buyers should adhere to it in their vendor negotiations.

Taste and Timing

Taste is hard to define and express, but most of us know good taste from bad when we see it. Good taste involves an aesthetic appreciation and a degree of sophistication that—in apparel, accessory, and some housewares categories—recognizes a purpose or point of view in the style and design of the article. In retail, the definition would surely include an avoidance of extremes, an appropriateness of the design to the target customer, and an assurance that designer items are, indeed, originals and not inexpensive knock-offs masquerading as the real things. Tasteful wares can still be trendsetters, without being garish.

One of the best summations we've seen recently comes from Spiegel, Inc.'s "Company Overview." Note that it does not go into great detail about specific price points, selection factors, or brand names—but it does give the reader an excellent snapshot of the person the retail buyers are aiming to please, her expectations and her taste level.

> Rather than having it all, today's woman is looking for moments when it all comes together. That's what we've learned about our customers through research, and why Spiegel creates products especially for her that are consistent with her lifestyle and style preferences. She wants to convey her own personality and style in both the way she dresses and decorates her home. Spiegel provides a broad, but focused product offering designed and organized to encourage her to express her individuality. We give her options—a complete outfit, a great must-have piece, or just the right item to solve a decorating dilemma in her home—and we offer her a convenient, dependable shopping experience. With solutions that make her life work, we can help her find one of those moments of balance and well-being.[3]

Another factor that impacts store policy is timing. The question of whether to take a leadership role in setting styles for your area, to be a close second, or to observe and wait until a trend is widely accepted, and then jump in must be decided in advance. It's okay to be a follower, not a leader, as long as you are consistent about it.

Other taste-and-timing-related issues that may be part of the policy guide: When should buyers risk an experiment with something really new? How quickly should the depth of stock be increased if initial sales look promising? How soon should something trendy be dropped before it stops selling?

Continuity versus Variety

The maintenance of regular assortments is a must for staple goods, and this is important for everything from convenience foods to men's fashion. Every retailer has its tried-and-true lines—classics that keep the customers coming back whenever they need, say, a pair of navy slacks or an unadorned cream-colored turtleneck. Most stores follow the policy of maintaining regular assortments for their bread-and-butter business and adding promotional merchandise by season to spark interest and prompt extra sales volume. The decisions here will be how much effort should be devoted to the regular assortments versus how much to display and "push" the promotional items. There is only so much shelf space, so a policy should be set.

The variety of product lines is another important consideration. Some stores carry large quantities of very few product lines; others carry a few items from each of hundreds of manufacturers. Logistically, this decision matters quite a bit. If the store is not a major customer of any supplier, the buyer loses clout with the suppliers. There are more orders to process, more (but smaller) deliveries to accept. It is more difficult to merchandise the store for a look and feel of continuity. Conversely, if too few suppliers are used, when one goes out of business, changes hands, or changes fashion direction, it could cause serious repercussions rather quickly in your store.

BREADTH AND DEPTH OF ASSORTMENTS

Time, space, and money are the limiting factors for most retail policy decisions, and nowhere is this more evident than in a store's relative emphasis on breadth and depth of the assortments within the product lines. For instance:

- Store A carries only the most popular selection factors—a few brands, a few styles, a few colors, a few sizes, at a couple of different price points—but keeps the assortment well stocked. Store A management has determined these are the items that are the most likely to sell.
- Store B carries a wide variety of all the selection factors, so that customers can inspect a number of different items that will meet whatever their basic requirements happen to be. Store B management is betting that this way, customers are more likely to buy more than one item, and feel like they're getting an extra "bonus" of satisfaction that there was so much to choose from.

Who is right? It depends on their assortment policies about breadth and depth. A clear set of policies in this area is critical. It determines the actual composition of the inventory and, therefore, reflects the retailer's sales philosophy.

Figure 4-1 illustrates three ways of composing the stock for a product limited to 16 units of inventory. Think of these sets of boxes as items on a shelf—display models of prepackaged men's dress shirts, for instance. The letters a to h represent a combination of selection factors that created different versions of the product—various colors, sleeve lengths, button-down or plain collars, and so on.

The first row, closest to the capital letters A, B, and C, is the **stock face** or **facing**—the first shirts at the edge of the shelf, and the first ones that the customer sees. The rest of the rows are back stock, perhaps a few on the shelf but possibly also in the storeroom. Do you see how even a small assortment of 16 pieces can be mixed and matched to serve different retail purposes?

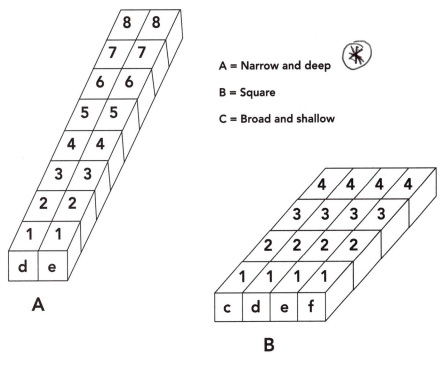

A = Narrow and deep

B = Square

C = Broad and shallow

Figure 4-1 Breadth versus depth in an inventory of 16 units. Letters represent different selection factors (such as different colors or patterns). Numbers represent number of units stocked of each different selection factor.

Obviously, within their limits of budget and inventory space, it's important for the department manager to make the following decisions:

- The width of the display, which is critical in respect to the depth that can be stocked
- The desired depth, which governs the permissible width

Now take a look at Figure 4-2. We know that some selection factors have different rates of acceptance, or sales velocity (i.e., some fly off the shelf, while others just sit there). The assortment can be configured to account for those variances. We'll simplify things by saying that the letters a through h represent eight colors in which the same shirt is available. Further, let's say the following:

- d is the best-selling color.
- e is the second best-seller.
- c and f are tied for third place.
- The remaining four colors (a, b, g, and h) appeal to only a few.

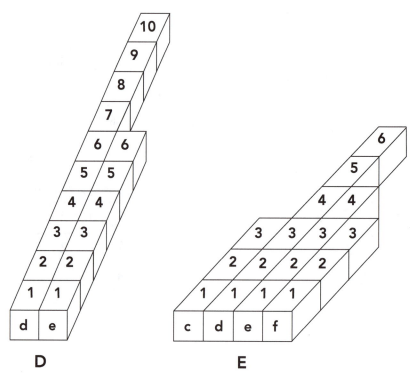

D

D is the "narrow and deep" assortment averaging 8 units of depth per selection factor.

E is the "square" assortment averaging 4 units of depth per selection factor.

E

Figure 4-2 "Model" stocks showing depth of each selection factor balanced to estimated sales. A "broad and deep" assortment would be represented by "G" stocked to a greater average depth. However, this would require a larger inventory allowance than 16 units. A higher inventory could be justified only if higher sales could be predicted.

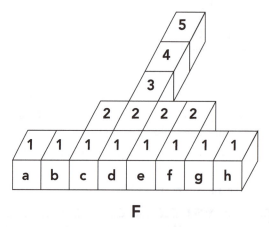

F

F is the "broad and shallow" assortment averaging 2 units of depth per selection factor.

The price-competitive buyer might stock d to a depth of 10 units and e to a depth of 6 units, as shown in display model E. Theoretically, this is the most efficient choice from a cost point of view. Later in the book, in Chapter 5, you'll see how faster turnaround can result from this type of display, since it is easier to stock and takes up less display space. It is easier to order, check, receive, price, and handle only two colors. Counting and keeping inventory control is simpler. Markdowns are minimal, since slow-selling colors are not stocked at all.

However, the buyer for a retailer known for its reliable variety and for high-fashion colors (to suit the most discriminating taste, of course) may carry all eight colors, as shown in Figure 4-1, display model C. Display model B represents the middle-of-the-road, a standard compromise in which only the top four sellers are stocked.

The buyer for display model C is well aware that 25 percent of the inventory is tied up in four colors that may yield only 5 percent of the total sales of that item, and that those four less popular colors will probably end up contributing the most to the markdown record of the product. But the buyer also knows the effect of those four colors, in window displays or in a department of otherwise "typical" colors. They have the power to stop people in their tracks or pull them over for a closer look—even if they end up buying one of the more popular colors.

Shallow stocking does require a more alert sales staff and frequent reordering. The ultimate test of a stocked display is its capacity to satisfy the demands of the one customer who happens to be standing there. If that person wants a shirt in color f, which is momentarily out of stock, the whole assortment loses some of its punch—although the customer may still accept one of the remaining colors and consider it a satisfactory substitute.

Determining Breadth

In the battle for patronage, breadth of assortment is an important non-price-competitive weapon. For many people, the variety itself is a sales magnet. It looks more exciting and attractive, and there's a better chance the shopper will find something interesting with a wider selection. The more a retailer's clientele is impacted (or even dominated) by mass thinking—that is, the less important differences in detail are, the more sense it makes for the buyer to emphasize depth at the expense of breadth.

However, for the more discriminating or fashion-conscious customer, a wider choice is required. This also applies to assortments made up of "mix-and-match" separates. It's difficult to explain on paper, but when it comes to apparel, the presence of high-fashion selection factors tends to lend an air of fashion authenticity to the whole assortment, even if it is made up primarily of the most popular two or three colors.

Company Image

Another consideration to influence a retailer's policy about breadth/depth balance is the desired image of the company itself—the attitude that consumers have about a retail firm in relation to their set of expectations. Together with the ambience of the store and the way the store communicates its philosophy to its target consumers (advertising, displays, and so on), the role of the merchandise mix is to meet the expectations the store has set.

In fashion or home furnishings, a store with a broad assortment policy might advertise central themes, looks, and ideas. Those with narrower assortments would be better off featuring individual items, backed by deep stocks of colors and sizes. A well-planned advertising strategy goes hand in hand with the assortment philosophy.

Timing of Selling Cycles

When selling anything that is subject to volatile fashion trends or seasonal changes, the opening assortments are wide and shallow. This is because many new selection factors appear on the market, and their degree of acceptance is not yet known. The buyer must use considerable judgment at market, culling out what may not sell—but the fact is, there are always items about which you just have a hunch and will want to add them to the collection early to test them. Then, when early customer response reveals likely concentrations of demand, the stock can be reduced in breadth and expanded in depth.

This process of narrowing and deepening continues into the peak of a season. Finally, toward the end of a season, most of the remaining regular stock should be concentrated in the lowest price lines and on the most popular selection factors. Pieces that can't be fit into this orderly liquidation process will remain as "broken" assortments, and they may be gathered with some specially priced promotional items (from vendors' overstocks) brought in to bolster sales volume late in the season.

Two theories of demand govern timing issues. First, customers of the higher-priced goods tend to buy in the earlier part of the season. Second, customers become less discriminating as the season advances toward, and past, its peak. They are more willing to sacrifice selectivity because they realize they've waited until mid-season, and they come in fully expecting that the stock may have been picked over.

An early-season assortment, and peak-selling assortments, may be called the elected model. Breadth and depth are chosen and reflect balance and realistic sales expectations. An end-of-season assortment has two components: a basic model (the minimum requirements of assortment) and leftovers that represent unbalanced overstock. The idea is to plan and price to minimize the latter, so the store isn't stuck with it.

Increasing Breadth

The breadth of an assortment may be expanded by adding product lines or by adding versions of product lines. The results of the two (seemingly similar) maneuvers are actually quite different. The first tends to bring additional, or supplementary, sales. The second brings complementary sales that may be shared with other versions of the product line.

First, the addition of new product lines is less likely to divert sales from the established assortment. When shoe stores added handbags to their stocks, they detracted nothing from the sale of shoes—handbag sales were wholly additional. In fact, the new product line was priced to bring traffic into the store and thereby increase the sales of shows. This **pulling power** will figure prominently in other discussions in the book.

The addition of other versions of the line means adding more selection factors to an established product line—color, material, brand, style, or price. This move will add to the total sales volume of the line, but most likely at a diminishing rate of speed. Each worthwhile addition has some complementary sales and pulling power, but within limits. For example, let's say a buyer began a winter season with a sweater assortment of six colors, selling at a rate of 144 sweaters per week, or an average of 24 per week for each color. If the buyer adds six more colors, will sales automatically double? Probably not.

What might happen depends on many different circumstances. The presence of the seventh color might add six sales a week to the category. (This is called the **net marginal productivity** of the seventh color.) However, this does not mean that the recorded sales would show six units for the new color. It might have sold at the rate of eight per week . . . but three of the sales credited to it might have been made from the first six colors, if the seventh had not been available. In other words, the new color is nice, but one of the "old" colors would still have prompted a sale. The new color "shares demand" with the old ones, depending on the whim of the customer or the ability of the salesperson to sell that customer a sweater, no matter what the color.

Statistically speaking, you might also assume that the new color had enough pulling power to prompt one additional sale of each of the six original colors, just because more people stopped by the attractive display to look. So you see, sometimes it's not as important *what* the customer buys; it's important *that* he or she buys.

An eighth color might sell at the rate of six units per week, with three "shared" sales, and one "pulling-power" sale, giving it a net marginal productivity of four. And what if the buyer jumps forward and adds more sweater colors? Let's say there are 10. It's possible that *all* of its sales are shared with the nine other colors, giving it no complementary effect. If it still produced an extra sale for the nine prior colors, its presence in the stock would have to be justified (or rejected) on the basis of that factor alone. An eleventh color might not even add pulling power to the assortment, thereby netting a marginal productivity of zero—and becoming completely unjustified.

Interestingly, somewhere in this process a peculiar phenomenon takes place. The addition of colors 12 and 13 may make the assortment so wide as to make it a "dominant competitor" instead of a "competent competitor." At this point, added colors may share almost wholly with prior colors, but the pulling power may increase sufficiently for the newest colors to still show rising productivity. This phenomenon, in theory, will continue briefly to the point of diminishing returns. By the eighteenth color, for instance, the marginal productivity has shrunk back to zero.

Figure 4-3(a) is a fairly simple illustration of the marginal productivity concept. A single variant of the product line sells at the rate of four. (It doesn't matter whether the rate is four per week, per day, or whatever . . . or whether the variant is a color, style, price, etc.) The marginal productivity of the second item is three. A third variant lifts the sales to 9, a fourth to 10, and the fifth shows a marginal productivity of zero. Put the graph in table form, and it looks like Table 4-1.

Figure 4-3(a) shows the total sales that accumulate as variables are added. The shaded areas indicate the net amount added to sales by each variant. Notice how the sales curve slopes upward at a decelerating rate until it flattens out at the fifth increment. Figure 4-3(b) shows the net added sales of each increment as its marginal productivity, starting with four and ending at zero.

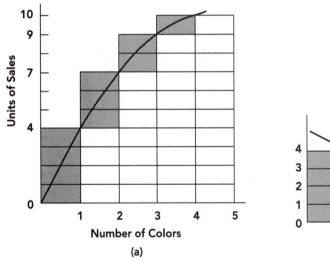

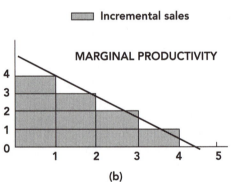

Figure 4-3 Sales accumulate as variables of an assortment are added.

Table 4-1 Another Way of Charting Marginal Productivity		
Number of variants in stock	Total sales of product line	Marginal productivity of the incremental variant
1	4	4
2	7	3
3	9	2
4	10	1
5	10	0

Figure 4-4 Total productivity of a dominant assortment.

Figure 4-4 shows the effect of the continuous addition of variants (incre-ments) to a dominant assortment. Notice that the first five columns on this graph are identical to those in Figure 4-3(a). At the sixth increment, marginal productiv-ity rises again. It climbs at the seventh increment, falls back at the eighth, and be-comes "zero" again as the ninth variant is added to the assortment.

What does all this mean? Adding variants behind the point of zero pro-ductivity does not increase the selling power of the stock—it merely creates a pseudo-assortment.

As you can see, marginal productivity is very hard to measure, but the smart buyer who wants to build an efficient and productive assortment must understand the concept. Will adding "one more color" produce enough added sales to defray the incremental costs?

Competitive Challenges

What constitutes a "competent" or "dominant" assortment depends on the merchandise, the retailer, and the competition. A grocery store with a small health and beauty section may offer one brand of nail polish in a dozen basic-but-popular shades. The warehouse and materials-handling teams can't be bothered with an open-carton or split-carton handling process to support the low sales velocity of added shades. The buyer works on the assumption that sales from these few shades offer the optimal profit situation.

A buyer for the cosmetics department of a department store or large drug-store may feel that it will take 40 shades of at least three brands to really be "in business." This buyer also realizes that most of the sales will come from a few of the basic-but-popular polishes; but the wide assortment better meets the reputation of the store as a cosmetic leader with all the latest products, and buffers it from competitive challenges.

Adding new products and new versions—like lowering price points—becomes addictive. It's fun and it keeps things interesting. But a high proportion of sales volume comes from relatively few core items in any product line.

This gets tougher when the product is something like shoes, in which any single style is available in 40-plus combinations of size and width! A chain shoe store may cut these potential combinations by one-quarter, or even by half, by carrying only medium-width shoes, with a second width (some narrow, some wide) depending on the style. The buyer who is committed to keeping the maximum number of options in stock will find distressingly low marginal productivity—but sometimes, the need to carry such sizes is dictated by store policy, to please that hard-to-fit customer.

As a general rule, all else being equal, the width of assortment in a given product line should vary somewhat directly with the number of product lines being carried. The profitability of the mix should be the main consideration.

The one exception to this rule may be discount stores where, in spite of many product lines, managers know that only a few items are the top sellers for their price-conscious clientele. Hence, they tend to carry deep and narrow stock assortments. (The rather colorful industry jargon for this theory used to be, "Thick on the best, to hell with the rest.")

The SKU Explosion

 The continuous hunt for new products; more precise demands by consumers; and producers who battle fiercely for greater shares of their markets, all combine to create a massive proliferation of SKUs (stock keeping units) in all segments of retailing. For example, consider Coca-Cola. Originally, there was one Coke in one size, an 8-ounce glass bottle, with one SKU. Over the years, **line extensions**—different versions of the same brand-name product—and various package sizes have been added. Today, there are dozens of SKUs, as each of these products is available in a variety of package sizes, from 12-ounce cans to 2-liter bottles to 24-pack cases:

Coca-Cola	Cherry Coke
Coke Classic	Diet Cherry Coke
Diet Coke	Vanilla Coke
Caffeine-Free Coke	Diet Vanilla Coke
Caffeine-Free Diet Coke	Diet Coke with Lemon
	C2 (low-carbohydrate)

It is unlikely that even the largest retailer would stock all these varieties in each size. If it did, each product's SKU would represent a separate entity in purchasing, inventory control, point-of-sale recording, warehousing, and so on.

Soft drinks are just one example. The exponential explosion of choice in almost every product category impacts stores heavily. A typical large, traditional department store stocks more than 1 million SKUs depending on its merchandise mix. So the buyer who determines the relative firmness (**demand rigidity**) of the customers' selection factors can pare down the least profitable SKUs and plan assortments that contain just the right mix of profitable ones.

Depth and Demand Rigidity

What determines demand rigidity? There are five basic factors:

- **Primary or intended use.** This is the basic use the customer expects from the product.
- **Secondary considerations.** These are "wants" that are substitutable if necessary. A woman who needs a gold handbag for a formal evening event may not care if it's adorned with sequins, beads, or simply made of gold fabric—as long as it's gold. However, the color *has to be gold*.
- **Typical purchasing habits that relate to the product.** Is it a convenience item, a necessity, or a specialty item? How "important" is it, overall, to the customer who seeks it?
- **Price lines.** Consumers determined to find a bargain aren't going to buy something that is not in their price range. Consumers who are willing to pay more are also more sensitive about other selection factors.
- **Urgency of purchase.** How soon do they need it? Is the formal evening event *tonight*? Is Mother's Day *this weekend*? As we've already discussed, customers who delay holiday and seasonal purchases usually realize they're shopping from depleted inventories and are therefore less selective.

We've also learned that the wants of the consumer are not always clearly defined in his or her mind, and that the elements in the stock may overlap when it comes to satisfying these wants because the customer, no matter what he or she is shopping for, may decide on (or be talked into) something other than what he or she originally intended to buy. The bed-and-bath department has an "adequate" (not huge) assortment of heavy wool and lighter electric blankets, because the customer who comes in looking for wool may be "sold" on the virtues of the lighter-weight, but just as toasty, electric blanket.

What all this amounts to is a bewildering variance of rigidity about their expressed wants as individuals. That is why we sort them instead into groups—to better gauge discernable patterns, which can then be used to construct an assortment. Why think about demand rigidity?

1. It is essential to plan a full assortment in each of the selection factors that are rigid—that is, the ones that they feel strongly about. The assortment may be less complete in the factors that are the most flexible. Stock control records and replenishment procedures are set up to facilitate

keeping up the assortments at the points at which the demand is the most rigid.

2. The physical stock should be arranged according to demand rigidity, especially in areas of the store where a customer culls through and selects his or her own items without the assistance of a salesperson.

3. Displays will be more effective (and the customer will be influenced to buy more than one item) because all the merchandise in a single location meets the most rigid requirements.

4. This type of planning helps determine how to set up unit stock controls. It is both expensive and time-consuming to analyze all sales and inventory by every possible selection factor; better to keep closer track of the items by rigid selection factors and handle the flexible ones less frequently. This facilitates prompter reordering of the most popular items in an assortment.

PLANNING SALES BY SELECTION FACTORS

The buyer must buy individual items by SKU, but it is first essential to plan the assortment on a broader basis. The central ideas or primary demands that make up assortments are known as **classification controls**. It is important for buyers to constantly review the individual products they select, to see if demand patterns are developing (or receding) around these common denominators. Following are some examples:

- Ease (or at least, less work) in performing specific household tasks
- Any type of fashion trend: elaborately embroidered sweaters, short or long hemlines, and so forth
- A specific, sharp sales increase for any particular product
- Better sales overall for a certain type of apparel—teen goods, or career clothing

The terms *classification* and *type* are often used interchangeably, but for this discussion, **classification** is the generic or end-use designation, and **type** refers to more specific selection factors *within* a classification. For instance, dresses are a classification. Within the classification, there are types of dresses: conservative, youthful, tailored, ornate, dressy, casual, and so on. If sales are analyzed in this way, the buyer may learn that 30 percent of the department's customers prefer dressy styles, but 70 percent prefer youthful styles, and the buyer can then adhere to those basic proportions in making assortment decisions about dresses.

The only caveat here is that you can't always equate actual sales with potential demand. The store may have sold very few tailored styles simply because few were carried in stock. Still, "typing" the classifications is a good beginning barometer.

Brands and Designer Names

Examining brand sales item by item is not enough. All sales of all items of a particular brand also should be combined to study the performance of the brand as a whole. This gives the buyer meaningful data with which to negotiate vendor contracts, as well as allowing for smarter assortment planning.

The tendency in some stores is to stock a dozen or so of a new brand or item if a couple of customers request it. This practice, while considerate, piles up a large stock of slow-selling odds and ends that eat up capital and shelf space and cut into the potential of proven best-sellers. Often, one or two brands in a price range will satisfy the demands of the majority of customers. Where slow-selling brands must be carried for one reason or another, it may be smart to track them as a unified group. This requires less stock than would be needed to represent each selection factor within each brand.

In fashion-related categories (furniture, housewares, apparel, accessories), designer names used to be true badges of distinction and hallmarks of top quality. In today's marketplace, their impact has been diluted—not only by the proliferation of lower-priced imitators but by the fact that some designers plastered their names onto so many products as to weaken the perceived benefits of exclusivity for consumers. One area of the department store is an exception. Cosmetics and fragrances are a highly profitable category, even with an extraordinary number of brands competing for market share. For the most part, however, a retailer's prestige no longer depends on how many exclusive product lines it can assemble and maintain.

Price Range

As mentioned, price is a very stable selection factor, so sales analysis by price will provide reliable planning guidelines. Overall economic changes (whether it's inflation, recession, prosperity, etc.) can result in wild fluctuations, however. Another sharp change would be technology-related—classic cases in past decades being the radical price downturns of microwave ovens and personal computers.

The one important note for assortment planning is that demand can be quite flexible *within a price range*. Part of your sales analysis might be experimenting with different "price endings"—the cents behind the dollars. It is a waste to price something at $12.95 if it can be sold just as effectively at $12.99 or $13.00. When pennies count, the difference is much more significant to the store than to its customers.

Color, Style, and Material

These three selection factors are not as stable as those previously mentioned, but they do change gradually enough to be somewhat predictable within broad groupings. For forecasting purposes, a fashion buyer can group clothing colors into three headings: black (or in the summer, white), the season's basic colors, and so-called **high shades**. In clothing, the relative importance of black the previous year almost always carries through into the following year. The same is true of basic seasonal colors. However, in the case of high shades—the trendy, high-demand "most fashionable" colors for a season—what is a must-have this year will almost surely not be in style next year. Early in the season, the buyer can experiment with a number of high shades and watch customer response. Some will catch on; others will be rejected. There are also demand cycles for different tints and tones of the "hot" colors. They may be rich and deep in the fall, pastel in the spring. Again, to make your judgment calls effective, you must know your target customer before the season begins.

With style details, like shoulder prominence, hemlines, fullness of skirts or slacks, it is more critical to watch the trends over a period of successive weeks or months than it is to look at the current sales percentages for a given week. Generic silhouettes of garments—and also the popularity of particular fabrics— may last for several years or, at least, several seasons. The central idea behind demand is more quickly apparent if, in the case of garments, sales can be classified as lightweight, medium-weight, heavy-weight; or large-pattern versus small-pattern.

Sales by Vendor

Finally, as mentioned in the previous section on "Brands and Designer Names," do not overlook the opportunity to view a vendor's performance as a whole. You will soon determine which manufacturer's styles sell best and at a reasonable profit, and which sell poorly or require constant attention to "move." Such a study is called a *vendor analysis*. Of course, what you may find is that even good resources can have a bad season. But without the analysis, the buyer is not a truly informed customer—of the vendor.

Size and Fit

The most rigid selection factors are size and fit, which makes the conflict between breadth and depth in an assortment rather complex. Fortunately, the planning concepts of stability and clustering make the problem more manageable.

The relative frequency of demand by sizes remains quite stable from period to period. Analysis of sales in a misses' dress category might yield the following size scale as a guide for future ordering:

Size	4	6	8	10	14	14	Total
Percent of Total	6	10	23	25	21	15	100

This is an excellent guide, but not faultless. Remember, always investigate whether (in this case) the weak performance of sizes 4 and 6 were the result of inadequate stock. Then, too, a check of the same information over a few different periods will yield an even clearer picture. Even specialized stores, like plus sizes or big-and-tall men shops, can use size scales as a determination of stock stability.

Figure 4-5 illustrates the concentration that commonly occurs in the demand frequency for a selection factor, called *clustering*. On a larger scale, it's the same principle as the shirts we looked at in Figure 4-2, only this assortment is based on a sales analysis of 15 styles of designer men's shoes, advertised as a group by a major department store. The numbers in the grid show how many of the styles were represented in each size, or size-width combination. Thus, all 15 style numbers were represented in the very popular size 9D and 14 styles were available in size 9B; but for the seldom-ordered size 9EE, only four styles were stocked; only one in 9E, and so on. The quantity for each style is not included on the chart, but the proportionate distribution of the styles illustrates the clustering of demand frequencies.

Width	AA	A	B	C	D	E	EE	TOTAL	%
SIZE									
5					1	1	1	3	0.6
5½					1	1	1	3	0.6
6					3	1	1	5	1.0
6½				1	11	1	2	15	2.9
7				1	15	1	4	21	4.0
7½				1	15	1	4	21	4.0
8			10	9	15	1	4	39	7.5
8½			10	9	15	1	4	39	7.5
9	1	1	14	9	15	1	4	45	8.7
9½	1	1	14	9	15	1	4	45	8.7
10	1	1	14	9	15	1	4	45	8.7
10½	1	1	14	9	15	1	4	45	8.7
11	1	1	14	9	15	1	4	45	8.7
11½	1	1	14	9	15	1	4	45	8.7
12	1	1	14	9	15	1	4	45	8.7
13	1	1	14	1	15	1	2	35	6.7
14	1	1	2		3	1	2	10	1.9
15	1	1	2		3	1	2	10	1.9
16					2			2	0.4
17					2			2	0.4
TOTAL	10	10	136	85	206	18	55	520	100.3
%	1.9	1.9	26.2	16.3	39.6	3.5	10.6		100

Figure 4-5 A clustering pattern may form in a wide scatter of men's foot sizes.

Let's look at the entire playing field the buyer had to work with. There are 140 different combinations of shoe length (size) and width (that's 20 lengths and 7 widths). The 20 lengths range from size 5 to 17, including some one-half intervals. The seven widths range from very narrow (AA) to very wide (EE). To fill this entire skeleton with only a single pair of each style in each size would require 520 pairs of shoes, in a total of 101 sizes! What's a buyer to do?

On the chart, notice that the most popular size range (the highest demand frequency) is outlined, and that's where the assortment is concentrated. There are 404 pairs represented in the 32 outlined sizes, 44 pairs are in the 11 outlined sizes in EE widths (where the store's figures may show a growing demand), and 72 pairs spread over the remaining 58 sizes of lower demand frequency.

The latter are the sizes that usually produce more remainders than sales, which stoke the markdown fires at season's end. It will also take heavy markdowns to clear them out of the store, because their market is relatively small. Lest you assume that the store simply is ignoring its male customers with special footwear needs, remember that this patron—who is well aware that his feet are narrower or wider, larger or smaller than the norm—customarily shops at a specialty store anyway for these items. So the merchant's time, space, and money can be better used to deepen the stock of sizes that will represent the heart of the demand. It's true that there will be some lost sales, but on the few occasions when someone makes a special request, a special order can be made to fill it, if that is the store policy.

Some retailers stock wide and shallow in an attempt to foster a reputation for having wide product selections—something for everyone. But few retailers can afford this luxury.

OTHER CONCEPTS OF ASSORTMENT

One of the broader but still effective concepts of assortment planning comes from Joseph B. Siegel, fashion merchandising authority and founding partner of the consulting firm Joseph B. Siegel and Associates. Siegel has a simple theory for planning seasonal stock:

- Five percent should be new, "cutting-edge" fashion. A store might have the reputation for broad assortments of apparel, but this small segment is critical as evidence that the retailer is a leader, not a follower. It tells the customer that the store is tuned into the latest trends. This merchandise should be displayed prominently to maximize customer awareness. It's admittedly high risk but, since only 5 percent of the stock is assigned to this group, losses are controlled.
- Fifteen percent should be "fashion right." These are the clothes with fashion ideas that were new last year or last season, and are now gaining broad consumer acceptance. This group should be advertised, with the major portion of the department's promotional budget focused on this merchandise.

- Eighty percent should be "fashionable." This is the solid, widely accepted merchandise that already enjoys popularity with consumers.

Siegel adds that markdowns in this assortment should come only from the "cutting-edge"and "fashion right" segments of the inventory.

Using Fashion and Product Life Cycles

From another common angle, a fashion cycle may be viewed as a selection factor or combination of factors that enjoy a period of high demand, followed by diminishing demand (that may happen quickly or slowly). At least, that is a commonly held stereotype. The cycle is often represented as a bell-shaped curve, as in Figure 4-6. The five stages look clearly defined on paper, but in the real world of fashion, they merge into each other. The "peak," for example, includes part of the "take-off" and part of the "decline."

This curve represents styles, but it also holds true for individual products—and buyers who want to stock a product in their stores must consider where it happens to be in its life cycle as they determine customer demand.

- In the testing phase, the product is introduced and takes its first tentative steps into the marketplace jungle. Sales are low, losses are low, but risk is high. The customer most likely to buy it is willing to spend a bit more money for it because it is "new." Many products, however, never make it out of the introductory phase.
- In the take-off phase, sales are picking up because competitors sit up and take notice of the new product, and the original consumers tell their friends about it. Profits are high, and more retailers want to sell it. This is also the point at which lower-priced "knock-offs" and/or legitimate variations of the product (called **line extensions**) begin to appear.
- At its peak, the product has reached the so-called maturity of its life cycle. Ironically, this is the point at which competition is the fiercest. The maximum numbers of retailers are carrying the product, and its selling price often drops, so profits begin to fall.

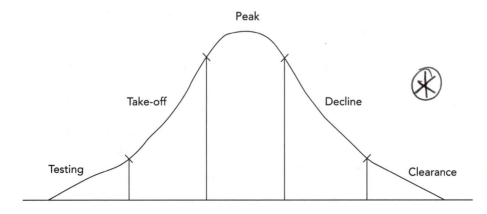

Figure 4-6 The rise and fall concept of a fashion life cycle.

- The product that begins a life cycle decline can either disappear from the market gradually or transform into a reliable staple item for which there is a reduced (but constant) demand. Either way, stocking the declining product is a relatively high risk for retailers, because it may sit on the shelf until...
- A major markdown makes it appealing to the bargain-conscious shopper who finally takes it home. Clearance is, of course, the merchant's last-ditch effort to unload the product rather than have to store it any longer.

SETTING ASSORTMENT POLICY

This chapter has covered the many facets of assortment planning, but it is important to note that the whole process begins with a solid set of store policies that guide and govern the retail buyers' actions. An old truism is that "a retailer gets the trade that he or she deserves." Just as policies are aimed at definite groups of consumers, the policies themselves will determine the groups that patronize the store.

It is troublesome to report that few retailers have detailed centralized policies, and even fewer have committed them to writing. What usually happens without this framework is that different departments evolve and cater to different types of customers, without building the overall store loyalty necessary to realize a profitable business.

The policies can be both clear-cut and flexible, and should provide an overview of the store's image, the marketplace, and the prices of goods to be sold. What kinds of topics might be covered? Here's a sample:

1. **The nature of the merchandise lines carried.** A policy of fashion leadership is more important to a women's specialty store than to a drugstore. This is not to say the drugstore has no interest in fashion—in cosmetics, it may want to be a leader. A written policy keeps everyone, from senior management to buyers to floor sales staffers, focused on the big picture.
2. **Characteristics of the trading area.** Although it is true that retailers select the customer groups they wish to appeal to, the choice may be limited by the general demographics of the trading area. Large areas have all kinds of room for all kinds of retailers; smaller communities may present limitations.
3. **Community need.** Demographic information may reveal the need for merchandise with special attributes for an underserved market. This is certainly true in large trading areas, but a store in a smaller community may do well to develop specialized stocks, or more personalized service, to compete with the less convenient big-city stores. An interesting example is the 2004 survey of grocery store managers compiled by the National Grocers Association, in which members around the United States were asked, "How do you feel grocers can best compete with Wal-Mart Supercenters?" By far the most popular answer (56 percent): Service.[4]

4. **Competition.** The creative way to best the competition is to compare the services it provides with the needs and wants of the trading area, and then buy those goods that evoke awareness and response. Remember: It is okay to copy the things that a competitor does right. What they *don't carry* or what they *don't do well* represent the possibilities for creative, distinctive enterprise.

5. **Pricing.** Decide what your target customers are willing to pay and try not to stray too far from that range. We mentioned earlier that a price line is just that—a range within which to work profitably.

6. **Available capital.** When policies change, it takes time to "walk the talk," making employees and customers aware of them. Broadening assortments, or venturing into newer types of merchandise, may not produce the quick results hoped for. Programs undertaken without adequate financing are destined to be a struggle, and possibly a failure. It is better to adopt policies that lead to fast turnover of stocks—narrow assortments of key selection factors—if the company budget is tight or the economy of the area is turbulent.

7. **Personal capabilities of the merchant.** To undertake the task of appealing to a sophisticated or highly discriminating clientele without sufficient experience is to court disaster. Whatever policies are set, they should be limited to what can honestly be implemented successfully. In the start-up phase of a retail business, this involves some real soul-searching.

Even stores that have been in business for years benefit from rethinking their merchandising policies and assortment planning tenets periodically, to refresh and refocus their efforts. As you've seen in this chapter, there is plenty to think about!

CHAPTER SUMMARY

Retailers and product manufacturers jump through a lot of hoops to get consumers to notice their wares over their competitors'. Differentiation is the term for making a product stand out from the rest. In recent years, one of the chief ways this is being done is through the creation of private-label or private-brand merchandise. The retailer has a hand in developing a custom product with a particular name on it, for exclusive sale by that retailer. Private brands are a successful and fast-growing part of the retail industry.

Before the retailer can decide on a private brand (or anything else to sell), extensive research must be done to determine what selection factors will have the greatest sales impact on the merchandise assortments—the groups of merchandise to be sold. Selection factors are those qualities that prompt the customer to select one item over another. Some selection factors—like the size or fit of a garment—are rigid; that is, the consumer would not be willing to buy the wrong size just to have the item. But most selection factors are flexible, at least to a certain extent. If a shopper comes in to buy a blouse of a certain style and color, if that style isn't available (or is available but in a different color), the shopper may well buy something else if he or she likes it enough.

Retail buyers use selection factor data to determine the breadth and depth of the assortments they select. Breadth refers to the number of choices (colors, styles, sizes) within an assortment; depth refers to the number of each item to be ordered for display and inventory. A couple of things are true about breadth and depth: first, that almost no store can stock *every* possible iteration (size, style, color) of every item; and second, the retailer should have written policies that clearly explain the store's image and expectations so that buyers have solid guidelines to follow when they go to market.

DISCUSSION QUESTIONS

1. What is a shallow stocking?
2. How would a buyer determine the depth and breadth of stock for a clothing department that featured mix-and-match separates?
3. How would a product development team go about branding a potentially controversial product—a line of genetically modified food—for public acceptance?
4. Would you agree to stock a new item in an existing product line based solely on its potential pulling power? Why or why not?
5. Reading the Spiegel "Company Overview," list five selection factors you think would be important for Spiegel's housewares buyer in order to satisfy that target customer. Now list five selection factors the apparel buyer might need to consider. (The two lists may overlap, if necessary.)
6. Think about the five stages of product life cycles, and from your own experience as a supermarket customer, name one product you've noticed in each "phase" of its life. Briefly explain why you chose them.
7. How should a buyer approach the launch of a private-label brand without angering the competing national manufacturers with whom the store already has good relationships?
8. Which type of store needs more breadth in its assortments: a shoe department in a department store or a specialty shoe store? Why?
9. Why does a buyer have to bother with determining the demand rigidity of selection factors if it is clear what the selection factors *are* for a group of buyers?
10. Add one or two topics to the list of assortment policies that you think should also be included in a store's written guidelines for buyers.

ENDNOTES

1. USDA Economic Research Service data (Washington, D.C.: Food Marketing Institute, February 2004).
2. *2004 Private Label Yearbook* (New York: Private Label Manufacturers' Association).
3. Excerpt from Spiegel Company Overview, www.spiegel.com, October 2004.
4. *NGA Marketing Survey 2004* (Arlington, VA: National Grocers Association's Grocers Research and Education Foundation).

CHAPTER

5

Planning and Control

In this chapter, we put the concepts and principles of assortment planning to work, and we turn from the fashion implications of buying decisions to the *financial* implications. We delve into the specifics of units and dollars—how much you can buy, in accordance with how much your company has to spend. The major topics include:

- How budgets are determined (and checked periodically) for a buying season or department
- Stockturn and how to determine the productivity of the merchandise as an investment
- Staple stock controls, or how stores ensure their basics and best-sellers are always available

- Factors to consider when dealing with seasonal merchandise
- How to buy even when the budget is very tight

TOP-DOWN VERSUS BOTTOM-UP

Merchandise planning is approached from two directions: "top-down" or "bottom-up." The **top-down** approach is so named because it begins with the senior executives or centralized office making sales estimates, either for a segment of the operation or a certain time period. The overall sales forecast is then divided into smaller segments, often by percentages being applied based on experience and judgment.

The **bottom-up** approach (also called a **built-up** plan) requires the managers of each individual store (or department, in a smaller store) to forecast what its potential sales should be for a time period—usually a quarter (three months). When the time period is over, the actual sales and expenditures are compared to the forecast and reconciled.

Figure 5-1 shows a top-down plan for a five-store chain of children's clothing stores. Top management has forecast sales of $225,000 for the upcoming quarter. This amount has been distributed down to the five stores (as seen in Plan a) and three departments (as seen in Plan b), to meet the planned sales total.

The bottom-up approach to the same budget is illustrated by Plans c and d. In Plan c, each store has been studied for its potential sales, and its forecast is entered on the plan. The chain total for this plan comes to $234,000—which is $9,000 more than the top-down plan. A comparison shows the difference is not great (4 percent), but it is centered in two stores. The original budget (Plan a) for Store A shows a sales budget of $3,000 more (about 6.5 percent) than the $45,000 allotted to it in the control plan. Store E shows a much wider discrepancy—$6,500, or 16 percent.

This will undoubtedly result in some debate. If store planners can justify their figure with convincing reasons, it may be accepted and the control (top-down) plan may be revised. Otherwise, the plans for Stores A and E must be revised, or a compromise must be reached to revise *both* sets of plans.

Now look at the sales of the individual store departments in Plans b and d. The bottom-up plan of $236,000 is $11,000 (nearly 5 percent) higher than the control plan, with the increase concentrated in girls' and teens' wear.

Plans e and f show how each department's sales have been distributed within Store A. Note that in the control Plan e, the sales total is exactly what the store's planned total was—$45,000 (from Plan a). That is because they were derived by starting with $45,000 and apportioning it down to the three departments, each based on past sales performance.

SALES BY STORES

Store	Plan (a) % Total Chain	Plan (a) Dollars	Plan (c) Dollars	Plan (c) % Total Chain
Total Chain	100	225,000		
A	20	45,000	48,000	20.5
B	16	36,000	37,000	15.8
C	20	45,000	45,000	19.3
D	26	58,500	57,000	24.4
E	18	40,500	47,000	20.0
Total Chain			234,000	100.0

Plan (a) is a top-down or generic plan which apportions $225,000 sales among five stores.

Plan (c) is a built-up plan of sales for each store which adds to $234,000 for the chain.

SALES BY DEPARTMENTS

Store	Plan (b) % Total Chain	Plan (b) Dollars	Plan (d) Dollars	Plan (d) % Total Chain
Total Chain	100	225,000		
Girls & Teens	30	67,500	78,000	33.0
Infants	50	112,500	112,000	47.5
Little Boys	20	45,000	46,000	19.5
Total Chain			236,000	100.0

Plan (b) distributes the $225,000 sales budget over three departments by estimating the normal percentage each would be expected to contribute to the total.

Plan (d) is a built-up plan for each department which adds to $236,000.

SALES OF STORE "A" BY DEPARTMENTS

Store	Plan (e) % Total Chain	Plan (e) Dollars	Plan (f) Dollars	Plan (f) % Total Chain
Total Chain	100	45,000		
Girls & Teens	30	13,500	16,000	33.3
Infants	50	22,500	23,000	48.0
Little Boys	20	9,000	9,000	18.7
Total Store			48,000	100.0

Plan (e) picks up the $45,000 budget for store A from plan (a) above, and distributes it by departments.

Plan (f) is a built-up plan by departments which adds to $48,000.

Figure 5-1 Top-down and bottom-up sales plans for a chain of five stores with three departments.

Plan f is the bottom-up plan, in which each department was studied and planned separately. Obviously, the department managers felt that girls' and teens' wear was selling well enough to warrant a budget of $16,000 instead of the $13,500 in the control plan. This was probably also the reason that Store A's overall sales potential was pegged at $48,000 in Plan c.

To summarize the basic budget examples, the bottom-up plan shows that the store's sales result from the detailed budgeting at the store level. This is just the reverse of top-down planning, in which the details of the specific plan result from goals already set by senior management.

Is there a right or wrong way to plan? In actual retail situations, good planners use both approaches to get two different perspectives. The underlying assumption (not always true, but a good barometer) is that wherever both sets of plans agree, they are likely to be reliable estimates. Buyers and merchandisers learn to work with probabilities, not certainties. However, one thing *is* certain in merchandise budgeting: When the control plans and the built-up plans do not agree, something is wrong somewhere. The two sets of plans should be reconciled to a point of reasonable agreement.

THE GENERAL MERCHANDISE PLAN

Figure 5-2 shows a common type of departmental dollar plan. We'll come back to it a couple of times in this section. The four abbreviations used in it are as follows:

Last year's performance (LY)   This year's plan (PL)
Revisions to plan (RV)   Actual performance this year (ACT)

Sales are always planned first. Then, by various methods, stocks (in dollars) are set for the beginning of each month. Probable markdown requirements are also entered in the months they should be taken. **Retail purchases** indicate the amount of merchandise that should be received into stock each month to maintain the proper inventory levels if the sales and markdowns occur as planned. The formula for computing **planned purchases** (also called **planned receipts**) is as follows:

Sales for the month
+ Plus markdowns for the month
+ Plus stock required at the end of the month (EOM)
      (or beginning of the following month, BOM)
− Minus the stock provided at the start of the month
───
Planned purchase for the month

Using Figure 5-2, here's an example for one month:

February planned sales	$ 48,000
Planned stock, end of February	170,000
Planned markdowns, February	+ 6,000
Total provision required	$224,000
Less planned stock (from	− 155,000
beginning of February)	$ 69,000

DEPARTMENT 4		Blouses and Sportswear						Store _____ Season: Spring	
Spring 19		Feb.	Mar.	Apr.	May	June	July	Total	% of
Fall 19		Aug.	Sept.	Oct.	Nov.	Dec.	Jan.	Total	Change
Net Sales	LY	45	55	53	60	97	40	350	
in $1,000	PL	48	60	58	65	106	41	378	+8.0
	RV								
	ACT								
Markdowns	LY	5	4	4	4	9	18	44	
in $1,000	PL	6	4	5	6	10	14	45	+2.3
	RV								
	ACT								
								EOM	
Retail Stocks	LY	157	172	176	184	208	166	162	**2ST
B.O.M.***	PL	155	170	178	185	212	165	160	2.16 ST
in $1,000	RY								
	ACT								
Retail Purchases	LY	65	63	65	88	64	54	399	
in $1,000	PL	69	72	70	98	69	50	428	+7
	RV								
	ACT								
Direct	LY	7	8	8	8	10	6	47	
Expenses	PL	7	8	8.4	9	11	7	50	+6.6
in $1,000	RV								
	ACT								

*Data in thousands   **ST = Stockturn   ***Beginning of Month

Approved _____
              (Buyer)

Approved _____
              (Merchandise Manager)

Figure 5-2 A department or classification seasons plan (in dollars).

A plan like this views the department inventory as a reservoir from which goods may be drawn as needed to meet customer demand as it fluctuates. Unfortunately, the reservoir usually has to run a little low. If it contained consistently large amounts of merchandise, that wouldn't be smart—it ties up cash and also the merchandise itself, which doesn't sell when it's sitting in a stockroom. Conversely, the penalty for letting the reservoir run too low is even more costly—loss of sales, disgruntled customers, expensive last-minute rush reorders, and frustrated employees who are trying to do their best to keep the shoppers happy. The ideal level is a delicate balance, then, between expected demand (outflow) and anticipated delivery (inflow) of merchandise. Together, this makes up the **rate of flow**. The amount of stock put into the reservoir (inflow) is roughly equal to sales, plus whatever may be required to cover markdowns and other shrinkage (outflow)—but the rate of receivings (rate of input) becomes key to management of the inventory levels and product mix.

Open-to-Buy Control

The system that regulates this flow of goods into inventory is known as the **open-to-buy** (OTB) control. In terms of dollars, it is the amount in the budget that the buyer is able to spend at any given time. The open-to-buy amount is determined (either by the week or by the month) by looking at the planned purchases for that period and subtracting the outstanding orders that will be delivered (and paid for) during the period. Again, Figure 5-2 shows the heart of the system. As you can see, the planned retail purchases (PL) for February are $69,000. However, as the season wears on, the most recent available actual figures (ACT) along with the revised future plans (REV) are used to project future purchases.

Let's say the planned numbers for April were revised:

- Sales were $52,000 instead of $58,000.
- The stock planned for May 1 (the end of April) was valued at $175,000.
- Markdowns for April were revised to $8,000.
- Actual stock on April 1 turned out to be $180,000.

How would we compute the amount that could be used for the planned purchases for April?

Planned sales	$52,000
Planned stock (end of April)	175,000
Planned markdowns	+ 8,000
	$235,000
Less actual stock (beginning of April)	−180,000
Revised retail purchase amount for April	$55,000

Contrast this with the original plan of $70,000 for April, as shown in Figure 5-2. If, for some reason, April 1 came around and $50,000 of orders had already been placed for April delivery, the OTB for that month would only be $5,000. But that $5,000 will be needed to realize the sales plan for April, and to provide a balanced inventory to go into the following month. As further orders are placed for April delivery, the OTB will inch closer to zero. If more than $5,000 worth of additional merchandise is ordered, the department will be "overbought" by the excess amount.

The accountant or controller's perception that the $5,000 is a "fixed amount," not ever to be exceeded . . . and a buyer's continual tendencies to order whatever they want without regard to the budget . . . are both wrong. The OTB amount at any time is not set in stone, but it is an extremely useful guide or diagnostic aid. If the OTB always seems to be less than what the buyer needs, it may indicate one or more problems within the system:

- Incorrect forecasting, or other planning errors
- Improper distribution of the merchandise mix, or other buying errors

- Unsuccessful promotions that should be analyzed for future correction
- Late receipt of goods, or other timing errors

On the other hand, if the OTB account always seems to have more money in it than the buyer is spending, the causes could be the following:

- Again, errors in planning or buying
- Unexpectedly successful promotions
- Failure to place needed orders in time

No matter what the problem, it should be analyzed and corrected. Unfortunately, the tendency of buyers who run short of OTB money is often to cut back on reordering, rather than question the figures and/or change the merchandise mix to get rid of the slow-moving stocks that are causing the problem. The nickname for this is "spinning the middle," because it results in better-than-average turnover of the "middle" or better-selling goods, while the "dead ends" turn over sluggishly. It may be that OTB in this case would be better termed "NTB"—*need to buy*.

Obviously, the profitability of the stock on hand depends on the nature of the components in the mix. So there are two types of plans:

- A **model stock plan**, which is an overview of the total amount of merchandise in the department on important dates or weeks.
- A **buying plan**, which is the schedule of items to buy, when to buy them, and when to have them delivered so that the model stock plan is fulfilled.

We discuss how to create these plans later in the chapter. How detailed they should be depends on many factors, but the most critical is that they take time to prepare, analyze, and follow. Deciding the degree of detail, then, store management should ask itself whether the value of the time spent will justify the cost of having every single item represented in these plans. It is a waste to prepare highly detailed plans for buyers who lack the time and/or capacity to use it—a buyer in a small chain, for instance, who works solo without an assistant or clerical help.

Looking back at Figure 5-1, we would need to subdivide the Plans b and d into smaller categories or classifications of merchandise. In some cases, plans might be developed by unit, for the month or for key weeks. However, plans like e and f may be left at the broader, department-level (in dollars) and subdivided by months. In a smaller store, where everything is on display and there's virtually no backroom stock, visual control and direct communication may allow less formal planning.

Sometimes, action is too swift for detailed analysis. A sportswear buyer at the peak of a selling season doesn't have the time to fit very specific individual items into a broad plan of price ranges, colors, and types of items. Any merchandise that requires stocking a lot of sizes (like shoes) heightens the importance of keeping down the number of other variants. The number of styles to be included in the model plan should be decided long before the opening of the season, so the buyer's job is simply to pick specific styles that fit the model. New styles that turn up later are carefully and sparingly introduced, if at all. One of the perennial problems is, when the buyer is caught up in the excitement of early market, to save enough of the OTB amount for some later "finds" if they come up. Some companies take the time to revise their model stock plans—at the start of a season, at mid-season, and again near its end.

One product line that illustrates steep demand curves and quick action is greeting cards. Sure, there are stable demand patterns for things like birthday and anniversary cards, and new stock numbers can be fit in smoothly, without any undue urgency about selling off all the "old" or discontinued cards. But at Valentine's Day, Mother's Day, Father's Day, Christmas? The demand curve changes, suddenly and completely.

There is a middle ground for planning and controlling stocks—not micromanaging by individual item, but not painting too broad a picture of a whole department. Many types of stores use standardized merchandise classifications—a sort of Dewey Decimal System, like the ones used in libraries—to assign a profit center, class, and subclass to track the sales and stock levels of various items by number. Every store uses it a little differently, but it is a good starting point with which to manage the universe of consumer goods within a department.[1]

Just today, for instance, the authors purchased some muffins in bulk at Costco for a school fundraiser. With this text in mind, the receipt was a bit more enlightening. The classifications by flavor were as follows:

60703 Almond Poppyseed   60735 Blueberry
60711 Chocolate   24311 Variety Pack (all three types)

The theory behind all merchandise classifications is that, as the subclasses become narrower, the items within them become more and more interchangeable to the consumer. In Figure 5-3, "Women's Gloves" is part of a demand center (260) that includes other types of accessories. Take a look at how the category is organized:

- The entire stock of women's gloves is subcenter 266.
- Under the subcenter, there are three overall classes: cold-weather gloves (267), all other fabric gloves (268), and all other leather gloves (269).
- Within the three classes, each type of gloves is categorized by its use or some special feature (it's lined or not, it's made of a certain fabric, etc.). The numbers that say "RESERVED" are open, so that if some other glove type is bought at some future date, there's a category it can fit into.

This system is flexible because it gives the individual merchant a lot of choice in how tightly to categorize the wares. A small store may elect to keep the classification records only on the first two levels. A medium-sized store may elect to carry some of its less important product lines at the demand center level, but subdivide the more important lines further. Even in the largest chain stores, once a product is logically identified as a member of a class and labeled with a code number, it can be tracked no matter where its physical location. Classification numbers are part of each item's **SKU number** found on its price tag. You'll learn more about that in Chapter 6.

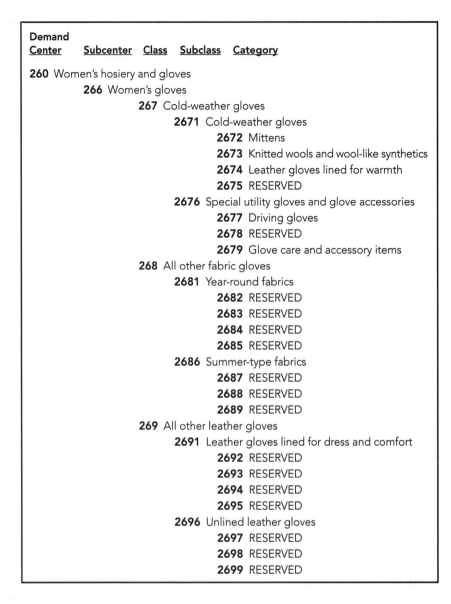

Figure 5-3
Classifying within the
merchandise group:
women's fashion
accessories.

MAKING THE MERCHANDISE PRODUCTIVE

An increasingly important consideration in planning the assortment, both by department and by classification, is to make each dollar invested in the merchandise productive, in terms of sales and profit. The customary index used to measure this is **stockturn**, short for *stock turnover rate*. This is a single number that reflects the big picture—a department's or product line's sales for a period of time, divided by the average inventory carried during the same period. For example, if the sales for a year in a department (or a classification) are $100,000, and if the average retail stock carried during the year is $25,000, the stockturn is 4. The most accurate stockturn figures are calculated either by week or by month, and nowadays, computerized inventory systems can do them at the click of a mouse.

The buyer's ability to reduce the average inventory without decreasing sales, or to keep the inventory nearly constant while sales increase, are both reflections of a higher stockturn. Either situation shows that every dollar of investment is providing more sales than it did before. If the buyer can get away with spending less on new merchandise but sales go well, all the better—the stockturn is good, so markdowns are being reduced and the merchandise in stock is probably fresher and more attractive to the customers. However, if the buyer is simply cutting back to save money, the inventory assortment may run low and actually reduce sales opportunities (and, of course, potential profits) because there's not enough merchandise in stock.

Good basic stock plans that truly reflect realistic planned sales are the best way to keep inventory low, but not *too* low. Other methods include the following:

- Reduce the number of price lines carried, if they are unnecessarily close.
- Avoid styles and brands that seem to duplicate each other.
- Concentrate on key items, eliminating the items and lines that don't sell especially well.
- Buy more frequently in smaller lots, if the extra ordering and shipping costs are not excessive.
- Carry smaller reserve stocks (if they are higher than what's really needed).
- Introduce and follow a system to avoid accumulating slow-selling items. Slow-selling stock is commonly controlled by these methods:
  - Mark the day or month of receipt on the price ticket of every item as it comes in, and check the stock at frequent intervals.
  - Set a period of time for each classification of goods, at the end of which anything remaining is considered a slow seller and dealt with accordingly. This means either marking it down or promoting it to get it moving.

Another way to measure the ratio of sales and stocks is a monthly **stock-to-sales ratio**. This is calculated by dividing the value of the total stock (at retail) at the first of each month, by the sales of that month. If the stock on February 1 is $20,000 at retail, and the sales for February are $5,000, the stock-to-sales radio is 4. The usual goal is to decrease the stock-to-sales ratio—not to increase it, as with stockturn.

A stock-to-sales ratio is an easy tool to use to estimate how much merchandise to stock. For example, if the stock-to-sales ratio for November is set at 3, and the planned sales for the month are $12,000, the buyer knows the department must stock about $36,000 worth of merchandise. Again, it's not a perfect figure, only an estimate.

A third and more sophisticated way to measure the productivity of merchandise is to determine the **gross margin return** for each dollar of investment at cost, abbreviated **GMROI** (gross margin for return on investment). For example, with annual sales of $100,000, let's say the gross margin realized by the department is $37,500 and the average value of inventory carried at any one time may be $15,000. The gross margin return per dollar of investment would be $37,500 divided by $15,000, or $2.50. These calculations may be made monthly, or even weekly. The goal is that, for every dollar the store invests, it must make an adequate margin to contribute toward expenses and profit.

STAPLE STOCK CONTROL

The focus in this area is to reduce the out-of-stock risks to whatever comfort level fits with the company's merchandising policy. There are two methods of doing this:

- The periodic inventory count, in which *stocks are counted as a means of determining sales*. The quantity of each item is counted at selected intervals. The orders received since the previous count are added, and when the total is compared to the previous period's total, the difference is the amount of sales of that item.
- The perpetual inventory system is a running record of stocks on hand and sales transactions. In this system, the *sales are counted to determine the stock on hand*. This type of system is almost always computer-based.

This discussion will guide you through the process of tracking merchandise and sales as if there were no computers—first, because you need to understand the logic behind the way the figures are derived, and second, because inventory control programs do require continual monitoring and modification in response to real-world business conditions. Styles change, sales results vary, vendors and items are added to and dropped from inventory, and so on. As a buyer, you may have a staff of assistants to do the data entry and crunch the numbers for you, but understanding the principles will help ensure better input and control, no matter how many assistants you have or how sophisticated your company's software. (We cover technology advancements in Chapter 6.)

There are several ways stocks are replenished, depending on the type of merchandise:

- Periodic or continuous fill-in, item by item. This may be called **continuous replenishment**.
- Fashion goods, which are subject to long opening commitment (a major initial order) and subsequent readjustment by reorders.
- Other types of stocks, which are subject to long commitment with relatively little reordering.

No matter what the system, there must be a logical procedure for reorders, in which certain data must be provided. The facts necessary for control of each staple item are as follows:

- A listing and description of the unit. This is like a snapshot of the product and all its ordering data: the price (what it costs the store) and size or pack (how many to a carton, etc.), any minimum orders required by the supplier, and its shipping weight (where freight is important). The sales unit is usually an individual item, but if it's something sold by the package or carton (socks, tennis balls, etc.), the package or carton is the sales unit, for control purposes.
- The probable **rate of sale** for this item, usually expressed in sales per week.
- The delivery period, or time it takes from placing the order to getting the item into the store and on the shelf for sale.
- The reorder period, which is the amount of time between orders. It will be more frequent for fast sellers, less often for slower-moving items.
- The **reserve**, or amount of merchandise to have on hand just in case the rate of sale increases unexpectedly.
- The current stock, both on hand and on order.
- The **maximum amount** of this item that must be on hand (also known as the **provision** of the item).
- The **minimum amount** of this item, that should trigger a reorder every time stock hits this level (also known as the **unit OTB**).

For the last two bullet points, formulas can be used to make the calculations:

The maximum amount	=	Projected sales for the reorder period
		+ Sales for the delivery period
		+ The reserve amount
The minimum amount	=	The maximum amount
		− The current stock on hand
		− The current stock on order

With all of this information in the database, the buyer can now prepare a built-up plan and reconcile it with senior management's top-down plan. To see the unit-stock plan in dollars rather than units, the buyer can calculate the average inventories and multiply them by the price lines. These figures can also be compared to the top-down financial forecasts.

A variation from the standard stock control plan is to reorder based solely on each item's minimum stock figure—that is, whenever the stock level of an item drops to this point, the buyer is notified that a reorder should be placed (or in an automatic ordering system, the reorder is triggered by computer). In this system, the length of the reorder period varies and becomes a less critical factor in stock planning.

So far, we've assumed for the sake of simplicity that all the units under control are homogenous—that every item in a stock unit is identical. But what about units that contain items of multiple colors, sizes, flavors, or some other major difference? If each of three colors, for instance, must be protected from being out of stock, then the maximum amount of units on hand will always be higher—and the stockturn rate always lower—than for the same sized unit of identical merchandise.

Calculating Stockturn with Staple Stock Control

In a perfect world, actual sales during the reorder period (RP) and delivery period (DP) would be exactly as estimated, and the reserve amounts would never be seriously depleted. In a perfect world, come to think of it, the reserve would not be needed! But this is the real world, where sales may be higher or lower than estimated. Over time, or over a great many individual items, the remaining quantity at its most critical or lowest point (just before a new reorder arrives) will average out—some high and some low—to the mandated reserve figure. That's why it is possible to predict the average inventory (or "average stock") and turnover for a given ordering procedure. The formula for this is as follows:

Average stock   =   One-half the reorder period sales quantity
                  +   The reserve amount

The stockturn rate is then calculated by dividing the estimated annual rate of sale by the average stock figure—using all figures from the same time period, of course.

Streamlining Stockturn Procedures

At this point, all the calculations are enough to make the creative, fashion-conscious student wail, "I didn't expect to have to be an ACCOUNTANT to do this job!" Fair enough. However, there are some hidden benefits behind the drudgery.

Much of the work involved in setting up initial assortment data, reorder frequencies, and reserve information, is a one-time job. Actually maintaining an established program is much easier.

Experience with a category of merchandise develops a sixth sense about its figures of performance. You'll be more instinctive about it, and more easily spot numbers that don't seem to fit, as time goes on. In many large companies, much of this work is done by planning experts or administrative assistants, guided by the knowledge and judgment of the buyer.

The small buyer, burdened with the many other responsibilities of running a business, often feels that he or she cannot possibly keep carefully itemized sales records or apply a formula to determine how much to reorder. And yet, no buyer's operation is too small to keep good records of the basics: how many of each item was received into stock since the beginning of the year (or some other control period), and how low the inventory must drop for an item before more are ordered.

The degree to which you streamline the paperwork (or data entry) involved in stock keeping, and how detailed your records must be, are functions of your own comfort level as well as your company policy (perhaps not in that order). Some buyers maintain a controlled ordering system without ever formally computing sales. If that is the case, however, someone is stuck with the task of counting the stock before any new order is placed.

MODEL STOCK AND BUYING PLANS

A **model stock plan** is a written overview of the optimum assortment that will best satisfy the customer demand a store expects during a specific time period. Some preliminary steps must be taken to create this plan:

- Decide on the selection factors that will be used to buy the merchandise. This literally means identifying all of the general characteristics that a customer would look at to either purchase or reject it—from the "nonnegotiables" like size and fit, to details like whether it has pockets.
- Map out the important target dates in the season, when model stocks must be constructed and available, and the lead times to get them ordered so they'll be delivered when needed.
- Calculate the sales figures for the months before and (from the previous year) after the target dates, both in units sold and in dollars. Check the figures against the department's budget and classification plans.

With this information in hand, the buyer should be able to begin planning. The detailed model stock plan will include how many items to have on hand (listed by major classifications, not individual styles).

The model stock plan is made first. Then, to implement the model stock plan requires a *buying plan*, in which the buyer goes into greater detail. In the buying plan, the buyer *profiles* the assortment, grouping the needs into subclassifications—sizes, styles, fabrics, colors—with amounts of each. The buying plan also details the timing of the orders. It includes an opening or initial purchase, in sufficient quantities to keep the store stocked until the reorder.

The buyer can start by taking the model stock plan and the preliminary data that was gathered and doing the following:

- Adding any sales *from the previous model* to the current plan
- Subtracting any purchases the buyer has already made, or any stock that is still on hand from the previous order

The result gives the buyer a realistic look at the current level of this merchandise category in this department. Let's say we're buying ladies' sweaters:

The **model** for November 1 in a certain price and type of sweater	100 units (sweaters)
Sales of this sweater during September and October	+ 150 units
Sweaters ordered for the previous sales period (September 1)	250
Stock now on hand	− 120 units
Stock to be ordered (OTB)	130 units

The picture can be filled in even further. A portion of the OTB to be ordered earliest would be scaled according to the size and color factors determined by the buyer; and, if the current stock on hand is unbalanced in some way, the new order should make up for that. If the buyer would normally order about 40 percent black sweaters but the stock on-hand contains plenty of black sweaters—the new order would be modified. The other option is not to order everything at once, especially if shipping is prompt and another order could be filled on short notice.

Now the buyer shifts from units and selection factors, to actual dollars he or she is about to invest. Figure 5-4 shows one approach to the task, again using sweaters as the product line. July and August are used as the lead time for a September buying plan. Cardigan sales for last year (LY) are used as a base for estimating this year's sales (TY). Note that the price lines ($30, $40, and $60) are an important part of the plan, indicating the relationship between units and dollars. Columns 1 to 5 are the numbers of items; columns 6 to 8 are their dollar values.

Selecting the breadth of styles that makes up the assortment is up to the buyer, within the policies set by the store. Some decide on basic percentages and apply them to the color selections—buy three colors and split the order into thirds, or buy 25 percent of the sweaters in black and split the other 75 percent of the order among the four most fashionable options (in the view of the buyer) for the season. The end result should be that if distribution of sizes and colors over the whole category is in line with the average customer demand, there's a better chance the product mix will satisfy most shoppers.

Some buyers do not find it practical to work out plans in this much detail. They'll arrive at a planned total—they know they'll need 237 units, for instance—divide them into the sizes and colors they've determined they will need and, from there, buy the individual styles based on their own experience and fashion sense. It's okay that there is a certain amount of educated guesswork in the buying plan. After all, it is made up of estimates that reflect the best use of available data and informed judgment.

Finally, the buying plans for each segment of the model assortment are assembled into a chart, known as a **Model Assortment Plan**—fortuitously, MAP—and yes, it is a map of sorts, a summary for the buyer to use at market. Items on the chart are checked off as the orders are placed to ensure that the model stock plan is met. But, again, in the world of fashion, flexibility is key. At market, a unique new vendor may have a no-reorder policy, so if the buyer wants the line, he or she must overbuy it right then; or the buyer tries to find a certain color but doesn't really like what is offered in that hue. In other words, in action,

Type	July and August					
	$30		$40		$60	
	LY	TY	LY	TY	LY	TY
1. Textured coat/jacket	30	40	50	50	35	35
2. Textured all others	40	30	40	50	50	60
3. Regular knit coat/jacket	65	65	90	90	60	60
4. Regular knit all others	65	65	70	80	85	95
5. Total units	200	200	250	270	230	250
6. Total dollars	6,000	6,000	10,000	10,800	138,000	15,000
7. Total—All prices		LY $29,800				
8. Total—All prices		TY $31,800				

Type	September					
	$30		$40		$60	
	LY	TY	LY	TY	LY	TY
1. Textured coat/jacket	40	40	50	55	35	40
2. Textured all others	40	35	45	55	55	65
3. Regular knit coat/jacket	75	70	100	100	60	65
4. Regular knit all others	70	70	75	110	85	100
5. Total units	225	215	270	320	235	270
6. Total dollars	6,750	6,450	10,800	12,800	14,100	16,200
7. Total—All prices		LY $31,650				
8. Total—All prices		TY $35,450				

Figure 5-4
Distribution of cardigan sales by type and price.

the plan becomes as follows:

• Adapt and adjust as necessary.
• No matter what you decide, place the orders promptly.
• If there are gaps, fill them in later, during the selling season.

Seasonal Stocks

A considerable portion of goods handled in many stores cannot be ordered by the methods outlined in this chapter. In many lines, vendors make what they make and sell it. They don't carry back stock. In these cases, the earlier the orders are placed with them, the better the quality and workmanship.

Seasonality affects virtually every type of retailer to some degree. Particularly in fashion merchandise, the end of a season brings a sort of product obsolescence simply because of the change in weather. This presents some very real problems in planning merchandise flow, and the buyer's challenge is to have peak inventories in stock to meet customer demand just prior to the historically high sales months, and to reduce them before the "troughs."

The impact of major gift-buying holidays will also require shifts in buying plans and the resulting promotional programs. The National Retail Federation estimates the six biggest U.S. buying-spree holidays, and their annual retail sales, as follows[2]:

Thanksgiving/Christmas	$219.90 billion
Valentine's Day	12.79 billion
Easter	10.49 billion
Mother's Day	10.43 billion
Father's Day	8.04 billion
Halloween	3.12 billion

As you can imagine, how well a merchant operates and merchandises during the annual Christmas season may well determine profitability for the entire year. Fourth-quarter forecasts about holiday shopping levels seem to vary drastically (from doom-and-gloom to things-are-really-looking-up), but for many retailers, the period between Thanksgiving and Christmas represents 40 percent of annual sales.

It's not just the floor salespeople who are working overtime—the merchandise should also be working hard too, in terms of being attractively displayed, well-balanced assortments. The sales period itself varies in length by almost a week, depending on how the holidays fall on the calendar. In 2003, there were 26 days in the all-important period from day-after-Thanksgiving to day-before-Christmas. In 2006, there will be 31 days in that period. When every day counts, this variable is significant.

While it is tempting to get caught up in the whirlwind of activity and excitement, this is realistically the time of year that calls for the highest level of control. Most seasonal merchandise can be phased out while the next season's wares are being introduced—but for Christmas-themed goods, the season ends abruptly on December 24th. Increasingly, stores are hauling out the holiday merchandise early and using the week after Christmas (when returns and exchanges are at their peak) to mark down their remaining holiday stocks. To bolster these unbalanced leftovers, retailers commonly buy manufacturers' closeouts or sale items, which can be sold at normal markups and still offer customers substantial savings.

PLANNING DATA FOR MODEL STOCK AND BUYING PLANS

In this final section of the chapter, we've reprinted two reports to illustrate the detail generated by a buyer's decisions.

The stock status report (see Figure 5-5) is a weekly report of the activity in the various price lines within a merchandise classification. For each price line (the column labeled "Price"), the following facts are reported, across the chart from left to right:

- The total units received
- The total number of sales of the item

	C1	Price	Total Rcpts	Total Sales	Total On Hand	Total On Ord	On Hand & On Ord	Projected Sales Next 4 Weeks	Projected Sales Foll. 4 Weeks	Sales Past 4 Weeks	% Inc. Past 4 Weeks	#1	#2	#3	#4	#5
TY	2	4.98						8	95							
LY												—	1	5	2	—
TY	2	5.98	1,669	1,313	356		356	235	82	198	11.0%					
LY			1,493	1,173	320					175		112	22	37	24	40
TY	2	6.90	2,124	1,693	431		431	175	92	162	7.0%					
LY			1,901	1,512	389					151		83	3	18	50	21
TY	2	7.98	123	95	28	36	64	45	1	32	2.0%					
LY			110	83	27					31		37	2	—	4	2
TY	2	8.98	336	296	40	160	200	138	160	99	1.0%					
LY			301	263	38					98		45	16	22	28	27
TY	2	9.98	535	406	129		129	57	3	46	4.0%					
LY			478	272	206					44		21	6	6	11	15
TY	2	10.98	313	257	56		56	29	15	18	1.0%					
LY			280	139	141					17		4	5	8	11	1
TY	2	11.98	533	346	187		187			102	3.0%					
LY			476	307	169					99		—	—	—	—	—
TY	2	12.98	1,199	763	436		436	355	34	276	2.0%					
LY			1,072	680	392					271		108	62	45	60	80
TY	2	15.00	525	374	151		151	109	5	81	1.0%					
LY			470	333	137					80		37	20	16	16	20
TY		Total	7,357	5,543	1,814	196	2,010	1,151	417	1,014	6.0%					
LY			6,581	4,762	1,819					966		547	117	127	186	174
TY		Markdowns	390	281	109			147	100	72	2.0%CR					
LY			401	277	124					74		89	6	21	16	15

Figure 5-5 Example of stock status report.

- How many are on hand, and on order
- The projected sales for two different upcoming four-week periods
- The actual sales for the previous four weeks
- The percentage of increase (over sales from the same period, last year)
- The sales by week for the same time period last year

With such complete data, the buyer is able to forecast sales for the coming eight weeks with considerable accuracy, plan at least a month ahead, and calculate how much to buy in each price line.

Figure 5-6 is an example of a unit net sales report. It tells us that there are two styles (of whatever the product is) at the same price ($5.99), which is fine except that

- One of them (Style 500) has sold a lot more than the other (Style 599).
- Even though Style 500 is outselling Style 599, the stock on hand for Style 500 is disproportionately large.

As a buyer, what would you do? Keep the large stock of Style 500 and hope that it continues to sell well? Or reorder more of Style 599 to better balance out the style and color assortments for the category? Think about it first, and then analyze it on paper.

You might use the formula earlier in this chapter for building each unit of sale up to its maximum or provision level, or you might determine a reserve amount for this category, to take care of unexpected sales and offer customers a minimum assortment of sizes and colors. To get OTB for the style numbers, take the maximum level and subtract the number currently on hand and on order. After doing the math, would your buying decisions be the same?

CHAPTER SUMMARY

Two types of plans dominate the retail industry—the top-down plan, in which senior executives (the folks "at the top") set goals and budgets for the staff to meet, and the bottom-up plan (made by the buyers, merchandisers, and/or planners) from a combination of past sales data and future projections. In any organization, the two plans should align closely or be altered to do so.

At any time during a month or a buying season, the retail buyer must know and be able to work with his or her OTB amount—how much money in the budget is "open to buy" goods to keep the store or department adequately stocked. When there never seems to be enough OTB money to make the purchases the buyer feels are necessary, the system has to be adjusted somehow to compensate for that. In the chapter, several options were discussed, and a few formulas were offered and explained to determine the maximum and minimum amounts of an item that should be kept on hand, as well as

CL	Ven	Style	Price	Current Week Rec.	Current Week Sales Tot.	Rec.	O/H	Sales Tot.	Season to Date #1	#2	#3	#4	#5	Remarks
2	124	1606	1198			37	24	13	6	1	2	3	1	
2	750	599	599		9	637	60	577	271	87	32	72	115	
2	932	2620	798		3	60	14	46	14	6	5	10	11	
2	932	2690	698		2	72	9	63	17	12	10	11	13	
2	932	2750	798		1	60	14	46	16	6	6	13	5	
2	932	3038	1198		31	217	70	147	62	14	21	21	29	
2	932	3050	1198		5	108	22	86	28	8	15	16	19	
2	1160	250	690			14	2	12	11	—	—	—	1	
2	1160	260	690			29	16	13	7	5		1		
2	1160	400	699		63	1560	339	1221	522	113	137	238	211	
2	1160	450	898			307	36	271	84	43	44	52	48	
2	1160	471	998		10	277	133	144	50	17	25	29	23	
2	1160	477	998		3	112	30	82	43	7	11	8	13	
2	1160	500	599	72	51	1032	296	736	323	52	70	141	150	
2	1160	481	998		47	146	66	80	20	11	16	18	15	
2	1160	2530	690		3	51	13	38	11	4	11	2	10	
2	1160	2708	690			66	1	65	24	9	9	11	12	
2	1160	2910	690			52	8	44	20	6	7	6	5	
2	1160	2930	1500		10	252	114	138	31	23	24	28	32	
2	1160	2932	1298		11	223	133	90	35	8	13	14	20	
2	1160	2960	1500			208	3	205	70	23	28	35	49	
2	1160	2962	690			38	11	27	7	6	2	9	3	
2	1160	2965	690	24		88	36	52	17	10	7	10	8	
2	1160	2966	690			8	6	2	—	—	—	1	1	

Figure 5-6 Example of unit net sales report.

different methods to determine how profitable ("productive") an item or product line is.

Buyers begin by creating a *model stock plan* that is just what its name implies—a model of what the store or department "should" look like to meet all the major demands and desires of the target customers, at the ideal dates for ordering and delivery. Then, a *buying plan* takes these ideals and boils them down to specifics—what color, how many, what price, by what date—to create a working document the buyer can take to market to keep him or her on task.

Seasonal and holiday merchandise has unique time constraints. Instead of treating these items as a necessary hassle that they hope will result in add-on sales, smart merchants can control this type of merchandise tightly to gain maximum profitability during busy sales periods.

DISCUSSION QUESTIONS

1. Can you name a type of business in which a manual perpetual inventory control system might work well? And even if your business had a highly automated inventory system, would you still have employees count manually sometimes? How often? Why or why not?
2. Classify to the subclass level some line of merchandise with which you are familiar. Or, using the Costco receipt data in the chapter, extrapolate the muffin SKU data that you know (and fill in others) to explain how these baked goods appear to be classified at the store. (In food items like this, is flavor a nonnegotiable selection factor?)
3. Why would you mark an item's tag with the date it was received at the store? For nonperishable items, does the "in date" really matter?
4. In what ways could an increase in stockturn reduce a retailer's operating expenses?
5. On your written plan for May 1, you're supposed to have 200 widgets in stock. Sales for March are estimated at 100; and for April, the sales estimate is 125. Delivery of new widgets takes one month. On March 1, your stock on hand is 170 and stock on order is 110. Do you need to order more widgets for April delivery, to sell in May? And if so, how many?
6. If your OTB amount never seems to be sufficient after the initial order to last the remainder of the season, this chapter listed several reasons for the problem. As a buyer, what can you do to remedy each one of those problems?
7. In your opinion, how soon is too soon to put holiday merchandise on display—not just Christmas, but Easter, Halloween, Valentine's Day, any of them? From your own observations over the past few years, do you

believe retailers do a good job of planning and merchandising their Christmas stocks in particular? Explain briefly.

8. If you were setting up a department store, would you group the women's fashions by size ranges—misses, juniors, plus-sizes, and so forth—or by classification (designer, separates, price ranges)? Why?

9. It's mid-season and you have a black sweater in the store that sells about three units a week. The current stock on hand is five of these black sweaters, with six more on order. The stock wanted on hand after the next order is received is 10 according to your plan. You know this manufacturer takes about three weeks from the time you order to get the goods. How many should you order?

10. If classification planning, SKU management, and computerized inventory control combine to do such a great job at categorizing, tracking sales, and prompting reorders, are department managers' and retail buyers' roles diminished? Or are they even more critical? Explain your thoughts.

ENDNOTES

1. One of this book's original coauthors, the late Joseph S. Friedlander, was a pioneer in designing classification systems in the 1970s. As chairman of the National Retail Federation's Merchandise Classification Committee, he worked for a number of years to develop a common language for manufacturer and retailer identification of groups of merchandise categories. The terminology has changed somewhat since then, but the system's basic concept and structure are still in place, working just as well as it did when first created.
2. Holiday consumer survey results by BIGresearch, LLC, Worthington, Ohio; for the National Retail Federation, Washington, D.C., September 28, 2004.

6

Technology and Internet Commerce in Retailing

You probably don't recall the days when computers were large enough to fill entire rooms of major corporations and were designed for repetitive, routine tasks to free up human beings' time for more productive activities. To say that things have changed is almost comical—in fact, this chapter will barely scratch the surface, since new technology reveals itself in this field continuously.

This chapter provides an overview of the most widely used forms of technology in retailing today. We'll limit the discussion to these topics *as they relate to the buying process*, or this chapter would be a separate book unto itself! They are as follows:

- SKU numbers, bar codes, and Radio Frequency Identification (RFID)
- Point-of-sale terminals and systems; Electronic Shelf Labeling (ESL)

- Quick Response (QR) and Efficient Customer Response (ECR)
- Electronic Data Interchange (EDI) and Extensible Markup Language (XML)
- eCommerce (or "e-tailing") and Internet marketing
- New frontiers—global data synchronization; Collaborative Planning, Forecasting, and Replenishment (CPFR) systems; and more

In the 1980s, retailers were increasing their spending on computer systems at twice the rate of sales growth. Retail software applications were relatively new (the first computerized scanner to be used at a supermarket was installed 30 years ago, in 1974) and everyone wanted to jump on the bandwagon. But now that we're all living online and hurtling down the Information Superhighway, the experts say many companies don't use technology very well or, at least, don't glean everything they *could* from the features and benefits of the systems they're using. (Our personal theory is that no one has time to master all the acronyms!) If your CRM and ERP aren't A-OK, or your POS system doesn't facilitate ESL or ILM, read on . . .

HOW TECHNOLOGICALLY ADVANCED ARE WE?

Forrester Research, an independent technology research firm based in Cambridge, Massachusetts, keeps close track of Information Technology (IT) developments in the global business world, doing specialized studies by industry. Forrester's prediction is that U.S. IT spending will grow to 7 percent in 2005, and continue at a similar pace through 2008.

Forrester also surveyed 52 IT executives at retail companies in North America, asking them what their technology priorities would be in 2004. The results offer an eye-opening picture of the hottest trends—and the budgets that will pay for them. Following are some highlights:

- 51 percent said their companies are increasing spending for Internet and eCommerce initiatives.
- Compared to other industries, more retailers (32 percent) said they are either upgrading to, or considering, RFID adoption. (More about RFID in a moment).
- 47 percent of retailers said they planned to purchase portal server and security technology.[1]

Retailers look at technological advancements in several ways. Since the 1980s, they've used computer-based programs like decision-support systems (DSS) to review past performance, analyze alternatives, and forecast results under simulated conditions, adding an all-important "what if?" dimension to merchandise planning. These programs have become far more sophisticated, giving companies the ability to provide faster and more accurate information at each level of business, and in partnership with suppliers. They have created limitless opportunities for multichannel (and international) marketing, with most companies selling on Internet Web sites along with their bricks-and-mortar stores and mail-order catalog components. And they have reduced labor costs by speeding up some jobs and eliminating others altogether. In short, they can be used as strategic tools in a highly competitive business climate.

There are also downsides. Introducing new systems can be confusing and expensive, especially for the small business. For larger retailers, eliminating those low-skill jobs may be profitable, but it is a source of anger and negative publicity in today's uncertain economy. At the other end of the scale, technology may require adding new kinds of specialized talent to the workforce, with competitive salaries and benefits. Some large companies now have a chief technical officer (CTO) in addition to a CEO and CIO, and/or executive-level logistics directors, all at six-figure incomes.

Retailers also worry that no matter what program or system they buy, it will become quickly outmoded and/or unable to integrate with what they're already using. Still, most are hooked by the promise that they can more easily track sales, automate the reordering process, and more—saving time and money. So let's take a basic look at how most retailers put technology to work.

UPC bar codes are part of many manufactured products. (*Source:* PhotoDisc, Inc.)

LABELING THE PRODUCTS

Long, long ago, there were . . . price tags. Yes, someone wrote the price on a paper tag or typed it onto a sticker and actually attached it to an item for sale. Except perhaps for yard sales, those days are gone. Most states do have laws that require items for sale to be price-labeled, but today's price tag is put to multiple uses, since it provides the retailer a lot more information than the price. Today, products are identified as follows:

- **SKU number.** The stock keeping unit, as we've already learned, is the individual identification number of a product that distinguishes it from other items. It is usually based on the classification of merchandise in an inventory control system, and on any flavor, package size, color, or other individual feature of the item. A SKU (pronounced "skyoo") is the smallest unit for which sales and stock records are maintained for the product. Even when it has a SKU number to identify it internally within a store or chain, the product probably also has a . . .
- **UPC code.** The **Universal Product Code** is the "bar code" we've all become familiar with. The pattern of lines and spaces of varying widths represents a code of numbers and letters that identify the product and manufacturer to a computerized scanner that reads the code. (See the photograph on the facing page, or open your refrigerator at home, and you'll find plenty of UPC codes to study.)
- **EAN code.** UPC codes are used in the United States and Canada, but EAN is an alternative bar code system used in 80 other countries. There are 8-digit and 13-digit EAN codes. The acronym stands for "European Article Numbering."

BAR CODE TRIVIA

Surefire icebreakers when you're standing in the supermarket checkout line? Well, maybe not . . . but, hey, they're interesting!

- The original idea for the bar code was a series of circular symbols, not lines. It was patented in 1949 by an inventor named N. J. Woodward.

- Today, there are more than 300 bar code **symbologies** (the fancy word for a bar code method or family), but fewer than 20 of them have popular applications.

- The blank space to the immediate left and right of the actual bar code symbol is called its **quiet zone**. The term for the width of the narrowest line in any bar code is its **X-dimension**.

- The part of the scanner that interprets the bar code is known as a **decoder**.

With all the line extensions and new products on the planet, it was bound to happen—the Uniform Code Council, the national organization that sets the standards for use of the UPC codes, estimated it will *run out* of new company prefixes for the 12-digit codes in 2005. The UCC is working with its European counterpart (EAN International based in Brussels, Belgium) to urge businesses to, at least, lengthen their codes to 13 digits to accommodate the EAN structure. The alternative for companies that want to do more foreign business is to expand their code to 14 digits, which will probably become the unified standard within the decade.

In addition, a joint effort called the EAN.UCC System®, the newly developed system that includes *all* current and future product codes, refers to them as **Global Trade Identification Numbers (GTIN).**

How does this impact individual retailers? The EAN.UCC organization declared that companies should be **2005 Sunrise Compliant**—that is, their equipment should be updated to read not only UPC codes, but EAN-8 and EAN-13 codes, with more changes to come. When suppliers change their code numbers, all the down-line systems in the supply chain must be updated. Computers must be able to recognize and process the new codes without kicking them out automatically as incorrect. A **Global Data Synchronization Network (GDSN)** has been created to set up "data pools" of product information that can be exchanged among trading partners.

Despite the increasing sophistication, bar coding and scanning save time. Employees don't have to manually tag the items, and cashiers don't have to enter the data at checkout. The exceptions—like baked goods, fruit, or anything that doesn't lend itself to bar code labeling—are known as **price lookups**, or **PLUs**. Their four- or five-digit code has to be punched into the system manually.

The problem is that this type of system is only as good as the data entry that goes into it. If an incorrect price is in the computer system, it is incorrect every time it's rung up—until someone catches the mistake and fixes it.

Multiple studies have been done about the accuracy of scanners, and thus far, they're not especially encouraging. Store surveys in both Oregon and Arizona reached the same conclusion—in 42 percent of retail scanning inspections, store systems failed to meet the "98 percent accuracy" requirement of correctly scanning 48 out of 50 items.[2]

In Pennsylvania, the Penn State College of Agricultural Sciences analyzed data in almost 400 supermarkets to examine the types of scanning errors:

- In 54 percent of the cases, the customer was undercharged for the item.
- In 27 percent, the customer was overcharged.
- In the remaining cases, the problem was that the item was not priced.[3]

Now you begin to see the dilemma for retailers. In addition to losing profit through inaccurate pricing, they are losing the ability to accurately forecast sales and reordering requirements based on correct data. In some states, they also risk penalties, and the resulting bad publicity. In Arizona, for example, a store can be fined $50 to $5,000 per month for scanner inaccuracies.

The Future of Product IDs

The biggest news in product identification is the use of **Radio Frequency Identification (RFID),** which is also known as the **Electronic Product Code (EPC)** and **Auto-ID**. You may have already seen this technology at work. One of its first major (and very successful) tests was to allow the use of prepaid toll tags for vehicles so drivers don't have to stop at toll booths. Railroad cars and livestock are identified with RFID data, as well as pets whose owners pay for special ID tags to track their whereabouts. Corporations that require security badges use RFID to create them.

In retail, RFID has been extensively tested at the case and pallet level for large quantities of items—and by the time you read this, it should be used on individual products in a retail store near you. Wal-Mart threw a big rock into the RFID pond when it announced that by January 2005, it expected its top 100 suppliers to deliver their merchandise with RFID tags in place. In 2004, Forrester Research estimated the edict would cost about $9 million per supplier to implement, and that only a few of the largest firms that had already committed to "starter" research would be able to fully comply. For most companies, January 2005 was just the beginning of a multiyear phase-in of the new technology.

In the meantime, technology marches on whether companies are in step with it or not. There are already "older-model" Class 0, Class 0+, and Class 1 EPC tags . . . and the new standard is expected to be the so-called Gen 2 tag. The Uniform Code Council founded an Auto-ID Center in 1999 to research the technology and begin setting some standards for its proper and ethical use.

A recent Harvard Business School newsletter article amusingly referred to RFIDs as "bar codes on steroids." The technology to make and program the radio-controlled tags (their trademarked name is **GTAG**™, for "global tag") currently accounts for 80 percent of the system's cost. In addition to a product's ID number, the tag can be programmed to include all kinds of additional information, from where it was made, to its route along a supply chain. Once the data is put onto the tag, it can't be added to or modified.

The RFID chip inside the tag is about the size of a grain of rice and includes a microscopic antenna. It doesn't put out any internal power, but it is activated when it comes into the proximity of a reader device (sometimes called **vicinity technology**). The tag doesn't have to pass directly in front of the reader to be scanned and recorded, and it can be read no matter what its orientation (upside-down, etc.) and through any type of packaging (cardboard, plastic, etc.). A single reader unit can scan hundreds of tags in one second!

The implication for retailers, once they adjust to the cost of this massive technology change, is that they will be better able to track and manage each and every item in inventory. But there are some downsides to RFID, over and above its cost. To name just a few:

- The companies pioneering the technology have already been in court, suing each other over patent infringements.
- The early demand for tags, software, readers, and so on may outstrip the supply, which keeps prices high.

- The tags don't always work perfectly. Label producers reported early failure rates of up to 15 percent. A radio-frequency tag may not be the best option for products that contain metal (which reflects the waves) or liquid (which absorbs the waves).
- Ironically, the tags can contain such huge volumes of data that companies may find themselves swamped with far more information than they can use, much of it repetitive. It will have to be filtered and refined quickly, or the speed and real-time capability of the system will be compromised.

There are two more points to make about RFID technology. The first is that as retail customers learn about it, they have real concerns about whether it might be invasive in terms of their privacy. A 2004 survey of 1,000 U.S. consumers found that, while most agreed RFID tags would be useful for things like preventing prescription drug theft and speeding up the checkout process, a significant number (65 percent) said they're afraid retailers will know too much about them—that they could be tracked through their product purchases, and their data will be sold to third parties, resulting in more junk mail and solicitations.[4] Some of the Gen 2 tag standard recommendations include a "kill feature," meaning the tag could be deactivated at the point of purchase.

Finally, RFID critics say it has been hyped so much that both retailers and consumers have unrealistic expectations about how incredible it is. Realistically, some of the benefits that have been promised are a decade away. Between now and then, companies are in for some very hard work, lots of highly technological study, and major expenditures. The retailers that succeed in using it will be the ones that focus *first* on defining a problem or task that needs to be dealt with, and then determining how (or if) RFID can be used to reach the desired results cost-effectively.

New Shelf Tag Technology

In addition to marking the products themselves, in some types of retail, customers also expect a shelf label. There are few greater annoyances to the supermarket shopper than picking up an item and not being able to figure out what the price is—or worse, having the POS system ring up a different price than what was on the tag, and the customer having to haggle about it with the checker.

Store employees spend a great deal of time putting up and correcting shelf tags, but this is changing. The newest generation of shelf tags uses the same radio-controlled technology as RFIDs. It is **Electronic Shelf Labeling (ESL)**. The new tag is a small liquid crystal display (LCD) that communicates with the store's computer system using low-frequency radio technology. The tag lights up with the use of a long-lasting lithium battery. Whatever price is in the master file in the store's computer is also shown on the shelf tag and at the checkout counter. Each label has its own "address" based on its bar code number; when the price is changed on the master computer, it automatically changes on the tag as well. Each tag can be tested periodically by the system to see if it works and if its battery is sufficiently charged.

The labels lock onto shelf fronts and can't be removed except with a special magnetic tool. Their manufacturers say they are easier to read, and obviously more adaptable, than the paper shelf tags.

RINGING UP THE SALES

When you purchase an item at most retail stores, you go to the checkout counter and a checker (salesperson, associate, whatever . . .) rings up (or records) the sale on a computer. The electronic scanner recognizes the product in the system and immediately accesses its price in the central computer system. The price is displayed on a screen for the customer to see, and recorded for the store on a **point-of-sale (POS)** terminal, or an **electronic cash register (ECR)**.

POS systems are used by large stores; ECRs by small stores. The difference lies mostly in the size and capabilities of the computer programs used in the store. A POS system can be programmed to track purchases and print out receipts, coupons, and special offers triggered by the purchase of certain items. The ECR is less sophisticated. It can do things like total sales by salesperson, but it is unable to provide more detailed information or perform inventory functions.

The normal cycle for a retailer is to have to replace about one-fifth of their POS or ECR terminals every year; the software can last as long as a decade before being updated. In the latter part of the 1990s, however, retailers in the United States slowed these purchases. This was partly because of an overall economic slowdown, but also as a cautious "wait-and-see" response to what would happen with RFID and other innovations. As of 2004, they seemed ready to buy again—to the tune of $3.2 billion a year by 2006.[5]

An independent business consulting company surveyed 172 retailers (including 14 of the top 30) to find out what kinds of technology they are most interested in as they replace older POS systems. Sixty-five percent said they'd be making buying decisions about new hardware or software within 18 months, almost half of them (48 percent) within the year.

- Real-time integration of the POS system with their other systems was extremely important to them. Almost everyone surveyed (90 percent) said that's what they need most for better inventory management.
- A majority of the respondents said they are very interested in new handheld devices for retailers that allow store managers to carry data with them as they walk around the store.
- Interestingly, the most important factor for selecting both POS hardware and software was not price. The top concerns were whether the system had "the best features" and fit with their overall business (78 percent), and the reliability of the system and reputation of the vendor (77 percent).[6]

In this global economy, the way a retailer's technology interacts with buying offices, suppliers, and manufacturers is key. More companies are investigating so-called **open POS systems** (like Java and Linux) that can be used with any hardware or software, as opposed to buying proprietary systems (like Microsoft products) that often include licensing fees.

One of the futuristic examples experts offer to illustrate RDIF technology is that someday, the POS terminal could be eliminated entirely in places like the grocery checkout line. Instead, a "smart" shopping cart equipped with a reader device will record each item as it is placed in the cart, and when the customer walks out the door, another scanner can read the total and charge it to a debit card or other account number preauthorized by the store. Americans already spent $128 billion in 1993 on self-service transactions, from automated grocery checkout lanes to ticket-buying kiosks for airline and movie tickets.[7]

Another popular function of POS software is its ability to allow retailers what is called **Customer Relationship Management (CRM)**. This is a fancy way of saying retailers need to be able to accurately track who their customers are and what they're buying, to be able to improve the relationship and personalize the shopping experience, thereby gaining loyalty. A store that sells both new and used merchandise (like videos or CDs, for instance) can be set up to track buying trends for both. Small chains that market inexpensive items to teenagers can quickly track trends. Supermarkets' use of so-called partner cards is another good example of CRM.

Experts are quick to point out that CRM is not simply a function of software. It's a combination of what the software can do and how the incoming data *about* the customers and their purchases is interpreted. Again, as with so many types of technology, it is only as good as the company's ability to *use* the data it provides. And no matter what the hardware or software systems, for "real" CRM, retailers are going to have to find a good balance between the convenience of automation and the keen eye and kind word of a human employee.

INVENTORY AND ORDERING

Computer systems for inventory are designed to support one of two basic purposes: **anticipatory buying**, in which primarily new and untried items (like clothing styles) are bought with the objective of their being sold out and replaced by other merchandise at the end of a season, or **replenishment buying** (as with groceries, hardware, and liquor) to restock specific items against a model stock plan. Many systems feature an **exception reporting** function, that triggers an alert when a particular SKU is selling at a different pace (either slower or more quickly) than its "normal" rate.

The previous section of text on POS systems mentioned different companies in a supply chain being able to communicate with each other by computer and, therefore, requiring technology that is compatible. This process is referred to as **electronic data integration** or **data synchronization**, and the system used to accomplish it is referred to as **Electronic Data Interchange (EDI)**. It is used to minimize routine business-to-business paperwork like invoices and purchase orders.

In 1981, Wal-Mart was linked by computer to only 1,000 of its suppliers; today, the figure has grown to more than 65,000. EDI has become commonplace as part of a larger concept known as **Quick Response (QR)**. It's a strategy that allows retailers and suppliers to form an alliance to manage their mutual inventories. This may mean the following:

- The manufacturer makes just enough items on demand to fill a particular order, meaning the manufacturer doesn't have to store a lot of stock awaiting orders. This type of plan is called **just-in-time (JIT)** production, or sometimes **lean production**.
- The **model stocks** developed by buyers for each product classification are shared with the vendor or manufacturer, with a minimum level at which a reorder is automatically computer-generated. Orders are smaller and more frequent, so the retailer doesn't have to store as much product. In some systems, the appropriate buyer (or perhaps the merchandise manager) must review the order before it is sent, sometimes not.
- The system may also be capable of delivery-related information. As an order is processed, the vendor's software can notify individual stores with the expected delivery dates for items in the order.
- The vendor is responsible for looking at the stocks and deciding when to order. This method is known as **Vendor-Managed Inventory (VMI)**. It's commonplace in the grocery industry—the vendor's sales rep stocks the store with product (and special displays and promotions as necessary) and uploads information to the store's computer system. Handheld computers are used for the on-site functions.
- The retailer can keep track of whether the money invested in each of its major vendors' lines is commensurate with the sales produced.

In the supermarket business, QR may be known as **ECR**, for **Efficient Customer Response**. Of course, these catchy terms involve a lot more than ordering by computer. The idea behind them is to foster a longer-term, more cooperative arrangement that is based on value-added services instead of price. It also minimizes the volatility of having to negotiate new business deals for every new season, and allows the partners to forecast and plan together, not just send invoices back and forth electronically. The goal should be a true partnership, entered into to save time, money, and paperwork. When competitive vendors service the same large retailer (like Sears or JCPenney), there's a certain trust level that must be maintained. Buyers can't help but learn some "insider information" about a number of competitors, and it's important to respect these relationships and never betray their confidence. In turn, the vendors who sell to competitive retailers must abide by the same unwritten code of ethics.

In terms of inventory management, what computers should provide the retail chain and its buyers is more common sense than high-tech, according to *The Retail Professional* newsletter:

- **Ease in building purchase orders.** This includes the ability to add new inventory, view receiving and sales history, and view the previous POs for a given item.
- **Comprehensive receiving information.** When merchandise is received, a good system will update the inventory, send the information to accounts payable, and print the price tags for the merchandise.
- **Clear, objective data and fast, accurate reports.** If you don't know exactly what your 10 best- and worst-selling products are this week, or precisely where you are overstocked or understocked, the system isn't doing what it should be.

Newsletter editor Jim Meisler's suggestion is not to expect to buy a system that immediately fills 100 percent of the business's needs. Instead, look for a reliable vendor with a good track record that will work with the company and update the system accordingly. It is also permissible to "test drive" the system through one retail cycle, to see how it performs.[8] In short, decide what you actually want a system to do before you shop for a system at all, and then be prepared to work with the vendor to fine-tune it to fit your needs.

The Future of Inventory Management

The latest technology in back-office functions like inventory management is the development of a new data transmission format called **Extensible Markup Language (XML)**. It is more flexible than EDI, which has become standardized. Extensible means XML can be "extended" to communicate computer-to-computer, and also computer-to-human. In computerspeak, it is known as a *metalanguage*—a language for describing other languages. (In the computer world, a *language* means the structure of an electronic document.) This allows computer programmers to adapt it to many different uses and types of documents. XML is also nonproprietary, which means anyone can use it without having to pay for the rights to do so.

What this means for retailers is if an existing EDI system is working well, fine. Data translates well between EDI and XML. But gradually, EDI systems are being phased out and/or merged with XML systems. Even if you know next to nothing about computers, the end result is that communication between partner companies will seem more natural and seamless with XML in place. And that may be all you need to know—leave the rest to the IT department!

DOING BUSINESS ONLINE

Excluding travel, online retail sales in the United States grew an astonishing 34 percent in 2003. Our purchases of general merchandise online are expected to total just over $151 billion by 2010, up from $75 billion in 2004.[9]

The businesses leading the way have been leisure travel and clothing, but books, video, and music sales have seen some of the largest year-to-year gains.

Internet marketing experts say existing, traditional retailers are the best positioned to succeed with online sales (also called *eCommerce* and *e-tailing*), because customers want to do business with retailers and brands with which they are already familiar. If an existing business has well-developed brand recognition and trust, it should also have higher online sales (called *conversion rates*) and lower customer acquisition costs. Brick-and-mortar stores must focus on making their eCommerce seem like just one more facet of business—simple, almost seamless to the customer, and capable of giving them 24-7 access to merchandise instead of just during regular store hours.

Consumers have also become more comfortable with online shopping in general. A 2004 poll of more than 1,700 online buyers found one-third of them said they planned to do even more of their holiday shopping online than they did the previous year:

- 89 percent planned to use the Internet to comparison shop; 86 percent use it to "research" gift-buying possibilities.
- 74 percent buy gifts for others online.
- 53 percent buy items for themselves online.[10]

Grocery appears to be one of the biggest industries poised for Internet success, but the logistics of home delivery are challenging. Still, half of consumers anticipate spending at least part of their food budget online within the next few years.[11] There are also exciting opportunities for small retailers online, in niche markets where they've built up loyalty for their unique product lines. As coauthors, we've bought a particular brand of coffee from Hawaii, lavender bath products from a farm in rural Idaho, and an out-of-print book from a shop in New Jersey—all without leaving home.

The person who shops at the same business in more than one way—online, by catalog, by store visits, and so on—is called a **multichannel shopper**. Your online customers' biggest fears are the security of their credit card information, and the annoyance of paying additional shipping, handling, and sales taxes. But overall, they appear more than willing to pay for convenience.

This means buyers and merchandise managers must consider a lot more than how their wares will look in store displays. Online retailing opens up a whole new venue for showcasing the merchandise. (Who could forget the Victoria's Secret online lingerie shows?) It also throws interesting new variables into the buying equations—when the whole world can see it, instead of just the people who come into the store, how many more will they buy?

So far, the merchants who have done well in catalog sales have adapted the best to eCommerce, because they've simply adapted their catalogs to "work" online. According to Peter Stanger, vice president of business-to-consumer topics for The Boston Consulting Group:

They enjoy the advantages of established brands, existing infra-structure, and extensive experience in selling to customers at a distance. They know they will succeed if they focus on the best customers, rather than allocate huge sums to attract customers whose purchases won't justify their acquisition costs.[12]

The Impact on Buying and Merchandising

BCG's report offers priorities for tackling both the strategy and operational challenges of Internet marketing, a few of which we'll paraphrase here, adding our own advice for buyers:

- **Create incentives to entice customers to go online.** The cost to serve a customer online can be lower than it is elsewhere, so the retailer should do whatever it can to actively encourage its customers to "try the Net." Buyers should insist that they are part of the design and updating process to merchandise the goods correctly.
- **Integrate online and offline channels.** The multichannel customer expects that "seamless" shopping experience, which means integrating all aspects of back-office functions and the technology associated with them: accounting, credit card acceptance, inventory, sales forecasting, product returns. If the merchant you buy for sells three different ways (in-store, online, and by catalog) there *should not* be three different systems to track goods internally!
- **Leverage offline scale.** A large retailer already has purchasing power, which only increases with online sales. This can be a definite bonus as a buyer, increasing your OTB budget. But remember, adding online capability can be expensive, so you've got to leverage the buying power you have in order to bring down your overall costs.
- **Use your distribution infrastructure.** This is one reason catalogers do so well at Internet marketing. They already have distribution systems in place. Adding a Web site means the retailer's distribution system must be revamped for different kinds of handling and shipping. This cannot help but impact buyers and vendors, deadlines, and contracts.
- **Manage channel conflict.** There is bound to be some infighting between divisions when a retailer sells in multiple channels. Someone will feel ignored—perhaps the brick-and-mortar store departments, perhaps some of the suppliers. Plan on it, and be part of the solution. You want them *all* enthusiastic about selling (or providing) the wares, in every venue.
- **Use your best customer to model future improvements.** You may think you know who you're buying for, but your "average customer" can change a lot when you open up the field to anyone who's got a computer. It requires a different type of market research and should focus on who's buying from the Web site.[13]

The other important consideration is that a Web site works completely differently than a store or catalog setup, in terms of merchandising. You will want to have input on what products are featured most prominently, what information or accessories are offered with the products, and so on. Let's take a blank screen and consider just a few of the points that buyers must ponder—decisions that are *not ever* necessary in an actual retail store.

- How many pages should the Web site have?
- How many items should be on a page?
- How prominently should the price be featured? If the item is marked down, how quickly can the page be updated to reflect the sale price?
- How many "views" of a single item should be available, and how does the customer access them? Who is responsible for providing the photos?
- How do you hide the item from view (at least temporarily) when it's out of stock?
- How will you group or categorize the items? There are no racks or shelves!
- How do you get the customer to view accessory items that "go with" others in different categories? Do you put the same item in multiple categories, on different pages?

Some of these questions are answered at least partially by the capability of the software, but others depend on what will prompt the best sales. As a buyer or merchandising manager, you'd better have some ideas!

Buying professionals are not expected to be technology experts. But one of the reasons to keep learning is to facilitate good working relationships with the people in the company who are the "techies," and to understand at least the basics of the systems and what they can do. It is also critical to insist on having input into the decisions that will impact your position and responsibilities, as well as those of the downline employees you may supervise—and to advocate for additional training whenever it is needed.

CHAPTER SUMMARY

This chapter summarized the most common forms of technology used in retailing, from identifying products with the newest generations of shelf labels and bar codes, to how sales are rung up, inventoried, and made online. Along the way, each type of technology meets one of two major goals:

- To save *someone* time and money
- To allow closer business relationships, as a result of increased sharing of information

These apply whether we're talking about the time savings of online shopping, or the Quick Response systems set up between a retailer and multiple vendors.

And you thought fashion was fickle? Now that you know something about the pace at which retail technology moves, you've got to wonder, "What does all this mean for retail buyers?" What it means is that the buyer and/or merchandising manager has fast and amazing tools at his or her disposal to help track purchasing patterns, fire off last-minute orders, and do market research about customers without leaving their desk. The output, however, is only as good as the input . . . and the retailer's ability to analyze and work with the data. The ones who do it best will not forget that both customers and coworkers, no matter how sophisticated their computer skills, are still absolutely human.

The good news-bad news part of new technology is that it can provide too much detail. Companies are tempted to overspend on systems that do things they don't even need; and sales data can be compiled in dozens of different ways. It is important to stay focused on the information that is relevant to your job and your buying decisions. Don't swamp yourself (or others) with material that is interesting but not especially useful.

Realize that even as you read this, new things are happening in retail technology. The best approach a merchandiser or buyer can take is to be open-minded about the changes and willing to learn about them—at least, enough to understand their impact on your day-to-day duties and those of your staff. Keep asking questions, and stay informed.

DISCUSSION QUESTIONS

1. Why do products need both SKUs and UPC numbers?
2. List three pros and three cons of having EDI capability with your suppliers and buying offices.
3. What basic "skills" would a computer system need to have for *anticipatory buying* versus *replenishment buying*? Which system, in your view, would have to be the more sophisticated?
4. What would be the minimum amount of technology a small, specialty retailer could have to operate successfully in today's business world—if they do not wish to have a Web site?
5. Why would a company want an *open POS system*?
6. If a retailer encourages customers to become multichannel shoppers, doesn't the retailer risk losing the shopper to any of thousands of other online merchants? How would you, as the buyer for that retailer, combat this?
7. Would you make the case for keeping grocery checkers, or replacing them with "smart" shopping carts? Briefly explain your choice.
8. Do you share the fears of some consumers that items like partner cards and RFID tags give retailers too much information about you based on your shopping habits? Is it just a hassle, or an invasion of privacy? Do you believe companies that say they don't sell the information to others?

9. How can a buyer whose employer *does not* have state-of-the-art technology best compete with one who *does*?
10. How many different acronyms for new technology are in this chapter? Why do you think this industry is so rife with them? Do you think all the catchy abbreviations make things simpler, or more confusing?

ENDNOTES

1. "Retail Industry IT Spending Profile—2004," Copyright © Forrester Research, Inc., Cambridge, Massachusetts.
2. 1998 retail survey results, Arizona Department of Weights and Measures, Phoenix, Arizona; and Oregon Department of Agriculture Measurement Standards Division, Salem, Oregon.
3. 1999 Analysis of Pennsylvania Scanner Certification Program (SCP), Penn State University College of Agricultural Sciences, University Park, Pennsylvania.
4. "RFID and Consumers: Understanding Their Mindset," a Cap Gemini Ernst & Young Study for National Retail Federation; in *Stores* magazine, March 2004 issue.
5. "Retail Automation Equipment: A Vertical Market Analysis of Usage and Plans for Wireless, Emerging, and Traditional Technologies—June 2002" (Natick, Massachusetts: Venture Development Corporation).
6. "Unlocking POS," joint research by IHL Consulting Group, Franklin, Tennessee; and *RIS News*, an Edgell Communications publication, Randolph, New Jersey, January 2004.
7. "2004 North American Self-Service Kiosks" (Franklin, TN: IHL Consulting Group).
8. Jim Meisler, "Computerizing Your Retail Business," November 1998, available at retailernews.com.
9. Research results copyright © Forrester Research, Inc., Cambridge, Massachusetts, as reported on the Shop.org Web site, August 2004.
10. "Online Holiday Mood Study 2004" by Shop.org and BizRate.com, Washington, D.C., September 2004.
11. "The Next Chapter in Business-to-Consumer E-Commerce: Advantage Incumbent" (Boston: The Boston Consulting Group, 4th Quarter 2000).
12. Quoted in "Retail Industry" column, on About.com, October 2004.
13. "The Next Chapter in Business-to-Consumer E-Commerce: Advantage Incumbent" (Boston: The Boston Consulting Group, 4th Quarter 2000).

Choosing Vendors

A vendor relationship is a lot like a marriage—for better or for worse, and some days are better than others. Vendor selection is a key element of the buying process, and as a buyer, you will have ample opportunity to discover and hire new vendors, as well as dealing with others who have long, firmly established relationships with your retailer.

This chapter covers the dynamics of the retailer/supplier relationship:

- Factors to consider in vendor selection
- Ethics and social responsibility in retail
- How and why to reevaluate current vendors
- Types of vendors to choose from
- How management policies impact vendor selection

We'll discuss domestic sources in this chapter; international sources in the following chapters. As in other chapters, the terms *vendor* and *supplier* are used interchangeably.

It is always smart to have the broadest possible market contacts, but a large portion of most buyers' purchases should be concentrated with a few key resources. If the buyer only has so much "purchasing power," some thought must be given to how to divide it between reliable partners and new prospective resources.

Your purchases as a retail buyer will fall into three groups:

- A **new buy** is a first-time purchase from a vendor. You may or may not have specifications for the product, and while you have done the "homework" detailed in this chapter, your company does not have a track record with this vendor.
- In a **modified rebuy**, the basic relationship has been established but the order itself changes, at least slightly. You might even be looking around at other vendors who could offer similar merchandise at a better price. In other words, you've had some experience with the original vendor, but your loyalty could still shift elsewhere.
- A **straight reorder** is routine replenishment of out-of-stock items—same sizes, colors, product count per case, and so forth. Buyers tend to let these go on autopilot, so to speak (and vendors love that!), because they are often computerized or handled by sales reps who visit individual stores. However, the items and stock levels should be checked periodically to see if modifications are necessary with changing seasons, economic conditions, and the like.

Herbert L. Seegel, a former president of R.H. Macy and Company (now part of Federated Department Stores, Inc.), compared vendors of nationally advertised products to the star players on a sports team. They can be counted on, game after game, to deliver high scores. But a good team needs more than its superstars—there's an important role for rookies, who bring new ideas, new playing styles, and new enthusiasm to the team. So it is in retail. Seegel believed it requires a combination of stars and rookies to make a winning team. Let's discuss how to recruit them.

CHOOSING A RESOURCE

Buyers select vendors based on their own evaluations of what the vendor can do for the retailer the buyer represents. Aside from fashion, brand names, ideas, point-of-sale materials, and anything else that is being offered, the decision ultimately boils down to this: *Can this vendor increase my company's sales and profit?* Of course, there are many more facets of the relationship to consider—but that's the primary one.

Exactly what can a supplier do to achieve this? The answer is a combination of attributes. For one, the supplier must be willing to help the buyer meet the budgets—for sales, markups, margin, contribution (after certain direct expense charges), and inventory turnover. This means the pricing of the goods, and the terms of the purchase, can be negotiated to the benefit of both parties.

In turn, the vendor must have the capability to actually meet the volume goals and shipping deadlines the retailer will demand. Depending on the type of merchandise, it should be made at least somewhat exclusive to one retailer in a particular trading area. In terms of marketing, the vendor must be willing to help with advertising and promotion in the quest for customer patronage. Above all, the merchandise must be suitable for the buyer's clientele—or none of the rest will matter much.

Suitability of Merchandise

Suitability is a factor partly because it is so tempting—in an exciting industry, at a colorful market with a fistful of cash to spend—to take chances and come back to the retailer with all kinds of interesting new items that seem to have a ton of sales potential. The key word here is "potential." The buyer must not lose sight of who the customers are and what they want to buy. Building relationships with vendors who also know your customer base and how to satisfy them gives you a solid base of merchandise from which to choose.

This does *not* mean you can never buy anything avant-garde. There may be room in the assortment for a new style, flavor, or color. But if the vendor does not offer products that either suit the preferences of a large portion of the clientele or have special appeal to a certain group, their trade potential with your store is naturally limited. The same is true for a vendor who may offer wonderful merchandise . . . but not at suitable prices for your customer base. More about pricing policies in a moment.

If a buyer knows exactly what is needed for a staple item (from basic department store turtlenecks to fresh lemons in a supermarket) **specification sheets** may be created. A "spec sheet" is a no-frills list of every requirement for a product, from how many pieces to a box or case to whether a food has been frozen, or, for clothing, what type of fabric it is made from. The buyer creates the list, which is then given to prospective vendors for their price bids. As a buyer, you will then be responsible for checking the quality of the merchandise when it is delivered against the specifications or samples. In a large multi-unit chain, store managers or department managers will do the checking, along with your own spot checks to back up their data.

The small merchant (particularly one who handles many convenience items or is located far from a major metropolitan area) may prefer to buy from a single wholesaler or manufacturer that handles a family of products. Food distribution giants, like SYSCO and Performance Food Group, are good examples of this type of arrangement. They can outfit almost any type of food-related business with everything from fresh produce and meat, to dozens of frozen items, to paper products—all delivered on the same truck.

Product Differentiation

Buyers of convenience goods, like most grocery items, often require vendors with highly standardized product lines, usually name-brand goods that have built their own reputations and long sales loyalty histories with customers. In most cases, however, the buyer looks for those suppliers who differentiate their products—partly to avoid direct competition, but mostly to obtain features of superiority or originality—even if it's only a matter of unique packaging. Most large retailers today have created their own brands for this very purpose, as we learned in Chapter 3 about the proliferation of private-label merchandise. Remember, buyers still must deal with vendors to produce those brands, and you will have some input into decisions about distinctive packaging, product sizes, and so on.

Buyers handle trendy product categories (especially housewares, furniture, and apparel) in two different ways. Some hop from one resource to another, picking and choosing every season from what they perceive are the hottest new trends and items. They are encouraged by senior management to spend at least part of their time at every market seeking out new, offbeat suppliers with interesting merchandise.

Others prefer to give business to vendors who are consistently good rather than occasionally spectacular; many retailers have a policy of buying only from a preapproved list of vendors. Both approaches are valid, and the former is definitely riskier. The probability is that the reliable vendors will, indeed, produce their share of spectacular successes over time. A third approach is to combine the first two, and split the budget—say, 70 percent for "old faithful" suppliers, and 30 percent for "new kids on the block."

In some situations buyers have no choice but to work with a supplier they consider below their standards. For instance, something that is flying off the store shelves *must* be bought, regardless of the performance record of its producer. No buyer would choose to be without merchandise that competitors are promoting vigorously and that is obviously achieving high sales levels. And sometimes, senior management has a couple of subpar vendors firmly entrenched—those long-time, handshake, golf-game business deals that surface in any industry. Management control over the vendor mix varies considerably depending on the type of retailer and the buyer's overall experience (or lack of it). Buyers work with them, gather data, and play a waiting game to prove the case that the relationship must change, or end. If the supplier's product line can be proven less distinctive than other better-qualified competitors, the case can certainly be made effectively. It just takes time and patience.

Timing and Delivery Policies

Depending on the type of product, **timing** may refer to elements of fashion leadership, the speed of innovation, or simply the speed at which merchandise can be made available for sale after the order is placed. In the world of apparel, all three are critical. How quickly is the vendor willing to offer samples for early inspection and product testing? Will the product be available in quantity throughout the year? When buying for retail clothing stores, this is important for areas of the country that may not start a trend but may adopt it eventually. The buyer can keep an eye on a particular line or style and, if it appears to be succeeding and getting a fair amount of popular press, can jump on board with a mid-season order.

Will reorders be possible? (In some high-fashion lines, they are not, which helps lend the mystique of exclusivity.) If they are not, the buyer may investigate so-called knock-off manufacturers, foreign companies that specialize in making look-alike designer items like shoes and handbags, but this is a very controversial move. The knock-offs may resemble the designer originals, but that is where the similarities end. (They are generally considered inferior in quality and are sold more cheaply because they were imported without the payment of U.S. Customs duties. There are certainly better ways of finding backup sources.)

Part of timing is the dependability of a vendor to meet promised delivery dates. Speed of delivery is most important when it is either difficult or inconvenient for the retailer to anticipate sales well in advance, and for retailers who are unable to pay for and warehouse large prepurchased quantities of merchandise. In such cases, buyers may prefer to deal mostly with nearby vendors or, at least, with those that have nearby warehouses or distribution centers. Another option, which we'll discuss later in this chapter, is to buy smaller lots from wholesalers instead of directly from manufacturers.

Distribution Policies

In this area, retailers and vendors do some serious negotiating. The buyer commonly strives to get a particular product line sold only in his or her stores, in his or her trading areas. But the vendor, understandably, wants to sell as much merchandise as possible. Those who make presold convenience goods will especially favor policies of wide distribution, and you can't blame them.

With well-known brands come brand policies, and if the brand is famous enough and has a big national advertising budget, the vendor generally makes the distribution rules. Many in the fashion world, for instance, will not permit the buyer to utilize the knock-off manufacturers mentioned. The more exclusive the distribution agreement, the more control the vendor has over how the product is promoted and even how it is displayed in stores.

Some suppliers will agree to a so-called selective distribution plan—they will sell their "name brand" to more than one retailer in a trading area, but only to outlets of a predetermined price and overall caliber. A department store's customers may see the same line of blue jeans in another department store, but not in a discount store. Another way suppliers increase distribution is by creating multiple brands for different types of stores. In the 1980s, for example, Hanes (the hosiery manufacturer, sold primarily in the "better" department stores) developed the L'eggs brand of packaged pantyhose to sell in supermarkets. The brands coexist nicely now, but when the announcement was first made, Hanes' department store orders dropped by 20 percent. The department store buyers perceived the availability of Hanes products in grocery stores as damaging to their customer image of the brand.

A manufacturer may produce the same product (or slight variations of it) under three different labels and sell it to three different retail competitors. If this is the case, the buyer will want to make his or her own retailer's expectations very clear. It is also fair to ask the manufacturer who else is buying the product.

Of course, a buyer has the option of getting exclusive or limited distribution in an area simply by purchasing everything the vendor has to sell in a particular line. And the vendor has the option of requiring "tie-in" sales—pressing the buyer to take some less desirable items in order to buy the top-of-line items, or requiring that the buyer purchase a certain (high) percentage of the items in a line in order to get the line at all. Now do you see why we call it serious negotiating?

Pricing and Payment Policies

The popularity of Wal-Mart, Costco, and other large, no-frills operators has become a worrisome threat to traditional retailers. As a buyer, one of the top considerations will be whether the supplier's "suggested retail price" is appropriate for your clientele, and sufficient for your company to profit with a decent markup on the items. There are two ways to make money in retail:

- By selling a few items at a high markup (the high-end, specialty, or boutique store, etc.)
- By selling many items at a low markup (Wal-Mart, dollar stores, etc.)

Where does this vendor's merchandise fit into the picture? All buyers are interested in a vendor's prices and terms, but for different reasons. In many fields, price lines are standardized among sellers, and the chief problem faced by the buyer is to get the best combination of all the attributes at the lowest possible fixed price. Is the vendor's policy to sell at market price, or at the following:

- **A market plus price.** This means the vendor asks a higher price for special, distinctive features of the product. (It's up to the buyer to decide if the features are actually noticeable enough to warrant the higher price.)
- **A market minus price.** This term applies to goods that are satisfactory for basement sales and discount stores but may not meet the requirements of a more discriminating clientele. It is a hallmark of wholesalers who buy remainders of different manufacturers' stock for resale with few additional "services" involved.

Credit terms are often the most critical in choosing a resource. As a buyer, you may be required to deal *only* with those who will grant credit. If you can pay cash up front, however, you can use it to negotiate a better deal. All buyers are also interested in getting prepaid freight terms—knowing what shipping will cost up front, with no surprises at the time of delivery. Freight costs can be extremely high in relation to selling price; these should be carefully weighed, and negotiated downward if possible, as part of the wholesale cost of the merchandise.

Ethical Considerations

In May of 2003, Wal-Mart decided to remove three men's magazines from store distribution, citing customer complaints (but offering no specifics about how many, or who complained). The following month, it added U-shaped "blinders" to obscure the covers of some popular women's magazines that often feature sexually explicit headlines. The moves had the magazine publishing world in a panic, since Wal-Mart accounts for 15 percent of single-copy magazine sales.[1]

Whether the retail giant was targeted, as some suggest, by extremely conservative and well-organized Christian groups, or whether it was a response to a sex discrimination lawsuit filed against Wal-Mart (ironically, the month before the magazines were pulled), the impact on vendors in the category was major and troubling. Can you imagine what the buyers' role would be in dealing with them?

Ethical issues run the gamut, but today they include a wide range of environmental and social issues—from the use of recycled products and packaging, to damage to forests or wildlife, to allegations of human rights violations in foreign manufacturing plants. Companies in most industries are expected to show social responsibility, through their donations, employee charitable efforts, diversity and empowerment training, and so on. What do your vendors do to "give back" to their communities? To their own employees?

In addition to how a company handles a conflict is how quickly it is handled. Ponder these potential dilemmas:

- One of your suppliers is accused of hiring sweatshop labor to make products in overseas factories for pennies on the dollar. National human rights organizations put the manufacturer on a "hit list" of companies to boycott. The product lines are not your top sellers, but they've been reliable and profitable, and the supplier has been easy to work with. (Remember the Nike scandal in the 1990s?)

- Let's say your own city council gets into the picture by condemning the supplier in local newspapers and on television. The mayor says the supplier is "stealing jobs" needed by people in your state, by having the work done overseas.
- What if the boycott is prompted by gay rights activists, charging that the supplier's hiring practices are discriminatory?
- What if the issue is product testing, and an animal rights organization claims the tests are cruel to animals and unnecessary?
- What if the U.S. Food and Drug Administration does not ban a food supplement your retailer offers but issues a news release saying its effectiveness is "questionable" and more testing will be done?
- What if a vendor offers you free samples for your own use? School clothing for your kids? A cash bonus when your stores sell more of the products than any other merchant in the area? And what if the vendor asks you *not* to mention this to your upline manager?

The point here is that buyers will face any number of potential ethical challenges. No one can prepare for everything, but if your company does not already have written policies about at least some of these issues, you should be involved in helping to create them. In fact, ask your vendors to see *their* company policies as well.

There are two reasons for having policies, procedures, and ethical standards in writing. Vendors know where they stand and what is permissible, making buyers' jobs easier. Buyers can shrug and cite "the rules" in graciously refusing questionable offers.

In addition, if a consumer should have a complaint about a product, both parties are likely to have to work together toward a resolution—or be named as codefendants in a lawsuit. The professional standards of each should be outlined as clearly as possible. Handshake agreements beyond what is written on the purchase order have a certain nostalgic flair, but they are no longer sufficient in today's litigious society. As an example, Wal-Mart is sued more than any entity other than the U.S. government.

Wal-Mart's battery of attorneys estimates more than 9,000 open cases, from enormous class action discrimination lawsuits to individual product liability injury claims.[2] You will want to be as certain as possible that the suppliers from whom you buy products will stand (with you) behind their safety and quality, and will be honest and fair in all of your mutual business dealings.

Assistance with Sales

In advertising and at the point of sale, there are great variations in the ways suppliers participate in selling their products. It is not uncommon for the supplier to pay for at least a portion of the retailer's newspaper advertising—more if the ad features a single vendor's product exclusively. When multiple vendors share the costs of large ads (full pages, full-color multipage flyers, etc.) it's called **cooperative ("co-op") advertising.** Depending on the involvement of (and cost to) the vendor, some will demand that their layouts and exact information be used; others specify only certain elements; still others make no demands at all about presentation. It is not uncommon for a vendor to ask for a **tear sheet**—an actual copy of the ad when it runs—before they agree to pay their part of the bill for it. We talk more about co-op advertising in Chapter 10.

The suppliers should be your subject-matter experts about their products, available to assist in training and merchandising. The smaller the store, the more the owner and/or buyer will depend on a supplier to furnish signage, counter and/or window displays, seasonal promotions, **endcaps** (displays at ends of aisles), fixtures, and so on. Large stores are more likely to require some uniformity in their displays, information that should be shared with the suppliers. But all retailers are partial to vendors who take an active interest in the sales process. As a buyer, you should look for vendor companies that will do the following:

- Attend an occasional sales meeting with floor sales employees to train them in product knowledge and selling techniques.
- Offer "leave-behind" product brochures and other information, either for the sales staff or to give consumers.
- Set up special promotions (sales, sweepstakes, holiday themes) in individual stores; or in supermarkets, arrange endcaps.
- Recruit and train "demonstrators" (like the cosmetic counter employees in department stores, people who give out food samples in supermarkets); and often, pay their salaries.
- Send out their own route salespeople (nicknamed "missionaries" in the trade) to check and rotate stock, fill displays, take orders, and make sure the supplier's products are well stocked and looking good.
- Provide efficient delivery, installation, warranty, and repair services for those items (like home appliances) that may require them.

There are some retailers who will argue that those who seek this much assistance from their vendors are abdicating their proper sales responsibilities. But why not take advantage of whatever means available if they assist you in selling the product? Buyers should just be aware of the strings that may be attached to the assistance. What is the vendor requiring in exchange—and how much control does it give the vendor in terms of display placement, length of promotions, and so on?

Other Considerations

A few other factors may impact your vendor selection decisions—miscellaneous on this list, but important nonetheless:

- **Recommendations.** The buying offices used by your retailers will keep you informed about their "preferred resources." Noncompeting retailers in the same buying group also often exchange information about best-selling items and lines, as well as "problem" vendors. And there is nothing improper about calling another retailer in a noncompeting market area and asking their buyers' opinions.
- **Convenience.** It may be as simple as choosing the most convenient suppliers—geographically, from regional market sources; or the ones that offer the easiest ordering, payment, tagging, and delivery terms.
- **Compatible technology.** The larger the retailer, the more they can require of their vendors in terms of technology. In order to participate in QR, EDI, and some of the other services mentioned in Chapter 6, vendors must be willing to adopt (or adapt) computer software and hardware so the systems can exchange data. With the advent of RFID tags, this will become even more critical.
- **Retailer's storage capability.** Most vendors offer price discounts for large orders, and some sources have large minimum-order requirements. As a retailer, you can only buy in quantity if your business has room to store the goods. Sometimes, the flexibility to place smaller and more frequent orders is preferable, even with the deeper discounts that bulk purchasing allows.

Weighing Vendor Selection Factors

So, there are almost as many selection factors for vendors as there are for the products they produce! Not all stores take all of them into account, but one way to jump-start the selection process (or to evaluate a prospective vendor against current vendors) is to create a report card, of sorts—a grading system with points assigned for each of your priorities:

4 for excellent	2 for fair
3 for good	1 for poor

Table 7-1 is an example that compares four vendors in seven key categories—key to this particular buyer, that is. Your own priorities may be different. But it's a fair way of making side-by-side comparisons of services.

Most buyers (and retail senior managers in general) find it profitable to analyze the vendor base periodically, to weed out the unsuitable ones and concentrate volume with the preferred ones. Technology makes this possible with up-to-date sales figures for each merchant with whom you deal. The ultimate measurement of their worth to you is the steady profitability of their merchandise. However, that is not the whole story. Even the strongest suppliers have off seasons and unforeseen problems.

It's not a bad idea to simply evaluate their overall dependability annually and discuss the findings with your manager. Keep your own notes about problems and concerns that come up. Whether you handwrite them in a notebook or make entries on a laptop, the details may be important in future

Table 7-1 A Vendor Comparison Based on the Buyer's Top Priorities

Buyer's Priorities	Vendor A	Vendor B	Vendor C	Vendor D
Suitability	3	2	2	4
Helps with ads and training	2	2	2	3
Distribution policy (more points for exclusivity)	2	2	4	4
Recommendations from references (other stores)	3	3	2	3
Computer compatibility (set up for EDI and ordering)	1	1	4	3
Credit terms (allows 90 days to pay and cash discounts)	4	1	1	4
Environmental/social awareness	3	3	2	2
TOTAL POINTS	**18**	**14**	**17**	**23**

decision making, and it is unwise to depend on your memory to recall dates and quotes. Check these benchmarks:

- Shipping goods correctly, according to sample or description.
- Shipping exactly as ordered, with no substitutions unless the buyer has been advised and agrees to the change.
- Uniformity of product in successive shipments. Do they appear to exercise some quality control?
- The authenticity behind the sales hype—what did the vendor tell you at market about how popular this item was going to be and why? Was it true?
- Accepting responsibility for defects and delivery snafus, and making adjustments promptly and graciously when necessary.
- Terms of the last "deal" they offered, so you can compare them to the next one.
- Efficiency and accuracy in billing.
- How much merchandise must be returned to this vendor? How much ends up being marked down to sell?

Using your notes, you can often pinpoint problem areas and work with your contacts at the company to get them remedied. Remember: It's a partnership.

Finally, browse on the Internet once in a while, using search engines to look at your vendors' Web sites. Read recent articles about the companies, also easy to find online. You may be surprised at what you learn—or more accurately, what you *didn't know* about them—that might help you in your negotiations.

TYPES OF VENDORS

We mentioned earlier that, in some cases, a buyer has very little input about the retailer's choice of suppliers. Senior management policy may dictate that product must be bought only from manufacturers, only from wholesale distributors, or perhaps only through a buying office. Here are the pros and cons of each option.

Buying from Manufacturers

Buying from the manufacturer (known as **buying direct**) has potential benefits for almost any type of retailer—but you may or may not get to realize these benefits, based on the type of retailer you work for and the way the manufacturer chooses to do business.

In the high-fashion industry, it is the norm even for the smallest stores to buy directly from manufacturers, or through their showrooms and market representatives. Involving a middleman or wholesaler would add too much time to the delivery of goods, which doesn't work well for trendy seasonal merchandise. Clothing is generally made in a very short time frame, right before a season begins. It must reach the market quickly to reach its maximum sales potential, so shipping straight from the manufacturer makes sense.

In other types of retail, only the chains that are able to buy in bulk can work directly with manufacturers. The manufacturer is prohibited by federal law from contracting with retail buyers to demand that they not buy competing goods, but there are certainly plenty of other ways in which buyers may feel their hands are tied by rather restrictive agreements. These "deals" typically include one or more of the following:

- A commitment to a large minimum order
- A steep sales quota as the "price" for permitting the retailer to retain the product line
- Some requirements for the amount of promotional attention the goods must receive
- A requirement to stick to their suggested retail prices

Despite the caveats, there are situations in which buying direct is optimum:

- When goods are perishable and must reach the retailer with a minimum of handling to avoid deterioration. (There are exceptions, as you'll see in the discussion of wholesalers.)
- When the manufacturer produces such an enormous product line that it is easy to place a large order and realize volume savings.
- Where the wholesalers carry competing brands of their own and neglect the manufacturer's product.

HOW THE TOP MANUFACTURERS STAY ON TOP!

A 2004 foodservice industry survey offers some interesting clues about what makes a good supplier, and a good supplier-retailer partnership. "Beyond the Basics" included the opinions of more than 470 foodservice operators and manufacturers about the companies they admire most for building solid relationships with their customers. The top three characteristics on customers' "wish lists" were as follows:

- **Innovation.** Provide actionable insights—that is, research that explores current and potential customers' desires and behaviors and translates them into innovative, actionable programs. For example, don't just offer new menu items and services; also offer new types of merchandising materials and programs to drive customer excitement and loyalty.

- **Solutions.** Use the research and insights to go beyond the "basic tactics" to benefit both partners' businesses. Manufacturers can and should help with supply chain and equipment issues, in addition to product presentation.

- **Added-value services.** Go beyond the basics of product training and specifications. Operators want to know how to use the products more efficiently and effectively. They need technical, culinary, and product expertise from the manufacturers.

The food and beverage manufacturers on the list are all heavy-hitting national brands, but vendors of any size could conceivably use the same methods to offer more and better information to drive sales, not just push product out their doors and into retailers' stores.[3]

TOP 10 FoodservicElite™ Manufacturer Rankings for 2004

Company	Ranked as "industry leader" by percentage of respondents	Percentage difference from 2003 survey
Tyson Foods	27.6%	+ 3.3
Coca-Cola	17.4%	+ 0.5
General Mills	14.7%	+ 0.4
Pepsi-Cola	12.0%	+ 2.7
Kraft Foods	11.0%	+ 0.9
Sara Lee	10.8%	+ 2.2
Kellogg's	10.1%	+ 0.7
Frito-Lay	9.9%	+ 1.9
Rich's	8.9%	− 0.8
Schwan's	8.5%	+ 1.6

- Where many retail stores in a concentrated area all carry the line and can be easily serviced by the manufacturer.
- Where there is a public merchandising warehouse that can do your retailer's storage and shipping functions without much cost overhead. In some cases, successful warehousing businesses replace the wholesaler.
- When the retailer wants to develop private-label brands or exclusive product features, and therefore works directly with the manufacturer for that purpose.

Buying from Brokers

Some manufacturers of nationally advertised products sell only through agents or wholesalers, creating their own network of regional representatives. In the food industry, for example, makers of specialty products often sell them exclusively through regional food **brokers** who are actually manufacturer's agents. They represent noncompeting lines, and since it is cheaper for the manufacturer to market this way than to set up a separate sales organization, having the broker do the job does not add much at all to the cost of the product. Brokers are still able to offer items to retailers at wholesale prices. Their fees are usually a percentage of net sales, and the amount will vary based on the type of product, the overall size of the merchant, and the types of services that the broker provides.

Again depending on the type of merchandise, brokers will pay personal visits to retailers' headquarters, set up sales and information booths at industry trade shows, have periodic "tasting" events (for food products), and/or maintain showrooms at regional markets. Many brokers' businesses are highly computerized, allowing retail buyers to "shop" and order online, although they realize that regular, personal contact nets better sales results. The whole idea is to allow the buyer maximum access to samples, and information about the product lines, in the easiest and most convenient form for the busy buying professional. After all, the broker is judged by how well he or she represents the manufacturers' products.

Buying from Wholesalers

The wholesale company is a **middleman** or **distributor**, buying from manufacturers and reselling to retail stores. Despite retailers' decreasing dependence on middlemen because of private branding, wholesaling is still a big business and most retailers rely on their local or regional wholesalers for at least a portion of their goods. Why?

- They are far more flexible than most manufacturers. They'll ship small orders to a single store, financed with liberal credit terms; or they'll agree to a major contract to provide many different goods and merchandising services to chain customers.
- They often represent smaller, unique manufacturers and provide guidance to "both sides" in forming new product-retailer bonds.

- They maintain a wide choice of staples, ready for immediate delivery. The best wholesalers really do attempt to be one-stop shops for retailers in a particular field, especially grocery and drug. In the grocery industry, the produce wholesalers also tend to have better year-round selections than individual growers, because they buy from multiple farms.
- They generally have invested heavily in technology, as they understand that time savings and convenience will retain their retailers' loyalty.
- They are extremely helpful, from making computer recommendations to advising on sales strategy, to providing merchandising assistance and advice on things like store and section layouts, fixtures, and promotional materials.

Wholesalers' prices are somewhat higher than manufacturers', but the extra costs are usually more than offset by value-added services, the speed of deliveries, and the savings from the retailer not having to store inventory.

Rack Jobbers and Drop-Shippers

These two unusual names refer to very specific types of retail support services. **Rack jobbers** have been around for years, ever since traditional supermarkets branched out from strictly food sales to other products, from housewares to cosmetics. They are assigned responsibility for these specialized sections of the store, and they visit individual stores to stock and price, clean, put up new displays, check inventories, and so on. The rack jobber company, by servicing many stores, qualifies as a high-volume purchaser (from wholesalers or manufacturers) and can pass the savings on to the stores.

Drop-shippers are manufacturers that agree to stock a certain amount of finished inventory, ready to ship it directly to the customer—not the store—when the customer places and pays for an order. The plan is well suited to furniture, major appliances, mattresses, and the like. The stores stock only samples of each item, cutting down on inventory and eliminating the hassle of having store personnel make the deliveries.

With the advent of Internet marketing, there is a new generation of drop-shippers that work a bit differently. They are gift, novelty, and specialty manufacturers (often small businesses, too small to hire brokers) that use mail-order and online retailers—more accurately, *resellers*—to market their products. The reseller advertises the item and, when an order is placed:

- The reseller notifies the drop-shipper by e-mail or fax.
- The drop-shipper charges the reseller (usually a direct charge to the reseller's credit card) the wholesale price for the item.
- The drop-shipper ships the product to the reseller's catalog or online customer.

The drop-shipper makes the wholesale price; the reseller keeps the difference between retail and wholesale price as profit. Most buyers will have limited contact with online drop-shippers or resellers but may negotiate with the more traditional type of drop-shipper for purchases of large, bulky goods.

CHAPTER SUMMARY

Perhaps now you can see why at the beginning of this chapter we likened vendor-retailer relationships to marriage. The selection of suppliers is a complex process that involves far more than who has the coolest new product line this season. The buyer is expected to have significant input in these decisions in most (but not all) cases, and there is plenty of legwork that must be done to get a view of the overall company, not just what it is offering for sale.

Always remember the litmus test: *Can this vendor increase my company's sales and profit?* This chapter detailed many of the facets of suppliers' businesses that should be examined—and then periodically reexamined, and also compared to the "track records" of other suppliers. Several of the requirements are not easy to quantify in terms of sales and profit numbers, such as the ethics of the supplier, the way it responds to controversy, and the level of technology commitments it has made.

The terms of vendor relationships will vary depending on the types of vendors. Buying direct from manufacturers has definite built-in challenges but may be appropriate. Good wholesalers can be counted on for wide product varieties and/or specialty products with flexible terms.

The research seems to indicate that the best vendors are those that offer as many service-oriented touches as possible—training, innovative display ideas and materials, and market research that includes meaningful conclusions and sales strategy, not just numbers. These are goals that, in a good partnership, you can often accomplish jointly.

DISCUSSION QUESTIONS

1. Would it ever be appropriate for a buyer of high-fashion women's apparel to purchase goods offered at a *market minus* price? Why or why not?
2. If you really like a manufacturer's representative personally and the lines sell well, but the manufacturer has some serious problems with prompt delivery and every invoice seems to be either late or inaccurate, how would you handle the situation? How much time would you offer to allow them to "clean up their act"?
3. After reading the chapter section on ethics, list up to five questions you would ask a new vendor about their sense of ethics in business.
4. Describe briefly how you would work with a "pushy" manufacturer who demanded more space into your retailer's newspaper ad.

5. If you were a store manager, would you support hiring rack jobbers, or would you prefer to have your own employees perform those duties to your standards? Briefly explain your decision.

6. If you were filling out a form such as Table 7-1, what would you choose as your own top six considerations for hiring vendors? List and number them, with 1 being most important to 6 being least important:

    a. In a medium-sized department store chain
    b. In a sporting goods store
    c. In a supermarket

7. Are there criteria other than those listed in this chapter that you believe would also be important to retailers?

8. Some retailers decide that a branded product line that represents, say, 25 percent of the items in a classification should produce roughly 25 percent of the sales for that classification, 30 percent should produce 30 percent of the sales, and so on. Let's say the products are men's shirts. Are there situations in which management might expect a greater share of the total? A smaller share?

9. As a buyer, how would you advise a small vendor who wants to know what she can do to more successfully compete with your larger vendors?

10. Would you be a proponent of dealing with many suppliers, each with their own strengths and unique wares; or just a few—one or two for basics, perhaps three for different types of innovative merchandise? Explain your rationale.

ENDNOTES

1. Barbara Love, "Wal-Mart Is Too Big and Influential to Ignore," *Circulation Management* magazine, July 2003.
2. Richard Willing, "Lawsuits a Volume Business at Wal-Mart," *USA Today*, August 8, 2001.
3. "Beyond the Basics," survey by Cannondale Associates, Inc. (Wilton, Connecticut) and Cognito, LLC (Cheshire, England). Reported in *I.D. Access* magazine, August 2004.

CHAPTER

8

International Vendors

If you question whether the world is getting smaller, or the borders of nations are blurring in the realm of international (and Internet) commerce, take a look at what is happening in retail. The global economy is here to stay, with all its pluses and minuses. For buyers, this can be both challenging and exciting. The exciting part is having a whole world of merchandise to choose from! The challenge is trying to negotiate its sale, shepherd it through the importing process, and get it into your stores . . . all with faraway vendors who perhaps don't speak your language or understand American business customs.

In this chapter, you can apply some of what you've already learned about dealing with suppliers as we venture into the international market. This includes:

- The proliferation and importance of imported products
- Gray markets
- Consumer attitudes about American-made versus foreign-made goods
- Finding international vendors and intermediaries
- Shipping costs and getting goods through U.S. Customs

To better understand the opportunities and challenges of international buying, it is important to start with a very basic primer on the global economy.

HOW "FREE" IS "FREE TRADE"?

Many U.S. companies already have major foreign connections—and you'd be surprised at how much "international trading" *you* actually do, day-to-day. Some of the most successful U.S.-based companies may have built their reputations with American owners, but they have since been sold to foreign companies in the increasing consolidation and globalization of business. Such firms are called **multinational corporations**. British firms own the most formerly American companies, including Ben & Jerry's ice cream; Dr Pepper/Seven–Up, Inc. (which makes two dozen beverages, from Sunkist to Snapple); Burger King; and Pillsbury. Mexican companies own CompUSA and make Oroweat breads. Investors in the Netherlands, Germany, Switzerland, and Japan are also major players in U.S. retail and manufacturing. The total amount other countries have invested in the United States tops $1.5 trillion.

On the U.S. side of the equation, Americans have long been aggressive overseas investors—some say *too* aggressive. Of the top 10 American-based companies with major overseas business holdings, five are manufacturers (Compaq, Ford, General Electric, General Motors, and Hewlett-Packard) and one is a retailer (Wal-Mart). Why the rush to leave the United States and conquer their respective industries worldwide? Two words: more customers. The biggest American-based companies believe they have saturated their home market. To spur continued growth, they must look outside the borders. China alone has 112 million potential customers—almost half the U.S. population—largely untapped, and concentrated in its 95 largest cities.[1] In October 2004, China got its first Hooters restaurant, which opened its doors in Shanghai!

The notion of **free trade** is based on the idea that the nations of the world should be free to trade goods and services with one another—a noble aim, to be sure, but one that has been fraught with problems, primarily because it's such a complex balancing act. It is almost impossible to synchronize the business dealings of any two nations such that Country A imports approximately the same amount of goods from Country B that Country B imports from Country A, under the same business rules and economic conditions. There are great disparities, for instance, between the major industrial nations and the smaller, lesser developed ones; and every nation's currency is valued differently, too.

The current problem is that the United States imports about 50 percent more goods than it exports. As an example, in 2003 U.S. automobile manufacturers sent 2,724 to China—2,573 passenger cars and 151 trucks and/or tractors—but China sent 24,758 vehicles to the United States![2] The financial impact when trade becomes "unbalanced" to this degree is called a **trade** **deficit.**

The United States is experiencing a record high trade deficit, and the main product categories involved are apparel, automobiles, electronics, and computers. We often see news headlines about a glut of foreign-made products in these categories. Even Wal-Mart, once the proud proponents of a "We Buy American" campaign in the 1990s, moved its worldwide purchasing headquarters to China in 2001 and today is the world's largest importer of Chinese-made products into the United States.[3]

The North American Free Trade Agreement (NAFTA) has been one of the most hotly debated attempts to encourage free trade between the three nations on the North American continent, by eliminating all tariffs on goods that flow between Canada, Mexico, and the United States for a 15-year period that began in the 1990s. As a nation, about 60 percent of our imports come either from China or Japan, but we now have record high trade deficits with both Canada and Mexico—we're importing (*from* them) more than we're exporting (*to* them).

A big part of the problem is that the prices of foreign-made goods are so much less expensive than the American-made ones—and their prices haven't risen much in more than a decade. Accounting for the inflation rate in the United States, dollar for dollar, imported goods are actually about 20 percent cheaper than they were in the early 1990s.[4]

"Why is that a problem?" you may ask. "American shoppers love a bargain!" Yes, but the flow of cheaper goods into the United States forces American companies to hold down their own costs to compete. And they do that by keeping salaries low, laying off workers, outsourcing jobs to other countries, and/or opening overseas offices—all controversial moves that reverberate loudly in the domestic economy and impact people's lives.

The good news is that there are some product categories in which the United States is exporting at a booming rate. Gemstones, cosmetics, household appliances, foods and beverages, animal feed, and industrial supplies are all being shipped to other nations at record levels.[5]

Trade Regulations

Government attempts to right trade imbalances and the economic havoc they can wreak are sometimes successful, and sometimes not. They typically require one or more of the following financial conditions:

THE WORLD TRADE ORGANIZATION

The gap between rich and poor countries remains large, and critics of free trade policies say they benefit the industrialized nations more than developing countries. The industrialized nations have the power to make the rules to protect their own interests; the lesser-developed countries (LDCs) don't have the systems in place, like manufacturing improvements and shipping infrastructure, to take advantage of the possible benefits of free trade.

At the core of the debate is the World Trade Organization (WTO), the sort-of United Nations for global trade. The WTO has 146 members, the most recent of which is China, admitted in 1999 after a full 15 years of hot debate. To be a WTO member, a nation must agree to the following:

- Trade on equal terms with all other WTO members, with the lowest possible tariffs.

- Make trade more predictable by following the rules and international trade principles set by the WTO.

- Foster healthy competition in the world marketplace by reducing or eliminating subsidies.

The WTO has big meetings that are known as **trade rounds**, in which details of the rules and principles are hammered out and challenged. As you might expect, the subject matter is often controversial. Add to that the fact that any decision must be unanimous, and you have the basis for some very lively discourse.[6]

- A **duty** or **tariff** is a tax levied by a government on the importation, exportation, use, or consumption of goods. (We'll explain them in greater detail later in this chapter.)
- A **quota** is a strict limit on the quantities of certain items that can be imported. Quotas limit the amount of imports, but they increase the prices of the items that do get into the country. At this writing (and it may change at any time as laws are changed), the United States has quotas that restrict the importation of bathrobes, bras, and knit fabric from China because the glut of those lower-cost products has impacted American producers of the same goods.
- A **subsidy** is a government payment to businesses in a particular domestic industry. Paying some of that business's costs allows the business to export its products more cheaply to other nations.
- **Sanctions** or **boycotts** are usually last-ditch efforts to force a nation to "clean up its act" in some regard by forbidding its merchandise to be imported into the country imposing the sanction.

We mention these terms because, as a buyer, you may hear them in your quest for suppliers from other countries, and at times, they may impact your ability to do business with them.

CONSUMER ATTITUDES AND BUYERS' RESPONSES

Now that you know a bit about the trade-related problems of the United States and its foreign trading partners, why buy overseas at all? There are several reasons buyers continue to do so. Of course, the primary reason is lower cost. Despite more than a decade of news about U.S. plant closings, outsourcing, and downsizing caused by foreign competition, American consumers continue their insatiable appetite for foreign-made products. Look at the checkout lines at places like Wal-Mart. Some may indicate some sheepishness about the apparent irony, but they'll tell you, "I don't care where it's from. I want the best quality I can find, at the lowest possible price."

A recent four-year study by Canada's well-respected Conference Board indicated that multinational corporations have outperformed their strictly domestic counterparts, in terms of sales, assets, and higher returns on equity. But at what cost to the U.S. economy? Multiple studies have been done on the loyalty (or lack thereof) of American consumers. Consistently, they cite factors like workmanship, price, and brand name as ahead of country of origin when deciding whether to buy a product. Another interesting finding: When faced with two similar items, a U.S. shopper would only be more inclined to "buy American" if the price was the same as the imported item. If retailers are supposed to be stocking merchandise based on the preferences of their customers . . . well? Can you put your sense of patriotism, or your concern for the U.S. economy, aside to make a foreign buy?

This point leads directly to the next—that for some types of goods, there *is* no longer an American-made market. VCRs and DVD players are made overseas. Many specialty food products, some fine wines, and ethnic handicrafts all have their origins in other nations.

The third reason for buying in overseas markets is that retailers who seek to attain fashion leadership are extremely competitive about ferreting out the most unique colors, trends, and craftsmanship. For buyers, having the whole world as your marketplace can be exhilarating, offering limitless options for differentiating their assortments from competition—as well as the opportunity to make exclusive deals with new vendors. Foreign cultures feature distinctive designs, beautiful handiwork, and very high quality in some product categories. In others, state-of-the-art technology is producing foreign products that are reliable, efficient, and low-maintenance—vehicles and computers, for example.

The combination of price, differentiation, and product quality means that goods of certain foreign countries have built reputations for superior value. They are good buys for the money.

Gray Market Merchandise

The U.S. Customs law defines **gray market** goods as "genuine goods manufactured in a foreign country, bearing a United States trademark and imported without the consent of the United States' trademark owner."[7] Also called **parallel imports**, the situation also arises when U.S.-based manufacturers sell some products to domestic wholesalers and the rest to overseas distributors at a lower price. The products themselves are exactly the same. Ironically, these cheaper goods are often simply re-exported by the practical overseas distributors. They end up back in America, at deep discounts and dollar stores, competing with their own "twins" in full-price stores. A $4 bottle of shampoo at the supermarket, or a $1 bottle at the dollar store: Which would the typical consumer purchase?

The products come through U.S. Customs to get into the states. The importing laws make it illegal to copy or simulate an actual trademark of a brand-named product—but that's not the problem with gray market goods. They're not imitations, but the real things! There's no attempt being made to fool consumers, so there's no deception involved.

American manufacturers and wholesalers have not been especially successful at stopping the flow of gray market goods, despite dozens of lawsuits over the years. They've made their contracts more restrictive, adding geographic restrictions about where products can be sold. (These are almost impossible to enforce, since the parties to the contract aren't the parties that eventually do the reimporting.) They've had better luck with placing restrictions on the licensing, copyright, and/or patent of a product; or proving that the gray market products are "materially different" than the "authorized U.S." versions of the items. A product that comes back to the United States with foreign language packaging and instructions, for example, is "materially different" than the same item sold in the States. Some courts have ruled that this could be confusing to American consumers.[8]

Despite all the wrangling, gray market goods continue to be purchased by discount stores that can pass the savings on to customers. Some see them as a necessary market force to balance out the fact that U.S. consumers generally pay more than anyone else for some types of goods; others see them as leeches that feed off the successful reputations built by brand-name manufacturers and are probably breaking the law, if not ethical standards as well.

BUYING FOREIGN GOODS FROM DOMESTIC SOURCES

You don't necessarily have to leave your stateside office to purchase foreign goods. There are four major types of domestic resources to assist you:

- The **import merchant** may confine the operation to selling a single class of goods or a number of related classes, including both foreign and domestic goods in order to broaden the line. Wine importers are a perfect example of this.

- The **resident sales agent** represents a group of foreign manufacturers and may or may not have merchandise stock on hand. If not, the agent is ready to handle the paperwork involved in bringing in the goods. (Again using wine as an example, an individual can be licensed as a "registered agent" or broker, and must sign for the products when he or she arrives in the United States at the Customs office.) Sometimes, the agent places the goods in a bonded warehouse, where no duty on them is due until the goods are actually withdrawn for delivery to the buyer.
- The **import commission house** represents a variety of foreign manufacturers, handling the importation paperwork and storing the goods. The commission house is paid by commission from the manufacturer for selling the goods.
- The major **buying offices** we learned about in Chapter 2 all have international offices, with representatives in other nations on the lookout for suitable items or lines for group purchases. Even if a retailer is not a client of a particular buying office, the group often has a wholesale division that offers some merchandise to nonclients. It helps the buying office pay the overhead of maintaining multiple offices and benefits retailers, too.

Advantages and Disadvantages

There are numerous reasons to use a domestic buying source, even for products made in other countries. First (and often primary for senior management) is that it saves the travel time and expense of the buying staff. The importer is usually highly experienced in the merchandise lines carried, has excellent connections in these markets, and is a skilled negotiator in addition to being familiar with trends in your area. Since he or she buys for a group of retailers, the larger-scale purchases may mean discounts for merchandise you could not have received on your own.

Regular credit terms are available. That's a huge improvement over dealing with an unfamiliar foreign producer who demands an irrevocable letter of credit, payment in full in advance of shipment, or other unreasonable terms. Your retailer will not want to tie up capital for a long time period before the goods arrive safely—and what happens if they don't? It is far easier to deal with a domestic seller in regard to quality, quantity, and timing of deliveries than it is with a foreign source. You hope returns are unlikely, but if they happen, to return them to a foreign seller is often impossible.

The import wholesaler customarily agrees to assume many of the fluctuating risks inherent in importing, from foreign exchange rates to calculation of duties, to foreign trade regulations and restrictions. The importer usually offers a firm contract price that is good for a certain time period, even if importing costs change. The importer also assumes the liability if a duty is paid at Customs and then reviewed by the Customs Service and increased. This is important because sometimes, as with other federal taxes, it may take months or years after the original paperwork was filed and the fees were paid, for the audit to take place and turn up new charges—long after the goods are sold and gone. If an additional amount is owed, the importer has 30 days to pay it.

Finally, in addition to the United States' own import-export laws and restrictions, the importer is familiar with the laws and the cultures of other nations. In a controversial and rapidly changing facet of the retail industry, it's a bonus to have someone else be the "expert."

Okay, now for the disadvantages. Importers are not the sources for exclusive or made-to-order merchandise. The prices they charge to cover costs, expenses, and profit may be more than the "landed" cost of the goods bought directly from the foreign resource. Reorders may be more difficult, because continuity is not the name of the game in this facet of business. Importers buy on behalf of groups of retailers, and there's no assurance the rest of the group will also want to reorder, or that the product line will still be available.

BUYING FOREIGN GOODS FROM FOREIGN SOURCES

Buying direct from businesses in other nations is becoming ever-easier in our global economy. The American buyer may purchase goods abroad directly from the manufacturers, or from a number of third-party sources whose roles are much like their U.S. counterparts:

- **Foreign export merchants** are wholesalers who confine themselves strictly to exporting and can usually provide faster delivery than is available from manufacturers.
- **Export sales representatives** sell the wares of certain manufacturers in their countries (or entire continents) but do not maintain inventory. These reps make periodic trips to the United States on behalf of the companies they represent to meet with buyers and merchandise managers.
- **Export commission houses** are the third-party "export departments" of foreign manufacturers and receive a commission from them on the volume of goods they sell. They may do some of the paperwork necessary to ship abroad.
- **Foreign freight-forwarders** are licensed by the U.S. Maritime Commission to arrange the shipping of goods on behalf of exporters. They are often hired by smaller exporters and manufacturers to be the "agent" for individual shipments, handling the documentation, labeling requirements, insurance, storage, and other services for smaller shipments that don't require a full container or full truck. They can combine or "piggyback" multiple shipments and split the costs between the merchants. (For oceangoing shipments, the jargon is "fishy-back.") Some freight-forwarders are associated with large shipping companies.

Language and business practices, as well as legal restraints, differ in foreign countries. In making contact with any of these resources, the buyer nearly always requires the assistance of a foreign buying office as an intermediary. It may be called a **purchasing agent** (if it's operated by American citizens), or a **commissionaire** (if it's operated by citizens of the host nation). Either way, they are locals and you are not! They are extremely helpful on market visits with everything from language and culture, to recommending sources for certain types of merchandise, to making storage arrangements for goods before shipment. Once a vendor-client relationship has been established in that country, the purchasing agent can handle shipments of sample goods and even take care of reordering for a busy buyer.

The largest retailers have set up their own foreign buying offices, and the U.S. Department of Commerce has also gotten into the act. Its U.S. Commercial Service has offices set up in more than 80 countries, in a total of 145 U.S. embassies and consulates, as well as 107 U.S. cities. Its BUYUSA.GOV effort (www.buyusa.gov) gives both would-be importers and exporters an opportunity to sign up to be matched with appropriate resources.

Buying abroad for retail stores is handled differently by different retailers. If a chain does an extensive amount of buying, there may be an international buyer or buying staff. Another common procedure is for a departmental buyer in one store to shop on behalf of all the stores in a chain for those departments, with the responsibility rotating among buyers in the group from year to year.

Advantages and Disadvantages

The advantages of buying direct from foreign sources are major. Prices are often considerably lower than those quoted by intermediaries. We've already mentioned the exclusivity of the products, which is important in remaining competitive. It also permits a higher markup than usual—certainly much higher than similar items obtained from domestic suppliers. However, for one-time buys, reorders are seldom assured.

Foreign manufacturers are known for their willingness to meet specifications of quality and style in order to be introduced to the American market. In the clothing business, sizes are different and must be adjusted for American measurements. It can be difficult to ensure the items are made to exact specifications, but it is not impossible, and samples may be requested in advance for a final check of materials and workmanship. Rapport can be developed that leads to long-range plans, and even financial partnerships in which the retailer puts up the money for expansion or modernization of a valuable manufacturer's facilities.

Working with overseas manufacturers in their own countries takes a lot of time and buyer involvement. A great deal of travel is necessary for the buyer, and the trips are long and costly. A detailed buying plan and carefully planned itinerary are important for you to meet your goals in such a concentrated time period. There is also the ever-present danger of overbuying, because the goods always tend to look more exciting in their foreign setting than they do back at home in the store.

There used to be long delays in obtaining out-of-country deliveries, but these have been overcome in large part by shipping by air instead of boat or truck. However, the norm is to place and pay for a foreign order far in advance of delivery. This ties up funds for the retailer. There are also unforeseen headaches in getting the merchandise through customs—partly due to the increased amount of security at airports and partly to congestion level at seaports. Great Britain's Freight Transport Association says the increase in global trade has resulted in most of the world's ports being clogged by the sheer numbers of cargo ships. In California, it can take up to a week for a container vessel to dock and unload, anchoring offshore until there is room to tie up at dockside.[9]

Unless terms are negotiated about the goods coming in at a certain port, the buying organization (i.e., the retailer) must assume the importing costs that would be borne by the importer or selling agent if a U.S. intermediary was used. Although some foreign manufacturers permit American buyers to purchase on an "open account" (an almost universal practice in the United States), most payments are made by means of letters of credit on a foreign bank. When the goods are shipped, the foreign seller presents a draft along with shipping documents to the bank for payment. The buyer negotiates a sales price in either dollars or the other nation's currency, whatever is most beneficial for the retailer considering the exchange rate at the time.

GETTING GOODS THROUGH CUSTOMS

In addition to an exporting source, an American buyer purchasing abroad must also have customs experts—either on staff, or by hiring a **customs house broker**—to shepherd the incoming purchases through the intricacies of getting through the U.S. Customs process. If you think Customs agents are only looking for drug smugglers, you've seen too many movies! That is only one of its many roles. The U.S. Customs Service has been in existence since the late 1700s, when tariffs were levied by the United States to raise money for the brand-new nation. It has been a prime source of income for the country since that time, second only to the Internal Revenue Service.

Today as a branch of the U.S. Treasury Department, Customs is now known as U.S. Customs and Border Protection. It is an enormous and extremely profitable organization that has become even more powerful with the terrorist actions and resulting security precautions of the 2000s. Customs agents are busy people. Every day, they perform the following tasks:

- "Process" (that's the word they use for it) 1.3 million passengers, coming into the United States on 2,500 planes, 550 ships, and 340,000 vehicles.

- Seize over 3,900 pounds of narcotics, $1.2 million in currency, $24,000 of guns and ammunition, and $368,000 worth of vehicles.
- Seize up to $500,000 of commercial merchandise.[10]

It is the latter category that should interest retail buyers. Customs is responsible for ensuring that all imports and exports to the United States comply with our laws and regulations. This includes what may (and may not) be imported, whether it is legally labeled and invoiced, whether it meets U.S. health and safety standards, and how much duty must be paid on it.

What in the world is a Customs inspector looking for when goods are examined? Here's the list from the Customs Service itself:

- The value of the goods for Customs purposes and their dutiable status.
- Whether the goods are properly marked with the country of their origin. (Special marking or labeling may apply, and certain articles are exempt.)
- Whether the goods have been correctly invoiced.
- Whether the shipment contains prohibited articles.
- Whether the requirements of other federal agencies have been met. (This refers to safety laws and others.)
- Whether the amount of goods listed on the invoice is correct.[11]

Gray market goods and commercial fraud account for much of the investigative work of the agency. Customs special agents track, for example, manufacturers in countries with export quotas who try to get around them by shipping their goods to "suppliers" in third-party nations. The "supplier" then exports them to the United States, passing them off as goods from the third-party nation instead of their true source. Unfortunately, this is not an isolated occurrence, as you can see in Table 8-1, which shows six-month figures for seizures of intellectual property, which means illegally or improperly labeled goods attempting entry into the United States. It makes the importation of legitimate goods into the United States more difficult, expensive, and time-consuming.

Goods from China are responsible for the most violations by far. They make up 58 percent of the seizures in the same six-month time period. South Africa and Russia are numbers two and three on the list, as the countries of origin for 7 percent and 6 percent of the seized goods, respectively.

Duties

The amount of duty charged for importing an item into the United States depends on two factors: exactly what the item is and the country in which it was made. Because the information on the import purchase order is used to determine the duty, it must be as specific as possible about these two important details—more specific than it might be for domestic orders. Incorrect or incomplete information will cause numerous problems and delays, and could create additional expense for the retailer. If the goods are covered under one of the textile quotas, the quota category number must be verified and stated clearly on the order.

Table 8-1 IPR (Intellectual Property) Seizures — Midyear FY 2004		
Commodity	**Domestic Value**	**% of Total Value**
Wearing Apparel	$ 27,752,256	43%
Cigarettes	11,513,518	18%
Handbags, wallets, backpacks	7,294,597	11%
Consumer electronics	4,545,795	7%
Toys, electronic games	2,305,296	4%
Batteries	1,733,403	3%
Media	1,626,559	3%
Watches, parts	1,016,783	2%
Footwear	988,115	2%
Identifying elements	798,686	1%
All other commodities	4,828,331	7%
TOTAL DOMESTIC VALUE	$ 64,403,339	
TOTAL NUMBER OF SEIZURES	3,693	

Source: U.S. Customs & Border Protection, Washington, D.C.

The duty rate of an item is tied to its classification number on a master list called the **Harmonized Tariff Schedule of the United States (HTSUS)**, and the rate varies (sometimes substantially) depending on the nation of origin. There are three rates:

- **General rates** are for countries with which the United States maintains so-called normal trade relations (NTR).
- **Special rates**, lower than general rates (or no duty at all) are granted for merchandise coming from countries involved in special programs to boost their trade with the United States.
- **Column 2** rates are for imports that don't fit either of the other two categories.

The importer is responsible for properly classifying merchandise before it is allowed to enter the country, which sometimes requires a lot more legwork than looking up an item number on the HTSUS list. There is also a classification requirement on the "exporting end" of the transaction, called the **Export Control Classification Number (ECCN).** The importer or retailer may challenge Customs if they disagree with the classifications of unique goods.

When a duty is charged, there are also three different types:

- **Ad valorem** is a percentage of the dutiable value.
- **Specific** is a particular, fixed amount per unit (per pound, per piece, per liter, etc.).
- **Compound** is a combination of ad valorem and specific (such as 10 cents per pound, and 35 percent of value).

Things get confusing when you realize that the dutiable value is what *Customs decides it is*, not necessarily the total on the purchase order! It is usually either the foreign value or the export value, whichever is higher—but again, there are three choices:

- The **foreign value** is the market price at which the goods would be freely offered for sale for home consumption, in their country of origin.
- The **export value** is the market price at which the goods are freely offered for sale for export to the United States.
- When neither of these two methods is applicable, the goods may be valued at **constructed value**, or cost of production—the manufacturing cost, plus general expenses like handling (but not shipping), and a profit margin.

Any shipment that is worth more than $2,000 in value also requires what is called a **formal entry** into the United States—the importer must post a bond to ensure payment of duties and compliance with the Customs rules, and can pick up the merchandise before the duty and processing fees are paid. The bond guarantees the importer is "good for" the amount. The formal entry process requires a number of documents be submitted, including a bill of lading, commercial invoice, the appropriate Customs forms, and so on. This makes it even more critical for the purchase order to specify the currency in which the payment will be made. Currency rates of exchange can fluctuate dramatically in the months between order and delivery, and the foreign buying office (commissionaire) should review all orders' documentation before they are shipped to prevent delays in Customs when the shipment arrives.

Landed Cost and Terms of Sale

The prices of foreign goods often seem too good to be true. The buyer must always be aware that numerous other costs are incurred before they reach the retail store. The final cost figure is known as the **landed cost** of the items—the total of price, packing and shipping, commissions, insurance, import duties, and miscellaneous services. The most accurate type of quote for a buyer to obtain from an overseas vendor is called a **CIF quote**, which stands for cost, insurance, and freight, since it offers the most complete summary of charges. Less desirable is the **C&F quote** (cost plus freight), which includes the cost of the goods plus transportation to the U.S. port, because any insurance on the cargo must be paid by the buyer's company.

Shipping costs are not based on value, but on the size of the container or carton, so lower-value shipments of bulky merchandise may add significantly to its landed cost. There are handy multipliers to use to simplify the calculation of landed cost, depending on the value of the U.S. dollar to the foreign currency of the importing nation.

Buyers shopping foreign markets may be given a list of multipliers for each type of merchandise to be purchased, based on average purchases by the importer from the same country, within the same tariff classifications. They won't be exactly right, but they should be close enough for a fair calculation. Buying offices or commissionaires in the country of origin can verify the figures, but it is the ultimate responsibility of the buyer to determine the approximate landed costs to port of entry before placing the orders. Further, remember there will be added transportation costs to get the merchandise from the dock or airport to the retail company's distribution or receiving center.

The terms of sale, or **trade terms**, are also different for international shipping. Within the United States, the custom is that goods are shipped **free on board (FOB)**, meaning the vendor pays the charges to a certain point. It may be to a certain city, or to a regional warehouse, which is specified in the sale agreement. The retailer picks up any transportation costs after that, to move the goods to individual stores. This gets more complicated when the vendor is across the ocean, so FOB terms are further specified. The vendor's price may include shipment to an inland port, to the port of export, or to a specific vessel at a specific port. The shipment may be **free alongside (FAS)**, which means the vendor pays for getting the freight "up to" the ship or aircraft, but not for actually loading it onto the vessel. A good, current summary of trade terms is offered by the International Chamber of Commerce in its *Incoterms* publications.

CHAPTER SUMMARY

Imported products compose a major, and growing, portion of the U.S. economy. Their impact on American manufacturing and retailing is substantial, and not always beneficial. However, there is no stopping the global economy, and for the retail buyer, it offers limitless opportunities to bring home unique merchandise at extremely attractive prices, with savings that can be passed on to bargain-hungry American consumers.

International merchandise should be chosen using the same selection factors and careful buying plan you'd use for domestic purchases. Planning ahead is especially critical because overseas buying is more complex than buying American goods; it is often done in the short time window of an international visit to the country, and the temptations to overspend in an exciting new environment are considerable.

International vendors should also be chosen using the same professional and ethical standards as your business sets for American companies. This process is also more complex, because it involves choosing intermediary or "middleman" services like foreign buying offices, agents, and commissionaires that must meet these standards as well. A U.S. retailer can get into serious trouble with the Customs officials for importing goods that don't meet U.S. laws and regulations, and so must depend heavily on importing professionals to keep up on the ever-changing duties, quotas, and other requirements.

The buyer is responsible for calculating at least a rough estimate of the landed cost for imported items, which includes adding all duties and transportation costs to the goods for a more realistic idea of what they will ultimately cost to sell. The type of price quote will vary by supplier, but it is an important key to what shipping and insurance costs will, and will not, be covered by the supplier.

DISCUSSION QUESTIONS

1. Do you think the ethical standards used to select foreign companies with which to do business should be different than for U.S. companies? Why or why not?
2. Are quotas a good idea to stop too much foreign merchandise from entering the United States? What would happen if we ended them all—do you think the market would eventually right itself?
3. If your company gave you a choice—buy American or buy foreign—and there was only enough money in the budget for one buying trip, what would you do, and why?
4. You are contacted by a domestic broker who has an unexpected shipment of bargain-priced goods and wants you to consider buying them for your retailer. What steps would you take to determine whether they might be *gray market* goods?
5. What factors should be considered in calculating the *landed cost* of a shipment?
6. Figure the landed cost of this purchase, both in Euros and in U.S. dollars. At this writing, the Euro is valued at 1.26 to the U.S. dollar:

Cost of merchandise	10,000 Euros
Bulk purchase discount	2 %
Packing	300 Euros
Shipping	500 Euros
Duty into U.S.	30 %
Commission for buyer's agent	6 %
Miscellaneous charges	$104

7. What is the role of a *commissionaire* in working with a retail buyer?
8. Do you think the U.S. Customs Service has too much power? Why or why not?
9. What are some of the ways smaller retailers can realize the savings of buying foreign goods?
10. Why would an exporter use the services of a *foreign-freight forwarder* instead of an *export commission house*?

ENDNOTES

1. Gwen Lyle, "Consumer Goods and Retailing in the PRC," in *Business America* magazine, January–February 1996 issue.
2. U.S. Department of Commerce, U.S. Treasury, and U.S. International Trade Commission, Washington, D.C., October 2004.
3. Jim Hightower, "How Wal-Mart Is Remaking Our World," in *The Hightower Lowdown* newsletter, April 26, 2002, © Independent Media Institute. Available at www.alternet.org
4. James C. Cooper and Kathleen Madigan, "U.S.: A Silver Lining's Menacing Cloud," *BusinessWeek* magazine, October 27, 2003.
5. "Record U.S. Trade Deficit in 2003," CBSNEWS.com, February 13, 2004. © CBS Broadcasting, Inc.
6. "A Century of Free Trade," Business Section, BBC News online, February 12, 2003.
7. Steven M. Richman, "Current Legal Issues Regarding Parallel Imports," *New Jersey Lawyer* magazine, October 1, 2003.
8. Information also gleaned from the case law summaries of Knobbe Martens Olson & Bear, LLP, a California-based law firm specializing in intellectual property and international trade law.
9. "Boxed in and Clogged Up," *The Economist*, October 14, 2004. © The Economist Newspaper and The Economist Group.
10. "How the U.S. Customs Service Works," available online at howstuffworks.com.
11. U.S. Import Requirements, U.S. Customs and Border Protection Service, Washington, D.C.

Translating Plans into Purchases

This chapter takes all the information in the text thus far—about assortment planning, sales forecasting, technology, and vendor selection—and crystallizes it into making the actual "buys" for a retail store. We discuss the following topics:

- Market locations and buying trips
- Selecting new items
- How items fit into the store's stock plans
- Buying job lots, irregulars, and "off-price" merchandise
- Developing product specifications
- Environmental considerations

The material in this chapter must be viewed in terms of current trade and economic developments and, of course, the type of retailer for which the   **165** purchases are being made. The shorter life cycles of the fashion industry, for example, will mean nothing to the supermarket buyer. The use of private labels may simplify, or even automate, the buying process for some items. And yet the vast majority of retail buyers continue to "shop" vendors' offerings, evaluate new items and lines, and make the ultimate decisions—to buy or pass. Even buyers for the largest retailers, whose emphasis is on product development, buy fashion and other categories from sample lines in the same way smaller retailers do.

Merchandise selection as a professional buyer is more a process of elimination than a glorified shopping trip. The one "perfect" item is not likely to pop up and announce itself, but to be discovered from among many that are "pretty close," or "nearly right." In one dress manufacturer's showroom, a buyer may see 30 styles in one price range of one classification to select one or two—and must then select the choice of colors. The supermarket buyer may view more than prospective new 100 items a week to choose two or three that will make it onto the store shelves. At a toy fair or housewares show, the buyer has two or three days to check out the wares of hundreds of vendors with thousands of items. In each situation, advance planning is critical to make the optimum buy.

There never seems to be enough time, space, money, or data to accommodate the requirements and intensity of the buyer's nonstop decision making. You may assume from all the new technology available that retail buying has been reduced to punching a bunch of numbers into a handheld computer and marching home with a merchandise order. Nothing could be further from the truth.

THE BUYING TRIP

There are lots of places to go when you're looking for things to buy! We'll group them by major type of venue: the market, the trade show or trade fair, and the manufacturing site visit. Any of these can be either domestic or international. Planning a buying trip begins a month or more before the buyer's arrival at these destinations, and in most retail chains of any size, a written buying plan must accompany the buyer.

Markets

In retail, a **market** is a single, huge complex where large numbers of vendors rent showrooms or have facilities in close proximity. The idea is that buyers can check out a plethora of merchandise without having to cover a lot of ground. Often it is merchandise of a particular type—an apparel market, a furniture market, and so on—but there are also wider-ranging *merchandise markets*.

The markets are located either in cities known for these industries, or in regional cities designed to serve stores in a particular section of the country. Examples of major market areas are New York City's garment district (for apparel) or High Point, North Carolina (for furniture). Smaller (but still massive) regional markets are located in cities like Atlanta, Chicago, Dallas, and Los Angeles. These are popular because of their proximity to smaller merchants in their respective regions.

Markets do not operate like retail stores and are not open to the public—only to retailers and buyers admitted with a special pass or proof of their employment in the trade. While a few merchants may have showrooms open daily, most of them rent space for a week or two at a time, and buying is done during "market weeks" that are publicized in advance.

As you might expect, almost every item looks good in the vendor's showroom. Some buyers spend their first day "at market" making brief, casual calls on key resources to get an overall feel for the merchandise and returning later to do their shopping. Other seasoned buyers shop one classification at a time, which makes it easier to compare lines and select a well-balanced assortment. It takes more time but serves to eliminate confusion when it's time to make final selections and write orders from notes and memory.

Trade Shows

Many seasonal staples and novelties, as well as clothing and specialty foods, are bought on periodic trips to annual sales-related events. For example, a toy show is held in New York City in early February every year, where toy buyers go to place their orders for delivery the following fall. The idea is that, with the Christmas season fresh in their minds, they are better able to plan intelligently for the next Christmas.

More than 2,000 major trade shows are held worldwide each year. Some are sponsored by industry groups, others by governments. U.S. vendors go to other nations to exhibit at trade shows, and international vendors come here. There are 70 annual trade fairs in African nations sponsored by their governments.

There is at least one huge trade show or exposition for every facet of the retail industry. The National Retail Federation's annual get-together is a major event. The Sporting Goods Manufacturers Association hosts "The Super Show" every year in Atlanta for buyers of sports products and apparel. The Footwear Distributors and Retailers Association of America has an annual spring conference.

In the food industry, just think of the free samples! The Food Marketing Institute has two enormous weeklong trade fairs, the FMI Show and the Supermarket Industry Show, both in Chicago. The National Association for the Specialty Food Trade hosts seasonal "Fancy Food Shows." There are trade shows for the Private Label Manufacturers Association, the National Frozen and Refrigerated Foods Association, and many more.

Manufacturer's Visits

It is always possible to arrange on-site visits with the product manufacturers, either on your own or through a buying office or agent. It is especially important to give them ample notice of your arrival in an area, informing them of your needs and making an appointment to meet with them and tour the facility.

Personal visits can be critical if your retailer is seeking custom-made products that require direct explanation and negotiation. If it's a trip to another country, be certain you have hired a translator in advance who is familiar with retail terminology if you are not extremely fluent in the native language, and read up on the social and cultural differences between your culture and theirs. You may be saving yourself embarrassment and even minimizing the risk of losing a deal by inadvertently offending your host.

SELECTING NEW ITEMS

Add the limitations of time, space, and funds with which every buyer is faced to the constant flood of new items onto the wholesale scene and you will see why a buyer is forced to be highly selective. Although some items are distinctly "new" in type or function, most are variations of existing items with a different color, design, feature, or marketing "hook" to make them more attractive, more reliable, or more convenient.

And yet new items are the lifeblood of retailing. They tell a customer a lot about the retailer's direction and reinforce for an individual whether the store is still in tune with his or her needs and wants. So it's important not to dismiss new "incarnations" of items without putting them to a couple of litmus-test questions:

- **Is it right for my target customer?** Buyers can't help but notice exceptional new styling, outstanding quality, and very attractive prices. Unfortunately, these benefits have no value whatsoever if the item itself is not compatible with the taste level of the target customer—which, of course, you have determined and fine-tuned before arriving at market.
- **Is it consistent with my company's image?** Yes, "image" is an overworked word in retailing, but for this discussion, it means the overall perception

people have of a store—its merchandise, employees, and service levels. If the buyer spends too much time or money on items that are at odds with the established store image, the results can be extremely disruptive to sales, display, advertising, and other departments. Items at odds include too much trendy merchandise in a conservative store, too much merchandise inappropriate for the age range of the customers, or the purchase of off-price goods to be sold at price points far below the norms for your store.

Unless these two tests are met, the items should be rejected without further consideration. Ruthless? No—intelligent, appropriate, and the mark of a mature buyer.

Narrowing the Search

The sales and buying plans (prepared in advance of the market visit) provide a framework or map that should automatically narrow the number of different comparisons in the selection process. The plan reflects anticipated customer demand by merchandise classification, type, price, and often other selection factors as well. However, it still leaves plenty of room for shopping with that final selection in mind.

The way to narrow down choices isn't easy, but it is simple. Scan the whole range of a vendor's offerings for ideas. Quickly eliminate any item or style that is clearly not suitable, leaving only either the suitable or questionable items. Remember that there will not always be an item that actually fits the plan at market. In this case, you can either change the plan or select something less suitable. And you're making these choices while you are also negotiating prices and "deals" with the vendor or a sales representative, some of whom apply more pressure than others.

Product Features

In the same way selection factors help a buyer prepare a plan, product features determine the suitability of each item *to that plan*. Considerations here include the following:

- **Specialty appeal.** The small or specialty store owner has an interesting advantage here over larger merchants. They know some of their customers personally and can come to market with the needs of particular individuals in mind. These customers will be strongly motivated to buy the item simply because they know it was chosen for them. This offshoot of personal selling is a major advantage of the small retailer. An item that is suitable to a limited group of customers will obviously have limited sales potential but may be important to round out an assortment. The preferences of this small group may be ignored by larger merchants in the trading area, and this offers a unique opportunity to the retailer who capitalizes on it. In terms of profit, the big share of a small market may compare favorably with the small share of a big market.

Teenage customers are a special conundrum. Their tastes change regularly and don't often make sense to adult buyers. A fad can start quietly in any section of the country and sweep across the land with electrifying speed; or it may be embraced by one group of teens and spurned by another. The fads aren't always short-lived, but when they're over, they're history—leaving retailers with costly markdowns. It will pay any store that courts the teen business to find ways to keep in touch with adolescent whims and needs. Their spending power is considerable—an estimated $95 billion per year, or about $3,300 per person, ages 13 to 19.[1]

- **Price line and taste.** Customers may also be grouped by the amount they are generally willing to pay for certain items. Price is an obvious distinction and retailers are well aware of its importance, as seen in the relative popularity of various prices in each classification of goods. However, the best-selling price lines may be more a reflection of the retailer's doing things the traditional way than the actual needs of the consumer. An item with broad appeal but somewhat high in price may be a valid experiment for the buyer, to encourage a bit of upselling in an otherwise slow category. This should be approached as an experiment, not a new mind-set.

The person who first wrote or said, "There's no accounting for taste," was perhaps a retail buyer. The buyer's own sense of aesthetics may be challenged by (for example) customers who persist in stuffing bulky furniture and heavy draperies into smaller rooms, but that doesn't mean the buyer can select what the customers "should be purchasing." The best practice here is to keep an eye on the social mobility, cultural influences, and new status symbols in a community that may create a demand for "better-designed" or more upscale goods, gourmet foods, and so on.

Then again, many products are basic and utilitarian—cleaning products, paper goods, household tools. In these product lines, the selection features are price, adequacy of quality for the purpose intended, brand preferences, and packaging.

- **Proven acceptance.** Is there a track record for the product? Something "new" that is only a minor variant of something "old" and successful represents an easy sampling decision. Unless the buyer suspects the attributes that made the "old" item successful are losing their vogue, the new may be sampled in considerable strength. The risk increases as the new product bears less and less resemblance to others of recent experience.

The typical bed sheet underwent a metamorphosis that illustrates the point. When the idea of color was introduced to a world of white cotton, it represented a radical departure from years of experience. To forecast public reaction, buyers must have had to think back to the introduction of color in other consumer goods (Vehicles? Clothing?) to note how well and how quickly they were accepted by shoppers. How were they advertised? How were they viewed by the fashion leaders in their communities? These are tough but necessary elements of decision making for buyers whose bosses require them to be early with innovations in order to maintain leadership status. When there aren't any trends, someone's got to make them by testing the market. Once color was introduced, a variety of prints—other than stripes and solids—were bound to be the next steps. These were minor variants of the original, tested product.

- **Current trends.** How does the item relate not only to successful items already in stock but also to observable trends for its category? Years ago, the housewares buyer was faced with a dilemma when stylish German and Scandinavian flatware first came to America. Housewares departments stocked a little of it at first, using the new lines to "trade up" their basic kitchen flatware categories. But the higher-priced flatware soon began competing with the lowest-priced "real" silverware—and buyers had to decide if there was a place for the new products in their bridal registries and upscale fine china departments.

  Some waited to see what competitors would do. The aggressive, decisive retailers made their own decisions. The new merchandise was sleek, simple, and functional. It fit well with an increase in casual living trends, and promised less work since it didn't have to be hand-polished like real silverware. It even survived the rigors of mechanical dishwashing. The choice to include it in the lineup of choices for interested customers was clear.

- **Significant and observable differences.** A great many items are suitable for a group of customers and reflect a current trend, but lack any feature that sets them apart from dozens of other, equally suitable products. Pass them up, at least for the moment, in search of a more distinctive item.

  In apparel, a good rule is to look for a feature that "does something" for the customer. It should enhance a good physical attribute, or minimize a poor one. Even classic simplicity can be an important element of appeal, as it can be "dressed up" or "dressed down," making it a better value. Sometimes the distinction lies in the brand name, type or color of fabric, or style, such as pants that have pockets versus pants that don't.

  In housewares, when silicon-coated frying pans appeared on the market, people learned not to use them with metal utensils, which could scratch the surface. The only alternative seemed to be narrow, wooden spatulas—until one buyer paired the pan with a wider, plastic spatula and created a sales-boosting difference.

- **Continuing utility.** The buyer should always try to picture the item after it has been in customer use for some time, and that's a dilemma. Some goods seem to have been designed for planned obsolescence, and the American consumer's appetite for change is considerable. Nowadays, how many customers buy furniture that they fully intend to hand down as "heirlooms?" However, the customer has not received good value for the money unless rational and emotional satisfaction is derived from *actually using* what they've purchased—and this is different than the satisfaction they feel *at the point of purchase*.

  Let's use flatware as an example again. The retail buyer thinks about the type of alloy used to make the *blank*, the piece of metal that becomes the fork or spoon, the percentages of nickel and chrome that will provide strength. The buyer is particular about the reinforcement points, the number of

A CHECKLIST FOR GOOD PACKAGING

1. Does it protect the merchandise in transit? In storage? On the counter, shelf, or other store fixture?

2. Does it conserve storage space and fit well into the store fixtures?

3. Is it a reasonable weight for the type of product? (If it's too bulky, the retailer may have to pay additional shipping charges.)

4. Does it reduce the opportunity for theft?

5. Is it attractive? Distinctive? Does it provide "eye appeal"?

6. Does it identify the product clearly—especially factors like size, price, and color?

7. If it is sealed, does it allow a reasonable degree of inspection by the customer as they shop—a cellophane window, a good illustration?

8. Is it functional? For some products, this will mean "Is it easy to open, close, remove?" For others, the question will be "Does it adequately protect the item against breakage?" If it can be displayed by hanging it up, is the mechanism for this purpose secure?

9. Does it provide adequate information about care and use of the product?

10. Does it have any uses other than actually containing this product?

finishing processes, whether the pieces are overlaid (extra silver added at key points of use), and so on.

In the lower price ranges, some standards may be lowered but not abandoned. It is fine to purchase low-end flatware to meet a certain market need, or for promotional purposes. But when the customer gets it home and finds that it gets dull or rusts in the dishwasher, or scratches easily, do you think he or she will care (or even recall) how little was paid for the set? In some product categories, the cheaper the price line, in fact, the more important it becomes that it is able to withstand rough usage.

- **Good packaging.** An increasing number of articles are sold in containers, and the attractiveness or utility of the package itself is often a major factor in customer choice. Well-designed packaging attracts attention and helps sell the product, so the buyer should consider the package as closely as its contents. If the former can be improved or customized, the buyer may make suggestions to the manufacturer and may refuse to buy if the suggestions aren't put into action.

- **Promotional opportunities.** Finally, think about the item in terms of how it can be advertised. What kind of publicity will be necessary to get it sold and what can it do for your retailer's reputation? Often, manufacturers offer an introductory advertising allowance to promote a newly purchased item;

or it comes with merchandising and display tips for the sales staff, or point-of-sale promotional materials. Will these fit your store's image and goals?

There are two points to be made here. The first is that you're not just buying for the consumer—you're buying for the salesperson, who must learn enough about the item to get excited about it and help sell it. The second is that a new item worth buying is worth promoting. Does promoting *this item* seem like something your store can do, and do well? And how will the manufacturer assist in that regard?

Weighing the Merchandise Features

Now that you've got a better eye for how to shop for retail stores, one way to put the individual factors to use is to weigh them, much as we prioritized the selection factors in Chapter 4 or the vendor criteria in Chapter 7. In this case, you might try assigning a grade to each item based on a 100-point scale of your own creation. For an item of clothing, it may be as follows:

Wearability, overall practicality in a wardrobe	30 points
A takeoff on an already successful style	20 points
Related to a current trend	10 points
Good taste or good design (as perceived by the customers)	20 points
Name brand or recognizable quality	10 points
Newness; originality of this variation	10 points
TOTAL	100 points

Then, based on experience, the buyer might establish a grading scale:

80 points or more	Best buy
60 to 79 points	Good buy
40 to 59 points	Risky buy
39 points or less	DON'T BUY!

The items on the "report card" for your store will vary depending on the clientele, the retailer's overall image, or the needs of a particular department. If the goal is to stress fashion leadership, for instance, the "newness" category may be given a weight of 30 points instead of 10.

Having your report card criteria handy provides an easy and fair way to assess a wide variety of merchandise quickly.

STOCK RELATIONSHIPS

Part of retail buying certainly is choosing items that can stand on their own merits. But the products you consider will be balanced with other stock, in the assortment, in the classification, and in the store.

- **Does it fit the buying plan?** Even if a buyer fails to select the "best" style, the fact that an item in the stock breakdown is needed to round out an assortment enhances the chance of that style being accepted by consumers. You can't decide on exact patterns and designs for men's ties, for example, until you get to market and see them. But you *can* come in with decisions already made about the types or sizes you'll need, the optimum price range, basic colors, and perhaps the fabrics you know will sell in your market. If the buying plan must be changed on-site, the decision should be deliberate—not because you've carelessly bought whatever looked attractive in three different showrooms. The price range is especially important, because it signifies your negotiating point.
- **Distinct difference from any article now in stock or on order.** Slight variations that are virtually duplicates of one another should be avoided, even if they are desirable from every other point of view. The goal should be to have every new style add to the assortment in the customer's eyes, adding new business instead of stealing from (the industry term is **cannibalizing**) the sales potential of something else.
- **Relationship to the vendor's line.** Some differences of opinion exist about whether a buyer should "cherry-pick" the best of a manufacturer's product line, or buy most of what is presented as long as it is reasonably satisfactory. We've already mentioned that it is desirable to concentrate as much of a "buy" as possible among several key suppliers, rather than buying an item or two from many different vendors. Many an upscale department store has made its mark by doing just that, aligning with designers that, in turn, add prestige to the store. However, more buyers—particularly in the mid-priced fashion field—prefer to "buy numbers" (individual items) rather than lines. They insist that it is their responsibility to present the best merchandise at market, regardless of its origin.

  This theory does not preclude them from developing key resources, but it might prevent them from getting bulk-purchase discounts.
- **Reorder ability.** Because profits are usually made on reorders of styles rather than on the initial purchase, it is important to determine in advance of purchase whether a reorder can be obtained, and how promptly. A special value or a short season may mean a finite number of goods, but the buyer should give preference to the items that can be reordered.

  The other consideration is that, if reorders are possible, the initial order can be smaller as a test purchase, to see how well it sells and determine if there is sufficient demand for more.
- **Competition with other retailers.** Whether competitors have already stocked the new item is an important consideration. Buyers are glad to consider the experience with the item by retailers in other areas, but are naturally concerned about the number and type of stores that have already purchased the line in their trading area—as they should be.
- **Shelf space.** The department for which the new item is being considered may not have enough space to display and store it in the sizes, quantities, and perhaps colors that may be required for a good assortment. In this case,

the buyer must decide if it's time to substitute the new line for an existing one, depending on the potential profit of each.

DECISIONS BY COMMITTEE

Taking all the factors on the last few pages into consideration may make the buying process more mundane, but the specific questions should make it easier to focus and simplify a staggering number of individual-item decisions. You will surely want to take a second look at some items, which is appropriate.

In the garment industry, the norm is to see the new line first on models, and then on hangers. The first glance centers, naturally, on general appearance and styling; the second, on detail—workmanship, fabric, special features. One way to ensure reconsideration is for the buyer to insist on writing his or her own orders, rather than allowing the sales rep (who is only too happy to do it!) to apply that subtle pressure. Compiling your own order gives you a final opportunity to think over each item, check it against the buying plan, and review terms and prices before the order is placed.

In some cases, it is a good idea to get another's opinion before making the decision. Calling on an assistant, a key store salesperson, the merchandising manager will provide another point of view, as well as underscore the importance of team effort. The buyer may be required to present a line of samples to a committee, or at the regular sales meetings of one or more stores in the chain, for input.

Some chains, especially in supermarkets, have buying committees that consider product selection from their various departments' viewpoints—how easy or difficult it will be to stock and warehouse; its profitability, distinctiveness, promotional value; and so on. They don't really concern themselves with the sales potential of the product—that's the buyer's job. Theirs is to take a real-world look at the product and how the store will have to deal with it on a daily basis.

BUYING JOB LOTS AND IRREGULARS

A **job lot** is an assortment of styles or products from unrelated lines that a vendor has been unable to sell at regular prices and is now offering at a reduced, flat price per item. The general rule for a buyer is to not buy a job lot unless it is priced low enough to ensure that the entire lot will be sold to the store's customers at a satisfactory markup. Because a job lot usually consists of merchandise of differing values, it is a good plan to sort it into price classes before buying, based on what you think you can actually sell it for.

For example, a buyer may be offered 100 children's Halloween costumes at a flat price of $8 each. Inspection and arrangement of the units by their "probable sales price" may convince the buyer that

20 can be sold for $19.95	(approx.) $400
60 can be sold for $12.95	(approx.) 780
20 can be sold for $9	180
TOTAL ESTIMATED SALES	$1,360
TOTAL COST	800
MARGIN	560 (or 41%)

If this is anywhere near the department's planned margin, it may be considered a good buy, because it provides a bargain selection for the customers. If it's not a high enough profit margin, the buyer passes on this job lot.

The danger with job lots of apparel is that a poor assortment is usually the result, especially in terms of colors and sizes, even though the styles and qualities may be excellent. So it is important to always place a realistic value on the expected revenue.

Another common error is to buy a job lot of out-of-season merchandise because it seems like such a great bargain. A manufacturer of winter sweaters may sell them for $16 apiece in January, when a few months earlier, each piece sold for $33.50 and retailed for $66. Late in the season, they can still be sold at $32.95—half the retail price, and still at a decent profit—to attract customers. The buyer's decision: Will they sell at half price? Or are the target customers already anticipating spring weather and spring styles?

The buyer must also consider the effect of the job lot's bargain price on other, regular merchandise in the store. If you've already got considerable stock on hand of an item that retails at $16.95, do you want a batch of very similar goods that can be retailed at $10? Introducing the lower-priced item may force a markdown of the regularly priced goods before it would otherwise be necessary. The better plan is to sell out a large portion of the regular stock before introducing a job jot.

One merchandise manager we know handles the situation this way in menswear: He has suit coats on hand that retail for $115. Their original cost to his department was $59.50 apiece. At mid-season, a job lot of similar quality suit coats may be bought wholesale at $39.50 each, and profitably retailed for $75. However, this would force a heavy markdown on the existing higher-priced stock.

The manager instead marks the new purchases at $89.50, taking a markdown of $25.50 on each unit of the higher-priced stock. He is making

- $30 profit on each of the original suit coats in stock
- $50 profit on each of the job lot coats in stock

After some sales at this price as the season wanes, the whole group may be reduced to a sales price of $75 and still provide an adequate markup.

Irregulars and Seconds

Certain amounts of imperfect and damaged goods are expected in manufacturing. Ideally, they are separated from the salable items during inspection or quality control and offered at a discount to retailers willing to charge less for them than for top-quality goods. The term irregular usually refers to an item with unobtrusive imperfections or in need of minor repair. Seconds and thirds refer to items with more extensive or apparent flaws. Very often, the performance or durability of the item is unimpaired—it just doesn't look so great.

It is the policy of some retailers to never, *ever* buy imperfect goods! They feel their image would be damaged by offering the public anything less than perfection. Other retailers allow such purchases in small, controlled amounts. Still others seek them out for deep discounting. But even those retailers whose dominant competitive weapon is low price should be cautious about promoting too great a proportion of seconds too much of the time. It creates the impression of carelessness in their overall quality standards as well as their business standards.

All advertising and signage must honestly and accurately reflect the exact nature of the offering: "Irregulars $6.99; made to sell, if perfect, for $12.95." All items must be clearly marked as seconds on the individual goods as well.

Off-Price Merchandise

The term **off-price** is confusing and inexact, just like irregulars and seconds. In a broad sense, quite a variety of retailers can be considered as "off-price" merchants: discount stores, dollar stores, warehouse clubs, factory outlets, deep-discount drug chains, and so on. Most often, off-price refers not to retailers selling at lower profit levels, but to merchandise being offered at a discount from its normal, regular price.

The reasons things end up off-price are many:

- Manufacturer overstocks or order cancellations by retailers
- Late deliveries of piece goods (the "pieces" used to make garments), which must then be manufactured and sold rather than being left as "pieces"
- Odds and ends leftover at the end of a season

Manufacturers also produce so-called **secondary labels**—merchandise similar in quality to their regular lines, but of different styling and at substantially lower prices. (Interestingly, one of the biggest secondary-label markets in recent years is the wine industry. Many top-quality wineries market pleasant, well-made wines at lower price points under a secondary label, to sell as restaurant house wines and in supermarkets.) In the apparel industry, manufacturers add off-price lines to keep factories busy and reduce cash flow problems caused by the peaks and valleys of seasonal production. The major advantage of buying from this type of planned production is the ability to select specific styles and colors. Some manufacturers show their secondary lines at the same time they show their regular, branded lines.

The buying office your company contracts with will be a prime source of information about off-price merchandise, perhaps passing along news about an attractive deal by e-mail or phone. When the timing is right, taking advantage of these can be profitable. In addition to being able to offer incredible bargains to customers, some fashion discounters are achieving inventory turnover of a dozen times a year, compared to three or four "turns" for a traditional department store.

There is, of course, also an opportunistic side to off-price retailing, in the form of jobbers who make a living buying closeouts and irregulars from manufacturers, and marked-down remains from retailers, to resell. Buying this type of merchandise presents some very real dangers, making someone else's unsold merchandise *your* problem. Take it on only if there is sufficient selling time in a season to dispose of the entire lot, and if the merchandise passes both of the litmus-test questions referred to earlier.

Buyers who have experience with off-price goods often buy them to gain extra sales in the last weeks of a season if there is still some demand for quality merchandise at reduced prices. Let's see how this can work using the example of 10 stylish sunhats, purchased at the start of a season for $14.75 each, that retail full-price for $30. After five weeks and an unseasonably rainy summer, only five units have sold—which would normally indicate it's time to mark down the other five. But there's plenty of warm weather yet to go, and the buyer is offered more sunhats of equal quality at an off-price deal of $9.75 per hat. She buys 25 of them and retails them at $20 each. The remaining five units of the original stock are marked down from $30 to $20.

Within two weeks, 25 of the total 30 units are sold at $20. The remaining 5 hats are reduced in price to $15, which clears them out of the store too. How does the buyer stand in terms of profit?

COST	5 units at $14.75	$ 73.75
	25 units at $9.75	243.75
	TOTAL COST	$317.50
SALES	25 units at $20	$500.00
	5 units at $15	75.00
	TOTAL SALES	$575.00
PROFIT ("Markon")		$257.50 (44.8%)

A decent profit was made, and lots of heads were attractively covered at bargain prices.

Off-price retailing was forecast to decline in the 1990s, but with the incredible amount of discount goods coming into the United States from other nations—and with Americans' keen eye for bargains—it has shown no signs of slowing. Outlet stores alone number more than 14,000, and there are more than 40 booming national chains, from T.J. Maxx to Loehmann's, that specialize in sales off-price merchandise.

SPECIFICATIONS, STANDARDS, AND PRODUCT TESTING

Buyers use product specifications in a number of ways. As mentioned, **specifications** are written guidelines for making an item, used as follows:

- At its simplest, specification buying is making requests to the manufacturer for minor changes in goods that they are already producing. Buyers may suggest enhancements to the quality of materials, workmanship, or styling; or they may ask that unnecessary selection factors be eliminated to keep costs down.
- A buyer can also take written "specs" to more than one manufacturer and ask them for competitive bids to produce the item.
- At its most complete, the buyer gives the manufacturer specific instructions for every aspect of a product, from raw materials, to colors and sizes, to packaging and wording on labels. The specs for packaging are every bit as exact as the specs for the merchandise itself. In the case of private-label merchandise, specs are a must.

The requirement for specification buying is usually major sales volume—a large enough order to make it worth the manufacturer's time to tie up production lines for a special order. Hundreds of items must be processed in order to produce them cheaply. An advantage other than price is that a competent manufacturer can become a valuable team member, with input on the specs and the production processes involved in meeting them.

Profitability is typically negotiated. The manufacturer may settle for a small fee per unit, since the large volume of the purchase lowers total cost ratios and gives the plant a decent return on investment. The manufacturer also is mindful of the prestige associated with being selected by respected retailers to do the work.

After the initial order is negotiated, the buyer's (or buying committee's) responsibility in the process is to provide quality control along the way, with inspections that may continue at intervals through the life of the contract. The idea is partly to ensure the quality of the products but also their uniformity. This can be more difficult than it sounds because it is sometimes hard to measure standards precisely. In the store, customers learn to count on a certain standard for their repeat purchases, which national brands pride themselves on setting, again and again. When a large supermarket contracts with a fruit processor for its own private brand of applesauce, and despite the specs, the buying committee declares it "too runny" and the apples pureed "too finely," problems ensue. Applesauce is not something that can be repaired!

Standards and Product Testing

With some types of products, there are state and/or national safety standards that must be met in addition to any of the retailer's specifications. Government agencies—the Consumer Product Safety Commission, Federal Trade Commission, U.S. Food and Drug Administration, and others—publish and enforce standards for many products and/or ingredients. The American National Standards Institute (ANSI) is a national nonprofit organization that coordinates and administers voluntary standardization systems for a wide range of industries. A buyer may include in the specifications that the items must conform to these standards.

Where more elaborate tests are required, a laboratory or testing bureau may be hired for a fee. From Underwriters Laboratories to NSF International (formerly the National Safety Foundation) to Consumers Union, their services may include the following:

- Helping companies set standards and specifications
- Aiding buyers in comparing competitive offers and checking vendor claims
- Conducting research to suggest product improvements
- Checking claims made in a retailer's own advertisements or displays
- Testing merchandise returned by consumers
- Updating buyers about legislation involving safety, health, labeling, and more

ENVIRONMENTAL AWARENESS

In Chapter 7, we discussed social and environmental concerns that may impact vendor selection, which are also pertinent to this discussion. The fact is that buyers and retailers *can* impact the environment by the choices they make. There are three considerations here:

1. More accurate forecasting of the prices of finished goods based on up-to-date knowledge of the prices of raw materials
2. Determining whether the raw materials are becoming scarce in order to seek substitutions
3. Eliminating products that may be either hazardous to the environment or potentially harmful to human health

For just one month (October 2004), the list of product recalls by the U.S. Consumer Product Safety Commission included the following: baby rattles, gas grills, toy cars, lighters, mattress pads, hot-water dispensers, children's chairs, toy washing machines, lunchboxes, work boots, bicycles, AC adapters for notebook computers, electric fans, lightbulbs, and heated towel racks. Two companies were fined for failure to promptly report safety-related problems, one a power-tool maker ($100,000) for defective handles on its spiral saws, and a toy manufacturer ($125,000) for children's drum sets.[2]

Not your problem? It is if you purchased 500 of them less than six months ago for your stores. And in legal action about defective products, the merchant is almost always sued, right along with the manufacturer.

On the other hand, merchants can make a name for themselves among some consumer groups for their adherence to environmentally friendly buying policies, or so-called **green marketing**. Whole Foods Markets is one such business, a grocery chain with 162 stores in the United States and Great Britain. From the company's Web site:

> We strive to offer the highest quality, least processed, most flavorful and naturally preserved foods . . . We believe in a virtuous circle entwining the food chain, human beings and Mother Earth: each is reliant upon the others through a beautiful and delicate symbiosis.[3]

The store buyer's concern for raw materials should not be limited to the products, but also to the way they are packaged. Biodegradable, nonpolluting, and recyclable are the watchwords here.

There are also ethical considerations in retailing. Should a store carry cigarettes, or advertise them in-store the ways the tobacco companies request, knowing the irrefutable evidence that smoking is a major cause of cancer? Should a store promote the sale of alcohol in an area with a high percentage of teen customers? Should a store carry food products that are genetically engineered, although the topic is controversial? It is wise to hammer out specific policies about these issues to avoid conflict and misunderstanding between senior management, buyers, and salespeople.

CHAPTER SUMMARY

Buying trips are some of the busiest and most intense times for retail buyers, but they can also be the most fun. This chapter mentioned some of the major market cities, described how "market weeks" work, and offered several ways buyers can organize their trips for the best use of their time. It is imperative that a buying plan be finalized to accompany the buyer, who might otherwise be overwhelmed by the choices and vulnerable to sales pressure to order goods that are unnecessary, inappropriate, or too expensive.

This is not to say the plan can't be modified if, upon arrival at market, the exact goods required by the plan are simply unavailable. The chapter offers quite a bit of detail and no less than 15 criteria for exactly how to sort through the limitless selections and create a report card of sorts to assist in decision making. It is important to look not only at the product and packaging, but at how the buyer expects it will fit into the stores' current offerings, and how much support the store will receive from the manufacturer or importer to help market it.

There is a role for damaged and off-price merchandise, but most buyers have to consider it carefully. It may or may not be the best quality, and if not merchandised intelligently, has the potential to drag down the profits that could be made on full-priced goods.

And finally, attention must be paid to the potential controversy and/or danger that any product may pose, from flammability to small parts that could pose a choking hazard for toddlers. The retailer's reputation will be on the line every bit as much as the manufacturer if a defective item is offered for sale.

DISCUSSION QUESTIONS

1. What deviations from a buying plan might be made at market when the offerings are not exactly what the buyer had in mind?
2. Offer an example of a product that has sidestepped its competitors by including a distinctive feature.
3. What are some examples of *limited group* offerings?
4. Establish a grading scale for two types of products: coffeemakers and men's ties.
5. Why do you think profits are usually made on reorders, not initial purchases of new items? Is this always the case, or can you think of exceptions?
6. Do you think it is ever okay to buy items that are not in keeping with your retailer's image—to "push the envelope"? Would you get permission first from senior management? How much of the budget and plan would you devote to an "experiment"?
7. In buying *irregulars*, do you believe you get what you pay for? Would you take the time for additional inspection if you thought you could bring back a real bargain for the store? Are your thoughts any different about *off-price* merchandise?
8. For what types of merchandise would a *buying committee* be more appropriate than an individual or department buyer?
9. For what types of merchandise do you think it is most critical to keep up on environmental (and/or social and ethical) issues about the raw materials used to make them?
10. Of the nine criteria listed in the section on "Product Features," briefly make the case for which one you consider most important in:

    a. A gas and convenience store
    b. A warehouse store
    c. An upscale department store
    d. A mom-and-pop gift store

ENDNOTES

1. Dawn Anfuso, Associate Editor, "Study Shows Buying Power of Youth," in iMedia Connection.com, iMedia Communications, Dana Point, California, September 8, 2003.
2. Consumer Product Safety Commission, Washington, D.C., October 2004.
3. From wholefoodsmarket.com Web site, October 2004.

C H A P T E R

1 0

Negotiating the Buy

The buyer's order expresses the buying decision in three ways:
It defines both the quantity and quality of the goods being ordered, it specifies the wholesale price for the goods, and it indicates any other conditions of purchase—packaging, tagging, delivery, promotional allowances, point-of-sale materials that will accompany the order, and so on.

While the word "negotiate" is often equated with bargaining for a price advantage—and surely there is some of that going on—retailers are often more concerned with other factors in making the best overall deal. So the first focus of a smart buyer is to, above all, *buy the right merchandise to fill the needs of the customers*. As we've mentioned previously, if it doesn't do that, it is not a bargain—at any price.

This chapter covers all the conditions of a wholesale purchase, and the buyer's responsibility in following through with the terms. They include the following:

- Price negotiation
- Types of discounts
- The services included (or not) in a final price
- Shipping and insurance options
- Advertising and markdown allowances

Of course, buyers are not insensitive to price. It is their responsibility to buy merchandise at the lowest possible prices while maintaining solid and honest relationships with the vendors that will help build mutually profitable businesses in the future. But, depending on the retailer's needs, negotiations may also include many other matters to be agreed on by both parties:

- The terms of the sale (dates, discounts, etc.)
- Quality guarantees
- Storage until needed by the retailer
- Delivery terms (when, how, and by whom)
- Transportation allowances
- Packaging, both for reshipment and for resale
- Additional services, like tagging the merchandise or putting apparel on hangers
- Reorder availability (and price guarantees on reorders)
- Return privileges and terms
- Promotional aids and allowances
- Markdown allowances

It is important to note that the lines between vendor and retailer are blurring, as technology allows them to invoice by computer, order by e-mail, and even access each others' sales statistics in some cases. But none of these helpful processes can work without the initial "deal." And that must be negotiated, human to human—preferably face to face.

THE SPIRIT OF THE NEGOTIATION

Good negotiators observe certain practices, and retail buyers are no exception. First, they go in with the "blessings" of their senior management, including a thorough understanding of what they are expected to achieve and the priorities assigned to the various goals. They analyze their own needs, goals, habits, and negotiating style and determine how these relate to the store's goals. And, if possible, they examine the same things about the seller, whether foreign or domestic.

Buyers recognize that the trust of the other party is essential if they want to come to a mutually satisfactory agreement. If they say they're going to do something, they follow through. In this way, they cultivate relationships, and even friendships, with ongoing business partners.

During the negotiation itself, the astute buyer is careful to explain the needs of the company and the logic of the agreement to be reached. The buyer also gives the seller every opportunity to talk, to express his or her own company's needs and goals, paying full attention to wording, gestures, and facial expressions. The buyer is quick to note the terms on which both parties already agree, and to limit the points of disagreement to as few as possible.

Bargaining at its worst is a way to wear down the opposition to try to obtain concessions not justified by the economics of the situation. Some buyers, who think themselves shrewd, promise big future orders (that never materialize) to get price breaks for a first order, ridicule a vendor for "pettiness" in holding out for a regular price, and threaten to end the negotiations with a boycott. This kind of behavior is not only unfair and unnecessary—it usually reflects worse on the buyer than the vendor. If by some chance the unpleasant negotiator gets his or her way, the manufacturer may do what the contract requires . . . but will lower the quality control standards slightly, or put the job last in a long line of priorities. There are dozens of ways to retaliate, none of them positive. An initial victory is not worth it, in the long run.

Bargaining at its best is tough negotiation. The buyer with a broad knowledge of customer demand, costs, deadlines, manufacturing requirements, competitive offerings, and the person sitting across the bargaining table can offer (and accept the other's) sensible ideas to come to an agreement that will be profitable for both parties.

Good negotiators often employ one or more of the following strategies during the bargaining process:

- They keep their limits hidden. That means they refrain from revealing at the start the most they will pay rather than pass up the deal. Instead, they let the seller go first, and quote a starting price. This strategy gives the buyer a clue about the seller's limit and may prevent turning the seller off immediately by offering a higher price than he or she would have accepted—coloring the rest of the negotiations.

  It sounds a little cheesy, but another way to hide a limit is not to show too much outward interest in the goods. Even if they are exactly what you need to fill out an assortment, if you "want 'em too, too badly," you are putting yourself at a disadvantage to admit it. Think of it this way: The limits in both the buyer's and seller's minds are not really fixed at the beginning of a negotiation. Both are open to suggestion, depending on how things go in the meeting. The seller who sees immediately that the sale is a sure thing by your enthusiasm for the goods is less likely to negotiate the particulars than one who feels he or she must convince you to buy. Psychology 101? Absolutely!

- The buyer avoids a long, drawn-out negotiation by indicating the importance of a prompt deal and the amount of time he or she has to give to the discussion. Of course, it's important to respect the seller's right to think over a proposition. If that is the case, however, the buyer can suggest a time limit: "I'd like to know your decision by the end of the week." Be firm, but reasonable.

- When, after some degree of negotiation, the amount that the buyer bids is only somewhat less than what the seller asks, the suggestion to split the difference is a good one. If the buyer offers 85 cents per item, and the seller is asking 95 cents, the deal may be made at 90 cents, provided that both parties benefit. Use this tactic carefully, though. If the suggested split is below the seller's limit, the negotiation may end right there.

- There are often multiple issues to be negotiated for a single buy, and the smart buyer negotiates them one at a time. Price usually comes first, then terms of sale and other arrangements follow. However, these matters are often interrelated, and price cannot always be the first issue *settled*, even when it is the first issue *raised*. The speed of delivery, or the store's upcoming promotion plans for goods of this type, may be overriding considerations. If it is difficult to come to a prompt agreement on price, suggest that you set it aside for the moment, and decide on the other conditions, then come back to it.

The ideal bargain brings profit to all—the buyer, the retailer, the vendor, and the consumer. Good negotiation is founded on the principle that each party must end up believing it has won; and good negotiators live by the credo, "If it's not a good deal for both parties, it's not a good deal."

PRICE NEGOTIATIONS

We should begin this section by acknowledging that not all buying situations even require haggling about price. A vendor's prices and terms are commonly fixed. However, buyers of large quantities for mass merchandising (and even small-scale buyers, if their needs are not typical) have an opportunity to negotiate special deals.

Alert buyers are always pressing for advantages in price and terms, but they distinguish between regular buying and buying of "specials." In regular buying to provide and maintain assortments, their success is more dependent on the purchase of the right goods at the right time in the right quantities. On the other hand, when specials are offered, price plays a more important role. Some stores do more business in specials than in regular goods, and their company policy for buyers may be to place price considerations above all other factors. Also, in the case of fashion goods already manufactured and subject to obsolescence, bargaining is necessary.

It may help at this point to compare the vendor's role to what happens in a retail store. Most retailers have a one-price policy. The goods are marked with a price and put on the shelves or racks for sale. People don't come in and bargain with the sales floor staff—they buy it, or they don't, at that price. If an article isn't selling after a certain time period, for whatever reason, it has not been accepted in the market at its original price. It may be lowered in price—to meet competition, or create a special sale, to reflect a falling market, or to clear out odd sizes in otherwise popular selection factors.

The vendor's business follows a similar pattern. A set price is determined for the goods being manufactured or imported. If they've made more than they need, if someone cancels or returns an order, if economic conditions change and fast cash is needed—the vendor marks down to clear goods out and make room for new ones.

Price negotiation seems to work well for new products or new versions of products. The vendor's estimate of unit costs depends very much on the quantity the vendor expects to sell, the average size of anticipated orders, and the methods of packaging and delivery. The buyer's opinion of the salability of the merchandise at different price points, the size of the order the buyer is prepared to place, and the conditions of purchase that they require all have a great deal to do with setting the vendor's price. The vendor who insists otherwise, sets a price and sticks to it, may be throwing a roadblock into the profitable distribution of the new merchandise.

Buyers use the following techniques to make their cases for better prices from their vendors, and they examine any so-called special offers carefully with these points in mind. We've grouped them by basic type of skill, knowledge, or result.

Do Your Homework

Estimate the retail value of the item. This is accomplished by viewing the item through the customer's eyes, deciding what the customer will pay for it, and subtracting the normal markup for this type of item to arrive at the wholesale price you should be charged for it by the supplier. Thus, an item that would cost $18 in the store with a customary markup of 37.5 percent ($6.75) should not cost more than $11.25 to buy wholesale: $18 minus $6.75. If it is more than $11.25, there should be a reason to justify the low markup—unusual volume opportunity, special features important to a certain group of customers, and so on.

The inexperienced buyer should consistently practice guessing at the normal retail prices of every item in the line, not only at wholesale but when browsing the competitors' stores. Look it over, make your best guess, and then look at the price tag. It will help greatly in becoming a fair judge of retail values, which can then be translated into cost equivalents you can use to measure quoted prices.

Learn to evaluate a quoted price by knowing the elements that go into it. Manufacturers' prices are often cost plus. Sometimes the material or labor costs are higher than necessary because of their own inefficiencies, or they may allot a heavy overhead or profit burden to the price. The smart buyer masters the costs of the manufacturing process and can estimate how much it should actually cost the seller to produce the goods. If the manufacturer quotes an amount that is far less than the estimate, there's a chance they'll skimp on workmanship or materials. If the quoted price is higher, there may be either production inefficiency or an attempt to rake in a big profit. Buyers do not have to share the estimate during negotiations—just have it as the target figure in their minds.

In practice, the buyer of fashion goods is often unfamiliar with the manufacturing end of the business, but the commodity buyer is an expert—contracting with mills for quantities of fabric and other materials delivered to a manufacturer who will produce the finished goods.

Compare price quotations. This may be done by shopping at market, checking out the lines of visiting sales reps, or keeping up on online offers and information bulletins. In retail, buyers don't ask for competitive, sealed bids as they do in some other industries. There are so many factors in making the buy that the lowest priced may not be the winning bid anyway.

The Robinson-Patman Act, which has been in effect since the 1930s, is one of several major federal laws prohibiting price discrimination and setting very specific rules for discounts and deals. It does allow a seller to legally reduce the price to a buyer when the seller is meeting the lower price of a competitor "in good faith," thus protecting the seller's business. So the buyer is on firm legal ground to inform one seller of the lower price offered by another, and to ask the higher-priced seller to meet it.

For seasonal goods, the remaining length of a season should impact the cost. There are several examples of this, including perishable items like produce and some packaged foods, as well as fashion merchandise. It is only logical that a reduced price should be negotiated for goods offered at "regular" price when their season is well advanced and demand will soon be declining, if it's not already.

Look for value-added services. Increasingly, manufacturers and wholesalers are giving retailers more for their money by offering floor-ready merchandise—already packaged, bar-coded, priced with a store-specific label, and even, in the case of clothing, on hangers. These may be included in the price, or for an additional fee per unit. The buyer's job is to analyze whether these services save enough time and labor in-store to justify their cost.

TYPES OF DISCOUNTS

The first question here should be a legal one—what qualifies as a discount, versus what is an unfair (and therefore illegal) agreement? The Federal Trade Commission's Bureau of Competition groups violations into two basic types: horizontal agreements (between competitors) and vertical agreements (between buyers and sellers). Following are examples of illegal horizontal agreements:

- Agreeing on price or price-related terms, like credit terms, when the agreement is not reasonably related to the way the companies do business
- Agreeing to restrict price advertising, or even non-price advertising, if it deprives consumers of important information
- Agreeing among each other to limit or restrict output, to drive up the price of an item by making it scarcer
- Boycotting a person or business as a group if the tactic is used by companies to force another party to pay higher prices
- Agreements to restrict each company's sales territory or to allocate customers, which are actually agreements *not* to compete

Vertical agreements tend to come under greater scrutiny if they involve pricing, although non-price agreements can also be unfair and therefore illegal. Following are some examples:

- A supplier and a retailer agreeing on either a minimum or maximum resale price of a product, especially when it means the price they are charging is noncompetitive
- A vendor cannot *require* you to buy one product in order to get another that you really want. This is known as a **tie-in** (as in, tying the products together for sale) and may be unlawful if it harms competition, or if it is a product you either *don't* want or could buy elsewhere if you wanted it, at a lower price.

In short, a practice is illegal if it restricts competition in some significant way and has no overriding business justification.[1]

Qualify for a quantity discount. Again, the Robinson-Patman Act permits vendors to sell goods of like grade and quantity at different prices, as long as the differences are limited to the vendor's cost of manufacture, sale, and delivery and/or the quantities sold. There are several ways to qualify for a bulk discount. One, as we've mentioned in other chapters, is to concentrate most of your buying with a few key suppliers. (In terms of loyalty, it also happens to ensure better service and other concessions.) You might place a blanket order, a firm contract for a major portion of items for a season. In this case, the buyer can usually specify sizes, colors, and other details.

Some suppliers allow the buyer to accumulate enough orders for a discount—say, if you order so much within a six-month period, you qualify for a discount on the total purchases during that period. Carpet manufacturers are among those who offer cumulative discounts, because they prompt reorders without a lot of sales time for the manufacturer. Fair warning: The Federal Trade Commission takes a dim view of cumulative discount programs unless the method of sale and the total quantities ordered clearly lead to manufacturers' savings that are at least equal to the concession. It is usually easier to prove these points in an individual sale than based on a group of sales over time.

Overall, it is probably easier to order less frequently and in larger quantities—as long as the retailer has the storage capability to house them until they are needed.

Carefully analyze the so-called free deals. It is very common for a sales rep to offer a "buy 10, get 1 free" sort of deal. The other common arrangement is to buy an amount of one product and get some other, unrelated product "free"—10 packs of gum with every 100 cigars, for example. In all such cases, the goods are not really "free," and they're only a bargain if the buyer can sell them profitably and create a bit of extra sales volume with no more promotional effort or expense. Either the gum or the cigars can go stale while awaiting purchase, so the best buy might have been the box of 50 cigars at the regular wholesale price.

Sellers use "freebies" in lieu of reducing quoted prices, or to force the distribution of items in the line that are in large supply. The buyer must always weigh these deals in terms of the profit opportunity they provide. Does it skew the balance of existing inventory? Require more shelf space that is already in short supply, or a special promotion to move it out of the store?

Cooperate with other stores to place joint orders. Smaller merchants, members of cooperative buying groups, and retailer-owned wholesale establishments all band together to buy in sufficient quantity to achieve volume discounts. There's often no appreciable savings in shipping and handling costs, but a better price may still result from buying in quantity. The group typically accepts the entire order at a central distribution point, and each retailer has some additional costs for getting it from that point into their own stores.

Buy through a wholesaler for a better discount. In many trades, wholesalers are granted special discounts based not on quantity, but on the important functions they perform by warehousing and distributing products. A manufacturer will almost always give a larger discount to a wholesaler than to a retailer. Getting this discount is tricky for retailers, because the whole point of the Robinson-Patman Act is to prohibit retailers from getting unfair price breaks that are offered to some, not all. On the other hand, buying groups of independent retailers can qualify for wholesale discounts *if they make their services available to nonmember stores* that don't compete directly with their members. Again, however, the rules are very strict about the group members not being competitors and not working together to "fix" prices.

Keep trade discount opportunities in mind. With staples that enjoy wide distribution, it is customary for manufacturers to show two prices on a list for each item—the list price and the *trade discount*. The latter are already lower prices, the lowest the vendor will go, and seldom negotiable. The retail buyer knows that these discounts are available to all buyers, and that they will vary in percentage depending on the oversupply or scarcity of the goods. The key is to understand what they are and how they are calculated.

The trade discount is a percentage deduction from a list price that *may be* a suggested retail price for the item. This discount is usually equal to the standard markup requirements for whatever type of retail trade it is. Thus, if an item has a 60-cent retail price, it may be offered to retailers at a 35 percent "trade discount"—that is, for 39 cents.

Other, functional discounts may be tied in for wholesalers, industrial users, and so on. Their discounts may be listed as "35 and 10," or "35, 10, and 5 off." These do not mean the same as "40 percent off" and "45 percent off," respectively. Instead, the discounts are "graduated" for an item that has a good, round list price of $100:

- The first discount is off the list price:

$$100 - 35 = \$65$$

- The second discount is calculated based on the new, lower price:

$$65 - 6.50 = \$58.50 \ (65 \times .10 = 6.50)$$

- The third percentage is taken off the most recent price:

$$58.50 - 2.93 = \$55.57 \ (58.50 \times .05 = 2.93)$$

List prices are often set considerably above actual retail prices. There are a couple of possible reasons for this. In some lines, the trade discounts have been larger than the markups many retailers require, and through competition, market prices have dropped "below list." Manufacturers (sometimes under pressure from unscrupulous dealers) deliberately set list prices higher than market prices in order to permit misleading price comparisons to the public that make some sales look more impressive than they actually are. This puts everyone in a tough ethical situation. It is *not* illegal to advertise list prices that are simply for identification . . . but it *is illegal* to use a list price for comparative purposes where it is not the local market price, or the retailer's own former price. (It's complicated, we know.) Further complicating the picture is that the rule is hard to apply in practice, because for many commodities within a trading area, there really is not an "accepted, regular retail price," especially for goods that are not easy to immediately identify and compare as similar.

Another reason to use trade discounts is to provide a ready mechanism for changing prices. If, for example, a manufacturer finds it necessary to raise some quick cash by discounting the entire inventory, they don't have to reprint the whole price catalog or reprogram the Web site. They can simply send out a notice informing the trade of an "additional 10 percent off" trade discount.

Assume Some of the Manufacturer's Obligations

We've already discussed the benefits of making product specifications to get exactly what you want from a finished product. Another advantage is that this relieves the manufacturer of most of the design costs, a fact that can be used to negotiate a lower price. The buyer must be certain in this case that the contract spells out how the manufacturer can use the design—exclusively for this retailer, or perhaps available to noncompeting buyers outside the store's trading area.

Cash-and-carry arrangements are also a way of assuming an obligation, as is the practice of ordering seasonal merchandise during out-of-season periods. The buyer who can forecast needs and order well in advance—earlier than competitors—may be rewarded with a discount. Even if the early order does nothing but transfer business from a busy season to a slow one, it helps a manufacturer level out the peaks and valleys inherent in the business. When a retailer or wholesaler also agrees to take delivery of the finished goods in advance of the season, the manufacturer benefits even more by not having to warehouse them. A buyer simply cannot afford to pass up a cash discount if possible. With some vendors' credit terms, it is cheaper to borrow money in order to pay cash for an order than it is to make payments to the vendor.

Many vendors allow payment in full over a very short time period (say, three months) to be considered the "same as cash," and they offer a discount if the order is paid for early. The trade term for this is **anticipation**. The savings here are less than what a pay-in-advance cash discount would provide, but still well worthwhile. Payment terms that allow anticipation are expressed in terms like these, which are known as **dating terms**:

- **3/10 net 45.** This means if the invoice is paid within 10 days of the date on the invoice, the retailer gets a 3 percent discount; however, the full amount is due within 45 days of the date on the invoice.
- **3/10 net 30 EOM.** EOM means "end of month." This means the 3 percent discount is available if the retailer pays in full within 10 days from the end of the month (EOM) in which the order was written. Another term for EOM dating is **proximo dating**.
- **2/10 net 30 ROG.** ROG means "receipt of goods." This means a 2 percent discount is available if the retailer pays in full within 10 days of the actual

A BRIEF LOOK AT THE ROBINSON-PATMAN ACT OF 1936

This law, enforced by the Federal Trade Commission, forbids any firm or person engaged in interstate commerce to discriminate in price when selling the same commodity to different purchasers *if* (and this is a critical point) the effect of the price difference is to create a monopoly or to lessen competition in the marketplace. Over the years it has been called the "Anti-Chain-Store Act," because compliance has focused on protecting independent businesses from being unable to compete with bigger chain stores that circumvented wholesalers to buy their goods directly from manufacturers for lower prices.

Attorneys say Robinson-Patman Act cases are difficult to prove and even more difficult to win, but there have been a few sizable (multimillion dollar) settlements in the last 20 years.

A few major points covered in depth in the law itself are as follows:

1. The act applies only to the sale of goods, not services.

2. A violation occurs when different prices are charged on goods of similar grade and quality, in sales that occur around the same time.

3. Generally, there is no violation unless there are actual sales to competing buyers.

4. Exceptions are made for so-called "functional discounts," when (as explained in the text immediately preceding this box) one purchaser pays a lower price because it performs different or extra functions in the seller's marketing system.

5. Exceptions are made to allow sellers to discount for quantity purchases, and for different methods of sale. The latter means, for example, that if a seller usually accepts payments on credit and delivers goods, the seller can offer a discount to those who are willing to pay cash and pick up the merchandise themselves.

6. To qualify as a violation of the law, the effect of the price discrimination must be to "injure" the competition. The plaintiff in a Robinson-Patman lawsuit must be able to prove that it suffered damages (such as lost profit or lost customers) because of the price discrimination.

As attorney Barry M. Block of the Ohio law firm Thompson Hine put it in a 2002 article, "Even a case you win is the last, or next-to-last, investment any business wants . . . The art of pricing isn't hard to master. Prices must merely be high enough to make a profit and fair enough to be legal."

Sources: Adapted from Encyclopedia.com, and the *Dayton Business Journal*, Dayton, Ohio, March 22, 2002 issue.

date the goods were received (in the distribution center or in the store). Again, the bill is due in full within 30 days, no matter what.

Anticipation on vendor invoices is a common practice among larger retail companies and can result in significant cost reduction. There's some controversy—mostly semantic—about whether a big discount like (8/10 EOM) is a "cash discount" or a "trade discount," but savings for paying promptly are savings by any name. No argument there! Of course, the higher the rate of anticipation and the longer the discount period, the greater the savings. It is a simple alternative to a short-term bank loan and should be used if the bank's interest rates are not as attractive.

Interestingly, some vendors are up front about their anticipation policies and state in writing on their contracts whether this is allowed and what the rate will be. Others don't mention their policies, and if you don't ask, you'll never know.

SHIPPING AND INSURANCE CHARGES

The standard practice among retailers is to regard the transportation and the transit insurance on incoming goods as part of the cost of merchandise. Nowadays, whether it comes from across the globe or across town, getting merchandise from a variety of out-of-town and out-of-country sources is a formidable expense. In some types of business, it adds 2 percent or more to the wholesale cost of an item; in retail departments where bulk and weight of items and packaging requirements are high relative to price (like the dishes and small appliances in housewares), the shipping costs are much higher. As we update this text, gasoline prices at the pump are well over $2 a gallon—so buyers should be doing whatever they can to keep transportation costs to a minimum. A few suggestions follow.

Ask vendors to either absorb the shipping cost or bear some of the risk while the goods are in transit. Just remember that the federal (and state) price discrimination laws make it difficult to obtain *any* shipping concessions unless they are offered to *all* buyers, or unless they are being made strictly to meet a competitive price of another vendor that might be geographically closer to the buyer's warehouse or store.

Let's say that two vendors are competing for the business of a Philadelphia buyer, one in New York City and one in Chicago. Both normally sell **FOB factory**, which means the purchaser pays transportation and insurance when the goods leave the factory. However, the Chicago seller may legally equalize the transportation charges by figuring out what it will cost him to ship to Philadelphia, versus what it will cost the New York vendor, and giving the difference back to the buyer as a concession.

The abbreviation "FOB" means "free on board," and it refers to the point at which the vendor is "free" of responsibility for the goods. The terms include:

- **FOB factory or FOB origin.** The vendor's responsibility for the goods ends when the truck arrives at the factory. The purchaser pays for the transportation and insurance from there.
- **FOB store or FOB destination.** This is the ideal for the retail buyer; the seller pays the freight charges and the title (and therefore, the legal responsibility) for the goods does not pass to the store until the goods arrive there.
- **FOB destination, charges reversed.** The buyer pays the shipping charges, but the seller insures the goods and/or takes responsibility for them during shipping.
- **FOB destination, freight prepaid.** The seller pays the shipping charges, but the buyer insures the goods and/or takes responsibility for them during shipping.
- **FOB shipping point.** The seller is responsible for the shipping costs to a certain distribution point (a central warehouse, a port or airport); the buyer takes responsibility and assumes shipping costs from there to the stores.

Figure 10-1 shows a number of types of shipping terms and what they mean, both for buyers and sellers, in terms of sharing costs and liability.

The other cost of shipping that really adds up is insurance. Here, too, *the buyer can negotiate who pays for insurance* or, literally, who "owns" the goods while they are in transit. It is usually cheaper to instruct a shipper to insure the goods at a minimum value, and to carry a blanket insurance policy to cover any loss over the minimum, than it is to have the goods valued at full price. On parcel post shipments, it may be less expensive to skip the insurance altogether and send them as certified mail. Savings can also be realized if a shipment that contains a number of packages is insured as a single unit rather than separately.

Check incoming shipments' transportation terms. If the shipment is prepaid and the buyer is charged as agreed, the charge added to the invoice should not exceed the actual cost incurred by the seller. That sounds simple enough, but when different people and departments do the ordering, the invoicing, accepting the delivery, and so on, it's easy for everyone to assume *someone else* double-checked the shipping charges for accuracy. If the order called for the seller to pay the charges, but the goods arrive "collect" or the charge is added to the bill, the amount must be charged back to the seller. If damaged, substandard, or unordered goods are returned to the seller, they should always be sent "collect," or the seller should be billed for the cost of having to return them. Freight bills should be audited after payment to be sure the charges paid were correct based on the product classification and weight reported.

Plan for the largest possible shipments, and route the shipments accordingly. Many factories have minimum shipping charges, so it is smart to ship the

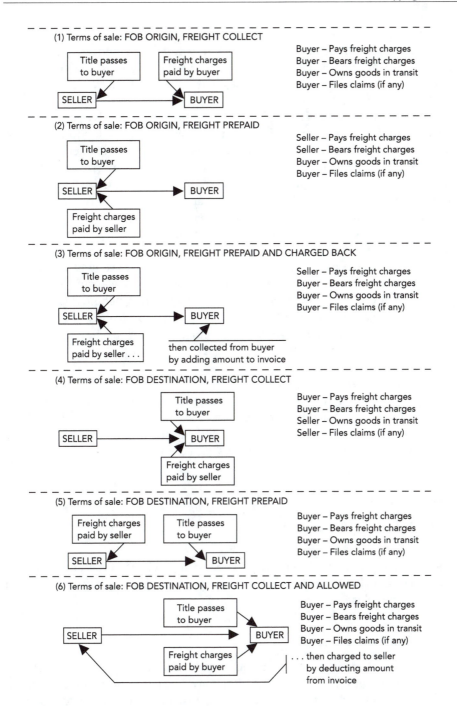

(1) Terms of sale: FOB ORIGIN, FREIGHT COLLECT

Buyer – Pays freight charges
Buyer – Bears freight charges
Buyer – Owns goods in transit
Buyer – Files claims (if any)

(2) Terms of sale: FOB ORIGIN, FREIGHT PREPAID

Seller – Pays freight charges
Seller – Bears freight charges
Buyer – Owns goods in transit
Buyer – Files claims (if any)

(3) Terms of sale: FOB ORIGIN, FREIGHT PREPAID AND CHARGED BACK

Seller – Pays freight charges
Buyer – Bears freight charges
Buyer – Owns goods in transit
Buyer – Files claims (if any)

(4) Terms of sale: FOB DESTINATION, FREIGHT COLLECT

Buyer – Pays freight charges
Buyer – Bears freight charges
Seller – Owns goods in transit
Seller – Files claims (if any)

(5) Terms of sale: FOB DESTINATION, FREIGHT PREPAID

Buyer – Pays freight charges
Buyer – Bears freight charges
Buyer – Owns goods in transit
Buyer – Files claims (if any)

(6) Terms of sale: FOB DESTINATION, FREIGHT COLLECT AND ALLOWED

Buyer – Pays freight charges
Buyer – Bears freight charges
Buyer – Owns goods in transit
Buyer – Files claims (if any)

Figure 10-1
Illustration of the effect of selling terms on distribution.

largest quantity possible at a time. Reorder schedules can be planned to exceed these minimums. If the terms are FOB destination, the destination can be a packing company or freight-forwarding company, which can arrange to receive and consolidate smaller shipments to minimize the costs from their facility to individual stores.

Routing a shipment involves selecting the least expensive type of carrier that will do the job promptly and safely. If a small shipment is necessary, it might be cheaper by parcel post than to hire a delivery service. If orders are placed well in advance, trains or buses will be less expensive than trucking companies, and so on.

No, none of these are typically a buyer's responsibilities. Large companies have logistics or operations departments to handle these functions, but the buyer's role is to be aware of the *costs involved*—because they impact the cost of the products. The fact is that most buyers inadvertently authorize considerably higher transportation charges than necessary, by instructing the seller to "rush" orders, or to ship the "best" way or the "cheapest" way. This is really an invitation to the vendor to ship the most convenient way.

An interesting and seldom-considered tactic is to work with a manufacturer to *improve packaging materials and methods.* In the interest of partnership, it behooves both parties to look at packaging options that are light but sturdy, and that fit better into boxes, cases, and other containers. Packaging is certainly part of making an attractive product, and the engineering behind it is big business. Every year, for example, the Pack Expo convention features hundreds of exhibitors of innovative containers, packaging, and packing/shipping materials. Perhaps you or your suppliers could get new ideas there.

Check all services to be provided or paid for by the vendor. Be certain you are getting everything you agreed on. Keeping up on the terms of the contracts you negotiated is part of your job as a professional buyer. You are not just checking paperwork. You are checking the honesty and organizational skills of your vendors, and the quality of your relationships with them.

ALLOWANCES

There are a few non-price items negotiated in apparel and certain other industries that are highly individual based on a certain vendor, a certain buyer, and a particular purchase transaction.

Advertising Allowances

Advertising allowances take several forms. Vendors may offer cooperative ("coop") ad programs, in which retailers may advertise branded merchandise in their local media, in store-named ads. Department stores use coop advertising extensively—the ad prominently features brand-name cosmetics, for example, but it is clearly an ad for the store itself. The store designs and places the ad, although the vendor may negotiate the right to view and approve it before it is run. The vendor then compensates the retailer based on a percentage of the amount of goods purchased from the vendor.

These allowances are usually, but not always, limited to a manufacturer's branded lines, and they may be used for purchasing newspaper space, television or radio ad times, and even to help pay for direct-mail ads or catalogs. The seller will typically require proof (receipts, copies of the ads, etc.) that the agreed form of advertising was actually *done* before issuing the credit. The coop arrangements are publicized among retailers—every store that carries this brand of cosmetics is offered the same deal, no exceptions—so the dollar amounts are not negotiated.

However, negotiations are more common when a medium- to large-size retailer places a major order for an upcoming season. The retail buyer, as part of the deal, may negotiate additional advertising dollars based on a percentage of the major order. In large retail companies, it is not uncommon for the buyer to be part of a team that negotiates this type of buy, along with the chain's sales or promotion director and the merchandise manager, meeting top-to-top with their counterparts in the vendor's sales organization. These meetings are probably the most fun and intense that a buyer will experience, as the topics cover far more than the buy itself. Together, the group outlines and agrees on advertising and promotions for the brand for a full season or more. The parties come away with a true game plan for how to spark consumer interest and boost sales for their mutual benefit. It may include the creation and/or shipment of point-of-sale materials and special display fixtures with the goods, to be used in the stores.

Pros and Cons of Advertising Allowances

If it is handled correctly, a cooperative plan has advantages for both retailer and vendor and can be a source of goodwill between them. The store is able to reduce its advertising outlay and can afford more or larger ads than perhaps it could pay for alone.

The vendor is assured that the products *are* being advertised. Promotion helps to move goods, and if the vendor can gain more of it by contributing to its cost, the vendor may consider the investment to be profitable. For example, say the vendor is offered either a 10-cent price reduction on 1,000 two-dollar items, or the chance to contribute $100 to the cost of a $200 ad placed by the retailer. The vendor must consider which of these moves will have the most beneficial impact on sales. The allowance should be part of the vendor's normal advertising budget, not an additional concession.

Retailers are often granted complete control of the kinds of advertising they undertake, although there is some advance agreement about featuring the brand name, particulars in the language of the ad copy, and perhaps the size of ad or cost of space. Sometimes, the two parties also agree on which days the ads are to be run, at what intervals they will be repeated, and so on. A few national-brand advertisers insist on their own ad design and their own copy; for broadcast, they may insist that the retailer use their own, nationally produced ads or, at least, hire a local advertising agency to do the job or insert a local tagline at the end. Large chains with their own creative design staff may resent that, but a smaller chain will benefit from having professionally produced ads it could not otherwise have afforded.

Federal (and some state) laws include requirements on ad allowances, to make them proportionally equal for all a vendor's prospective customers. However, it is the large retailers that most often take advantage of them. Either the rules for the allowance are so complex or the amount available (based on sales or quantities ordered) for a smaller store is *so* small that the smaller store does not bother to apply for the funds. The Federal Trade Commission asks that vendors develop an alternate plan when these cases are brought to its attention, but for the most part, the small merchant decides an ad allowance is out of their league, or too much trouble, and does without it.

Meanwhile, a trend among larger retailers is to contract for radio or television time, or multipage newspaper or magazine ads, and then to parcel the time and space and resell it to their various manufacturers. The retailer, by purchasing the time or space in bulk, is able to negotiate a better price than single-ad costs. But manufacturers show some resistance to this idea, in which the retailer plays more a predatory than a partnership role with them. Harkening back to the Robinson-Patman Act, as we have so often in this chapter, the parties can get in a lot of trouble if the retailer buys advertising at a lower cost (either because it's local or because it's purchased in bulk) and sells it back to the cooperating manufacturer (or some manufacturers, but not others) at higher single-ad or national rates. Remember, the law requires that everyone play fair with everyone else when it comes to prices.

For a buyer, the risk of taking advertising allowances from the "big guns" is that instead of promoting the chain's best merchandise at a price, the retailer focuses on promoting the lines on which the biggest payback can be obtained. Soon, the ads themselves show the pattern—certain items are consistently given more space than they deserve, dominating the ad copy. The store loses its reputation for unique finds by always promoting the same powerhouse name brands.

Ultimately, there is also an impact on the consumer. Allowances are one way to keep retail prices a bit higher. Rather than reducing prices to move more goods, the seller and retailer are using funds to promote the goods more intensively at their current prices. The consumer is, in the end, the one who pays for the extra promotional effort.

Markdown Allowances

Another area for active negotiation is so-called **markdown money**. The vendor and buyer agree on a percentage of the total purchase that may be used by the retailer to reduce the net cost of markdowns on merchandise. Vendors may offer markdown allowances for the buyer to order a specific style or item—something the vendor really wants to get out into the marketplace and sample, or something "high-risk," or even something that hasn't sold particularly well in the past. Buyers can also request a markdown allowance, for goods that have been selling poorly in their stores.

Markdown money is given in the form of a credit at the time of purchase and is not tied to the actual selling performance of individual styles or items. It is simply the manufacturer's "financial acknowledgment" that, if an item does not sell and the retailer has to mark it down, the manufacturer at least helps take the sting out of the potential loss of profit, by covering some (not all) of it. The risk is still shared, but to a slightly lesser degree.

Consignment Selling

Speaking of unsold merchandise, you may also negotiate whether a vendor will accept returns, if they are made within a certain time period. For very new, untried merchandise that the buyer agrees to experiment with, this may be an option because it shifts more of the risk to the vendor. The deal can be a **consignment** arrangement, in which the retailer accepts the merchandise, puts it out for sale, but only pays for what actually sells, when it sells. In consignment sales, ownership of the product passes directly from the vendor to the store's customer. The store simply acts as an agent for the vendor.

The other option is to agree to a sale with return privileges **on memorandum**. The term doesn't mean anything in particular, just that there is an agreement (presumably a "memorandum") that the retailer pays for the merchandise and returns whatever does not sell within a certain time period for a credit or refund, less a small percentage restocking fee. In this case, the product is owned by the retailer, not the vendor, because the retailer pays for it like any other order.

From a retail buyer's standpoint, consignment has the advantages of eliminating markdowns and increasing stock assortment without having to invest more money. Often, these deals also include the assistance of the vendor's route salespeople, who rotate the stock, keep the merchandise looking good, help with training, and generally serve as the vendor's emissaries in the field. Interstate Batteries has secured a reputation at the top of the automotive battery industry by selling strictly on consignment to service stations and auto parts stores, stressing service and regular route deliveries.

Consignment and on memorandum sales also work well in making deals with small vendors, like artists and craftspeople. Some college bookstores operate by ordering large quantities of textbooks in advance of a term or semester and negotiating the return of unsold copies.

Slotting Allowances

In the grocery trade, the **slotting allowance** began in the 1980s as a proliferation of new products and line extensions began to compete for a finite amount of supermarket shelf space. This is one industry in which it has become common, but incredibly controversial, for manufacturers to offer price concessions in exchange for prominent displays and supporting shelf space for their wares.

Today, the term is applied to a range of related trade practices. Each of these types of payments is made by a manufacturer to a retailer:

- Lump-sum payments in connection with the introduction of a new product into the retailer's warehouses and stores. These typically take the form of an amount per store, and are sometimes called *new item fees.*
- Ongoing payments, either monthly or annually, for favorable placement on store shelves; sometimes called *shelf fees.*
- **Renewal fees** are payments to remain on the retailer's shelf. These are nick-named "pay to stay" fees.
- Payments are also made to increase the amount of shelf space a product line gets in-store. These are called **facing allowances**.
- **Market Development Funds (MDF)** are paid for endcap displays and to fund promotions and merchandising programs for the products. The nick-name here is "street money."
- **Failure fee** is a payment to make up for a new product that doesn't end up meeting its predetermined volume targets.
- **Free fill** is the term for a retailer requiring that the supplier provide a certain amount of new product for free, in order to promote it.[2]

Does the word "insidious" seem to apply to any of the catchy terms? Little wonder that it can cost a manufacturer $2 million to persuade a national supermarket chain to stock a new product in its first year.

In recent years, both the Federal Trade Commission and the U.S. Securities and Exchange Commission have probed this business practice—the FTC for unfair trade restrictions, and the SEC for accounting improprieties. An FTC study of five product categories released in November 2003 revealed the following:

- Manufacturers spend a total of $9 billion annually on slotting fees.
- For a product in a single store, the fees range from $2,313 to $21,678 per item, per year, but there is considerable variability in the amount of fees paid and the likelihood of having to pay them.
- In the ice cream category, only 10 percent of the manufacturers earned enough in their first year to cover their slotting fee costs.
- The fees make up a major portion of the revenue earned by the store for some products in their first year on the market.[3]

Despite the controversy surrounding them, slotting allowances have been considered essential to gain market exposure for new products. Companies that have challenged them so far in court as restrictions of trade have been largely unsuccessful. But some major players—who refuse to play this particular game—may provide impetus to change the status quo without legal intervention. Procter & Gamble refuses to pay slotting fees, and Wal-Mart refuses to accept them.

CHAPTER SUMMARY

If, as the old saying goes, "everything has a price," then the skilled retail buyer is charged with negotiating that price on the best terms for the profitability of his or her employer. Learning negotiation skills is a huge part of being a successful buyer, and it begins with understanding what goes into determining the price of an item in the first place.

For the vendor, the unit cost includes the quantity they expect to sell, the average size of anticipated orders, how the product will be packaged, and who will pay for insurance in transit and delivery. The buyer's point of view includes how well the item is expected to sell (depending on its eventual retail price), the size of the order the buyer is prepared to place, and the conditions of purchase—speed and cost of shipping, whether the item can be reordered if necessary, how much the vendor will chip in for advertising and markdown allowances, and what additional services may be included. This chapter has summarized the most common terms and issues that will come up in negotiations.

In terms of pricing, there are numerous opportunities for discounts, from ordering in quantity to paying before the due date on an invoice. Individual percentage amounts may seem small but together, they can add up to substantial savings. Whenever special or out-of-the-ordinary discounts are offered, however, the buyer must evaluate them carefully to ensure that federal price-fixing and antitrust laws are not being violated.

By being fair, knowledgeable, and honest, you can be a sharp negotiator without bullying or intimidating the vendor—and you should expect similar courtesy in return.

DISCUSSION QUESTIONS

1. What are the advantages of ordering out of season?
2. If *anticipation* terms are calculated to be about 6 percent a year, are the savings large enough for most buyers to take advantage of it today?
3. Do you think the Robinson-Patman Act works against the small retailer it was designed to protect from price-fixing, by making some types of discounts illegal?
4. Do you see a cash discount device as essentially a reward for prompt payment, or as a penalty for late payment?
5. An invoice for $500 with the terms "8/10 EOM" arrives in your store's accounting department. It's dated August 6. Compute the amounts the

store will owe if it is paid on September 10. How about September 30? October 30?

6. How do you think negotiations would be different in making a private-label deal as opposed to buying a shipment of national brand-named goods?

7. How might the shipping terms be different if you were negotiating through a wholesaler for an overseas shipment of goods rather than a domestic shipment?

8. Some retailers seek neither advertising allowances nor markdown money from their vendors. Why do you think they choose to pass up these benefits?

9. For what types of products, or in what situation, would you think it might be smart as a retailer to negotiate a *consignment* deal with a vendor?

10. Are some types of *slotting allowances* "fairer" than others? Why, or why not?

ENDNOTES

1. "Promoting Competition, Protecting Consumers: A Plain English Guide to Antitrust Laws" (Washington, D.C.: Federal Trade Commission).

2. Tim Columbus, attorney, Collier, Shannon, Rill & Scott, PLLC in NACS Online, newsletter of the National Association of Convenience Stores, Washington, D.C., 2004.

3. "Slotting Allowances in the Retail Grocery Industry" (Washington, D.C.: Federal Trade Commission, November 2003).

CHAPTER 1

The Buyer's Order and Vendor Relations

This chapter examines the services and support that vendors and retailers provide to each other in business partnerships, working together on long-range plans and programs to the benefit of both. After the negotiation is complete, the order must be placed, and the relationship continues with the follow-up and service aspects of the sale.

Many buyers wait to get back from a market before placing their orders, to give themselves a bit more time to think about their decisions and how they fit the buying plan. Increasingly, the order process itself has been computerized, so order placement can be done with the click of a mouse—but luckily, it still requires a human buyer to make the decisions, input the data, and send the order across town or across an ocean. That process, and what **205** happens afterwards, is the subject of this chapter. We will discuss the following:

- Order placement and accuracy
- Types of orders
- Follow-up and receipt of goods
- Typical vendor services
- Protecting yourself from unethical practices
- Retail education and regulation

As we write this, total retail sales in the United States topped $919 billion in the previous quarter—that's more than $300 billion a month—and the goods all had to be ordered by someone.[1] It's a big job!

THE ORDER FORM

Most manufacturers and/or distributors have their own, standardized order forms that they provide to smaller stores. When most orders are small and the form is carefully scrutinized, the plan works fairly well. Because each company's order form is different, though, there's always the risk that some essential notation will be omitted, leading to controversy later. The other danger is that the fine print may contain a condition the buyer would rather not agree to—but was too busy to notice. So in the large store or chain, it is most common to have a standard order form that provides all the necessary protection to the buyer. Vendors are notified that no agreement is valid unless it is submitted on an official order blank, and are instructed on how to fill it in properly.

The store form also acts as a check on every order placed, since it is numbered and the controller keeps records of the numbers. In many stores, each form must be accounted for by number, and no goods are accepted unless there is a corresponding purchase order number associated with them.

The buyer's order, whether on paper or by computer, is useful in several different places:

- At the vendor's business, who fills the order
- At the store's central order or accounts payable department, to compare it with the vendor's invoice for the goods when it arrives
- With the buyer, who keeps a copy for his or her own records
- At the department (or computer program) that keeps unit control data to track sales, charge the buyer's OTB account for the purchase, do forecasting and assortment planning, and so on

- At the receiving department, to look for the incoming shipment and mark it with retail price tags when it arrives

Can you think of anyone else who might need a copy? In this high-tech age, there are good and bad points to having everything on computer. An advantage is that almost anyone can access the file if needed. A disadvantage is that almost anyone can access the file if needed! Safeguards must be built into the system to prevent unauthorized changes to the order after it has been finalized, and to authenticate an order and the appropriate electronic signatures to prevent fraud and placement of "phantom orders" for payment to fictitious vendors.

With the growth of multi-unit operations, order forms have increased in number and complexity. It's not uncommon for a store to have half a dozen different types of forms, depending on what is required on them—one for apparel (that has room to list sizes), one for goods that don't require size information, one for furniture (where finish, fabric, and color must be listed), one for special order merchandise, and so on.

Many invoices require the buyer to indicate the retail price on all but the original invoice that goes to the vendor. This forces the buyer to consider the retail price at the time the goods are ordered, instead of having to decide on it when they come in. It also makes it possible to mark the goods promptly upon arrival, without having to wait for the buyer to decide on the retail price. While this does save time, it sometimes results in the buyer not being attentive to inspection of incoming goods—they're already going to be priced anyway. Since the original order, something may have happened in the market, perhaps with a competitor, that would warrant a change, however slight. It is smarter to require a buyer to recheck prices when the goods arrive, and again when the invoices for the goods arrive.

What's on an Order Form?

No matter what the order form looks like—how fancy, or whether it's a paper form or an online form—its purpose is to summarize all the essential information that all parties require in completing the sales transaction. In no particular order, these are:

- Name and address of the store.
- Name, phone, and e-mail info of the buyer (or another store contact).
- Delivery destination for the goods, if not to the store.
- Order number or invoice number on the form.
- Number of the department that will be selling the merchandise, if the store is departmentalized.
- Classification number(s) of the item(s) ordered.
- Date of the order.
- Name, address, phone, and e-mail contact info of the shipper
- Credit terms, including when payment is to be made and what cash discounts (if any) are available for early payment.

TYPES OF ORDERS

Advance order—A regular order, but placed for delivery at some future time, rather than for quick delivery.

Back order—An order, or a portion of an order, that the vendor has not filled on time but intends to fill as soon as the goods in question can be manufactured or procured.

Blanket order—An order that covers the store's requirements for all or part of a season, but not indicating specific shipping dates or the details of size or finish. The store places requisitions against blanket orders as the goods are needed.

Open order—This order is placed through a buying office, where the office fills in the name of the vendor it believes is best suited to fill the requirements specified by the store's buyer.

Regular order—An order placed by the buyer directly with a vendor for stock requirements, giving full specifications about the amount of goods and time of shipment. In chain stores, the requirements by unit for each store may be indicated. Also called a **stock order.**

Reorder—An order for additional quantities of goods purchased before.

Special order—An order placed at the store level, for a single unit to satisfy the demands of individual store customers.

- Date of shipment, and a cancellation date if the order is not shipped within a certain time limit. (Terms like "at once" and "as ready" are not specific enough and should be avoided.)
- Method of shipment: carrier to be used, whether delivery is to a consolidator or freight-forwarder, and where title for the goods is to pass.
- Free delivery point ("FOB" terms).
- Descriptions of the merchandise (including style and lot numbers, colors, sizes, finishes, etc.).
- Quantity ordered.
- Unit cost price of each item.
- Any discount amount, and what type it is (trade, quantity, functional, seasonal).
- Total estimated cost of the order. (We say "estimated" because the buyer has committed to a certain number of units at unit prices and would not be bound by a simple math error; and the cost may change if some items are not available.)
- Signatures: the buyer, often the merchandise manager, and sometimes the vendor or a representative of the vendor.
- Standard instructions and special instructions: warranty statements, advertising allowances, and any standard contract language as required by the store's legal counsel.

Contract language often includes a line or two about the store's freedom from obligation if the order is not fulfilled exactly as written, or that in accepting the order, the vendor agrees that the goods they are providing meet all federal and state laws and regulations about this type of product. Special instructions may include a mention of any value-added service the supplier intends to provide: labeling, samples, certain numbers of point-of-sale materials to be delivered with the goods, and so on. (See Figures 11-1 and 11-2.)

In many stores, the signature of the buyer is the only one that must appear on the purchase order to make it binding on the store. An order signed by the buyer indicates the store's offer to buy, in the quantities and at the prices specified. In exchange, if the vendor gives the buyer a signed confirmation or acceptance of the order, the order becomes binding on both. Even if a vendor's representative signs the order form—say, at market—most vendors feel the terms are not binding until they look over the form and send an official confirmation. By e-mail, it is easy enough to do so quickly. Then again, some suppliers just ship the goods based on a purchase order and don't bother with written acceptance.

The signature of the merchandise manager is also required in many stores. This does not indicate that the merchandise manager wants to second-guess the buyer's decisions, but that he or she has an obligation to keep up on this part of the store's activity. Merchandise managers keep the OTB records and control order placements against them; and they have a responsibility to make suggestions and provide a check-and-balance function in the buying process. Of course, new vendors should be notified that outgoing order forms require two signatures. Otherwise, they will assume that the buyer's approval of an order is sufficient, and they may ship goods that haven't been fully authorized by the store.

ORDER FOLLOW-UP

Prompt delivery is as important to a retailer as low price. Sales will be lost if goods do not arrive as planned, and some items—like fashion merchandise—may even depreciate in value between the time the order is placed and when the goods are received. So, in order to ensure on-time shipments, the buyer creates an organized follow-up system. Orders are arranged by due date, and vendors are contacted a few days before the due date to see how things are going and reconfirm the shipping terms. In the case of fashion merchandise, stores that use buying offices may assign this duty to them.

Follow-up *is not* "hassling the vendors." It is smart to make contact with them during seasonal peaks when buyers are clamoring for goods. In the apparel industry, goods come through a factory in a multitude of sizes and styles, and they're grouped by orders (with an attempt to fill early orders first). The buyer who is on top of the game can sometimes "steal" a style that the manufacturer

PURCHASE ORDER

THE ABOVE ORDER NUMBER MUST BE SHOWN ON ALL INVOICES AND PACKAGES.

RESOURCE CODE

DATE

TERMS:

RESOURCE: _____

ADDRESS _____

CITY _____ STATE _____ ZIP _____

SPECIAL INSTRUCTIONS

LABEL INSTRUCTIONS
☐ MFG. LABEL
☐ STORE LABEL
☐ BOTH
OBTAIN LABELS FROM:

WHEN SHIP:
AS READY ☐
STARTING
COMPLETE
AUTOMATICALLY CANCEL
AFTER
Without Written Notice

INDICATE BY LETTER IN THE FIRST COLUMN OF EACH SECTION, THE SIZE RANGE BEING USED

STORE CODE

MERCHANDISE INDICATED BELOW SHIPS TO STORE SHOWN ABOVE UNLESS OTHERWISE SPECIFIED IN SPECIAL INSTRUCTIONS.

ALL SIZES OF A COLOR MUST BE SHIPPED COMPLETE IN ONE SHIPMENT.

LENGTH - INSEAM
WIDTH - SLEEVE

SHIPPING INSTRUCTIONS
☐ UPS
☐ UPS BLUE
☐ P.P.
☐ EXPRESS
☐ FREIGHT
☐ AIR FREIGHT
☐ OTHER

INSURE
☐ YES ☐ NO

REORDER LEAD TIME IN WEEKS (CIRCLE ONE)

CHECK SEASON ✓
SPring
SUmmer
TRansition
FAll
HOliday
BAsic
PRomotional

1 2 3 4 5 6 7 8

CLASS | STYLE | DESCRIPTION | COLOR CODE | | RETAIL PRICE | QTY. | UNIT COST | TOTAL COST

→ TOTAL →

_____
AUTHORIZED SIGNATURE

1. We are not responsible for purchases unless made out on this order form and duly authorized by a responsible signature.
2. If the terms specified on this order do not appear on, or agree with, the seller's invoice as rendered, seller agrees that purchaser may change the invoice to conform with this order and make payment accordingly.
3. Merchandise arriving after date specified, or not as ordered, is subject to refusal or return of part or all without prior notice, at vendor's expense for both incoming and outgoing shipping charges.
4. In the event the seller is unable to deliver any part or all of the merchandise called for by this order, seller agrees to notify purchaser immediately.
5. Goods received on or after the 20th of the month will be paid as if billed the 1st of the following month.

Figure 11-1 A sample purchase order form used by retail buyers.

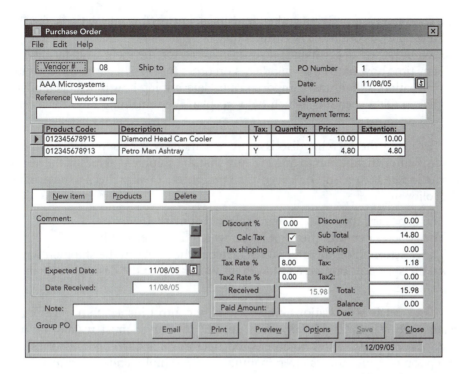

Figure 11-2 A sample online purchase order form used by retail buyers.

had laid aside for shipment to another buyer who just hasn't gotten back to them. But the main purpose of follow-up is to *get the goods you ordered*. If the vendor says they've already been shipped, ask for a bill of lading number or a tracking number that will allow you to trace the order if it doesn't arrive. Otherwise, how would you know if the vendor is telling the truth—or just putting you off for a few more days?

Checking Incoming Orders

After the goods and corresponding invoices have been received by the store, orders must be checked against them to make sure the vendor shipped exactly what was ordered, and that all conditions on the order form have been met. The usual practice is to compare merchandise with invoice, and invoice with order copy, rather than to compare the order with the goods. Here again, technology can help somewhat, for scanning tags and counting items. But human involvement is necessary, and it is the buyer who has the final say on questions like, "Is this really what you ordered, or not?"

In small stores, the buyer is responsible for this checking process; larger stores have an order-checking department. The reason for the centralization is threefold:

1. Frankly, some buyers cannot be depended on to do anything more than a cursory check. They allow too many discrepancies between order and invoice to slip by.

2. The buyer's time is too valuable to be spent performing what is, for the most part, a routine clerical function.

3. A centralized department makes it possible for the store to determine at any time how much merchandise is on order for each department. This information is of primary importance in determining how much each buyer has in OTB accounts, which helps to plan the remaining buys for a time period.

Receiving the merchandise is a process that involves several distinct responsibilities, in addition to making sure that the shipment agrees with the information on the order. The buyer often performs a quality check to determine the following:

- The goods are the identical items selected at market.
- The goods agree with the samples on which the order was based.
- The description on the order form matches the goods in the shipment.
- All the specifications were followed (if applicable) in the design of the merchandise.

Large retail organizations employ quality control inspectors to check for established standards of workmanship, but the buyer must usually be depended on to check style and other subtle factors for apparel or accessories. An exception is if the store is given manufacturer's samples and can compare the goods to them. The buyer can also arrange to inspect the goods on the manufacturer's premises just before they are shipped. Standardized goods typically do not require inspection for quality.

Then there's the quantity check—counting each item by SKU number, color, garment size, package size, and so on—and comparing these with both the original order and the incoming invoice. In case of discrepancies, it is usually the buyer who decides what action to take.

Finally, there is the pricing step. It is the buyer's job to ensure that all price tags and tickets contain all the required information, not only dollar figures but SKU numbers and any other classification data for stock keeping purposes. This is especially important now that wholesalers and other vendors routinely offer to do the tagging themselves as part of their service. It is presumed that all stores in a chain will sell identical goods at identical prices, but this is not always the case. The buyer and/or merchandise manager can allow regional differences in price if local conditions warrant it.

Order Cancellation

The buyer should have the final say in decisions to cancel orders. At some point, if an order has not been received and the vendor's failure to meet a deadline (or sufficiently explain the delay) has become clear, this decision must be made. Otherwise, the order file or centralized order department becomes clogged with "deadwood," odds and ends that preclude their ability to close out orders and outstanding balances.

If an order is still on paper, or in the computer as "active," it is handled that way by the system. This limits the buyer's ability to purchase other merchandise, since it is included as a financial commitment instead of in the open-to-buy account. For example, consider a buying limit of $5,000, for a buyer who has $4,800 in committed orders and only $200 left in OTB for a department. It may be that, of the $4,800 worth of orders, $500 is nothing but deadwood, awaiting cancellation. If the buyer checks invoices periodically and clears out the problem orders, the OTB in this case increases to $700 of usable funds for the buyer.

Sometimes a buyer has the opposite problem—goods show up at a store or warehouse with no accompanying order form. They may have been shipped in error. The buyer's order may not have been transmitted to the individual store or warehouse; or it was transmitted but the person who usually checks the e-mail was on vacation. A vendor might have shipped based on oral agreement, hoping that once the goods arrived, they would not be rejected. (You'd be surprised at how many vendors send unordered merchandise and cross their fingers with this in mind.)

In any case, the retailer must have a policy about what to do with merchandise for which no order is on file. A few stores return it at once, with the vendor paying for the return shipping COD. Most check with the buyer, who prepares an immediate written order if the shipment was authorized but the paperwork had not been done. This is considered an extremely poor way to handle incoming stock, however, as it encourages the vendors to be as lax about shipping as the buyer was about doing paperwork. Until an order is in hand, the store should not check in, inventory, or display the goods in question. If an order is wrong and store personnel do anything that indicates it will be accepted for sale, legally this is considered an act of ownership. In this case, the store could be required to keep, and pay for, the entire shipment.

Even when it is completely justified, order cancellation is a touchy subject. The returned order must usually be accompanied by some paperwork, either a cancellation form or a note from the buyer explaining the return. It is sent back collect (with the vendor picking up the return freight charges). As part of a professional follow-up system, the buyer can make a phone call or send an e-mail message to let the vendor know the goods are being returned, and to try to determine what happened or clear up any misunderstanding promptly.

WORKING WITH VENDORS

This brings us to the love-hate topic of vendor relationships. It is natural to focus on differences and stressful situations when teaching this subject, because it is often through conflict that lessons are learned. But it would be wrong to categorize either buyers or vendors as "good guys" or "bad guys." For the most part, the two groups get along well and even become friends, in the professional sense. They become accustomed to dealing with one another, learning to respect each others' judgment and market skills and to accept advice. They know that cooperation and negotiation will build business faster than antagonism and constant complaining. If problems arise, usually both parties want to work at fixing them.

The fact is that, as in any industry, some buyers are more business-savvy, better organized, and more personable than others; and the same can be said for vendors. When they don't get along, or when each constantly tries to gain an advantage at the expense of the other, these efforts tend to result in higher distribution costs. And that helps no one.

Codes of Conduct

For a large chain with a group of departmental buyers, a code of conduct document is often developed for store policies about a number of specific activities. We've discussed many of them at length in previous chapters; the idea here is to agree on and abide by a written policy about each.

- **Price concessions.** In general, buyers feel they have a right to demand the lowest prices they can get. Many don't even realize that it is unlawful to seek or receive prices *so low* that they are, in fact, discriminatory. One way to cover this is to make it a standard condition of every order that the price granted is in no way discriminatory under the Robinson-Patman Act. Another option is to make it a policy that every buyer insists on fair and equal treatment in price comparisons to competitors.
- **Advertising allowances.** We covered the many facets of advertising allowances in Chapter 10. Based on those criteria, the store should set a policy that determines how it will handle ad allowances, and how much control the vendors will have in ad content and placement in return for their allowance dollars.
- **Meetings with sales reps.** Many buyers (and also buying offices) find it distracting when vendors' representatives feel they can drop in anytime to chat or show samples. It is a common policy that sales reps are seen only during certain hours, or that they must call ahead for an appointment time.
- **Advancing seasons.** A practice that stems from keen competition in the apparel and accessories trades is the so-called **advancement of seasons**, when both vendors and retailers cut prices before a season is over, even if customer demand has been active. This is accompanied by the promotion of next season's line, perhaps long before there is a normal customer demand for it.

While it is understandable to want the excitement of previewing a new line, such early markdowns usually prompt unnecessary losses for both stores and vendors. There may be a need for a general (but somewhat flexible) policy about the proper times to institute seasonal clearances and to offer a new season's goods.

- **Style piracy.** Again from the fashion trade, this issue has arisen as a matter of controversy between vendors, but the complaints are frequent enough to mention it. Often, a vendor claims that buyers take its samples or make sketches, then get some other, less expensive manufacturer to reproduce the article at a lower price. Whether or not this is true, your company should have a policy that prohibits buyers from attempting it.

Later in this chapter, we discuss ways that buyers can protect themselves from unscrupulous business practices they may encounter in the retail marketplace.

VENDOR SERVICES

Now let's discuss what vendors (supplier, manufacturer, wholesaler, importer, and so on) should be doing to uphold their end of the retail relationship. We'll cover a number of topics, and with each of them, the buyer should ponder the following questions:

- Will this service or this particular event increase sales in my store or department? Or will it simply transfer demand from one product (already in stock) to another?
- If the cost of this service is part of the price paid for the product, is the actual savings to the store greater than the increase in the cost of the merchandise?
- Is the supplier in a better position than my store or company to develop and run effective promotions for the product?
- Does the seller have my store's best interests in mind with these promotional tools? Could the programs perhaps run counter to the interests of the store?
- Have I reduced my store's ability to function as a purchasing agent for our customers, because the vendor is promoting specific products over competing products that we also sell?

The answers to some of these questions may seem obvious, but a buyer is usually under great pressure to reduce operating expenses—and a cost "hidden" in the price of the merchandise for a "special service" may escape criticism by management.

In the case of supermarkets in particular, the service most retail buyers would pick over all others is reduced prices. But there are plenty of other ways that vendors can help their customers. Let's briefly examine just a few.

A SAMPLE STORE POLICY ON BUYERS AND SALESPERSONS ACCEPTING GIFTS AND FAVORS FROM VENDORS

- No gift of any kind, regardless of its worth or the circumstances in which it is given, should ever be accepted. Any other approach inevitably creates confusion and potential problems.

- Luncheons with a vendor or his or her representative as a part of a regular day's work are an accepted and often valuable part of the buying process. Although such meal situations are not to be solicited, they may be accepted on an occasional and reasonable basis. They should also be reciprocated as a token of company appreciation, not with a "one-to-one" approach, but simply as a periodic gesture of goodwill. In the central office, reciprocation is made easy with the cafeteria facilities available in the building.

- Meal-related expenses must be reported in the month in which they are spent by the buyer, including a notation of the lunch guests and the merchandise they represent.

- Favors (such as golf dates, theater tickets, dinners, and gift certificates) should be accepted on a very infrequent basis and only if they are reciprocated in each instance. The reciprocation need not be a return of exactly the same favor, but it must be comparable and adequate in value in the buyer's judgment. Again, this must be detailed on the expense report in the month in which it is purchased.

- The social aspects of the buyer-source relationship are, in and of themselves, not necessarily unhealthy or contrary to the company's interests. If handled the wrong way, however, they can be insidious or unethical, and can lead to abuses.

Some buying organizations do not have policies as strict as this one. They do not, for instance, regard a small end-of-year "thanks for your business," a Christmas or anniversary remembrance, or new baby "congratulations" gift as out-of-line. However, they do expect buyers to be aware of—and to avoid—any favor or gift that might prompt them to feel an obligation to give preference to the vendor in some way as they conduct their daily buying and sales activities.

Sales Programs and Promotions

Buyers generally welcome, and even expect, the promotional assistance of manufacturers and distributors. The forms these promotions take depend largely on the type of merchandise. With convenience and impulse goods sold under brand names, the buyer can expect such things as specially designed countertop displays, posters, window display kits, and merchandising racks for store aisles; preproduced ads for radio, television, or print to boost name recognition in the market; and so on. As an example, soft drink companies give special deals on fountain equipment (or give it to the stores outright) in exchange for having the machine prominently feature the company's leading brand—and of course, pouring its products from almost all the fountain valves.

For fashion and variety store goods, the materials are usually designed to assist in window and store displays, to educate salespeople, and to provide care and use information to the customers. (Information on fiber content and care instructions must be provided by law for most textile goods.)

The usefulness of some promotional material is probably questionable. Stores receive so much of it that if they displayed it all, no one would be able to walk down an aisle! Small stores use them the most, because they substitute for independent planning and execution. It is important to note, however, that the cost to vendors for all types of promotions is substantial. Each deserves to be evaluated on its own merits—and used, if it fits with the store's image and marketing plans.

Gifts, Coupons, and Rebates

There are a couple of important notes about freebies and rebate programs. First, from a strictly legal standpoint, the manufacturer or distributor of goods cannot give things away if the quantity, value, or frequency of the give-aways is used as a form of price discrimination among competing retailers. Second, it is considered deceptive advertising to call a premium "free" or a "free gift" if its cost is actually included in the price of another article sold in connection with it. In some states, the pricing laws forbid premiums if they are used as a way to sell goods below cost.

Nonetheless, manufacturers often—very carefully—plan "buy one, get one free" sales (nicknamed "BOGOs" or sometimes "BOGOFs"), and sample give-aways, often in connection with new merchandise. Recently at the supermarket, we've seen some interesting promotional packaging of upscale Progresso brand canned soups—four-can packs at a special price, touting its low carbohydrate content for dieters who are counting carbs.

Another device is the manufacturer's **coupon**, a printed promotional offer used by shoppers to redeem a cash value or free item at the point of sale in retail outlets. You've surely seen them and may even use them in your own shopping. Coupons require bar codes on them in order to be able to scan them, which allows them to be handled more efficiently at checkout and also makes the store's coupon sorting and administration duties more efficient. The store sorts the coupons and returns them, with a summary and invoice, to the manufacturer for reimbursement. The retailer may be offered a small commission for the bother of handling coupons and waiting for the money.

Most stores think couponing is a hassle, but it's not going to go away anytime soon. For product manufacturers, a well-designed coupon is a valuable and effective marketing tool, since it serves a dual purpose—moving items off the shelf, as well as delivering extra advertising value at minimal cost. They complement other marketing techniques by encouraging repeat purchases, building brand loyalty, and attracting new customers.

Lest you think today's shopper is too busy to bother with cutting them out, sorting them, and using them at the stores, think again. In 2002, of the 335 billion paper coupons issued, 3.7 billion were redeemed, for a savings of $3.1 billion.[2] Studies have found that most of us don't have time to plan our shopping the way we'd like to, so we make most of our buying decisions on-the-spot, at the store. In-store coupons can simplify those decisions.

The newest trends in couponing pair it with technology. Electronic coupons are spit out at checkout along with the customer's price receipt, triggered by an in-store system that is programmed to print coupons based on what the customer has just bought—if dishwasher soap was purchased, the coupon is for a competitor's brand of dishwasher soap, or a two-for-one offer on the next purchase of the item. Since they are highly targeted, electronic coupons have significantly higher redemption rates. The disadvantages include higher distribution costs (the printers, paper, and ink), the design of the coupon (not especially attractive, and not in color), and that it is redeemable only at the store or chain where it was printed.

An even bigger trend is online couponing. Consumers downloaded 242 million coupons in 2002, up from 111 million in 2001. Only 7.6 million of them ended up being actually redeemed, but the advertising value of the offer, and the perception of savings it creates in the mind of the consumer, make it a valid choice for manufacturers looking to stand out in competitive categories.[3] Statistics show that middle-income families—the target customers for most merchants—are the most likely to use computers and are also the most likely to clip paper coupons.

Online coupons generally are single-product, so the customer doesn't have to buy multiples of an item to realize the savings, and their expiration dates are usually longer (almost five months, compared to three months for the typical newspaper coupon). An interesting benefit of online coupons for the manufacturer is its ability to number each coupon and track its use. Customers who sign up for an online coupon service register with their name, e-mail address, family size, and other identifying statistics to "match" them with the types of coupons they want. When they end up printing out and using the coupons, the numbers can be traced to who redeemed them and where.

There are plenty of online coupon sites to sample: BabyResource.com, CoolSavings.com, Ecentives.com, SmartSource.com, and Yes-Its-Free.com, to name a few. The other huge consideration for manufacturers is that online coupon distribution and redemption costs less—an estimated $50 million per year—than the $2 billion spent annually on newspaper coupon advertising.[4]

A third important promotional aid is also a type of coupon. The manufacturer's **rebate offer** asks the consumer to send in a rebate coupon with a specified proof of purchase to the manufacturer. The payment (either a small check or a free item) is made directly to the consumer. Rebates offer consumers another strong motivation to buy. Savings from regular prices must be clearly identifiable, and it's up to the retailer to make certain this is the case, by correctly displaying the rebate information and having the rebate forms readily available. The savings must also be sufficient to justify the inconvenience to consumers of preparing and mailing the rebate document. Rebates are far superior to vendor-subsidized markdowns, because the retailer receives the full retail sales amount at checkout while escaping the administrative burdens of coupon redemption.

PACKAGING AND LABELING

The trend toward self-service and the technological advances in packaging have led most buyers to recognize that many items take on greater value if they are displayed in a well-designed package. This is especially true for items like some pet foods, cosmetics, cleaning supplies—things that have very little eye appeal by themselves benefit from a catchy name, colorful container, and attractive graphics. Packaging also saves selling time, since the package can be used to describe the contents, provide at least some product instructions, and so on.

Vendors and retailers today work extensively together on packaging, and the retail buyer is often the one to analyze the merchandise and request package improvements, or total repackaging for a particular chain of stores. Unit packaging is more efficiently accomplished in bulk at the manufacturer's facility than at retail, except for perishable goods like meats and produce, and even in this area, some vendors prepackage. Some of the large multistore buyers who develop private brands have special packaging departments that design the packages, have them produced under contract, and deliver them to the sellers who make the goods.

Labeling

Getting goods ready to sell also involves labeling them. The package can also work as a label, of course, but for products not readily unit-packed (such as clothing), labels must be attached directly to the merchandise. And have you noticed that, on a typical shirt or sweater, there may be four or five different, small labels and tags containing different information? Vendors of branded products have attached labels for years to do the obvious—emphasize their brand names. But today, a number of federal laws make it mandatory for a seller to label merchandise, and for the labels to remain on the goods until after resale to the consumer. Briefly, the laws include the following:

- The Federal Food, Drug, and Cosmetic Act requires that certain information be divulged on labels or packaging, including net weight, names of ingredients (in decreasing order of prominence), and in some cases, warning labels.
- The Fur Products Labeling Act sets the standard wording for naming and describing furs, and requires that the label identify a fur as "used" or "reused."

- The Federal Textile Fiber Products Identification Act says most textile products must be labeled with the fiber content, the percentage (by weight) of different fibers (in case of mixtures or blends), the name or registered number of the sponsor (manufacturer or retailer) of the product, and the country of origin if not made in the United States.

  Brand names used in juxtaposition to generic names are not to appear in larger type, and if the retailer wants to remove the tags when the items are purchased, they must be replaced with others that contain the same information.

- The Flammable Fabrics Act requires that highly flammable fabrics be kept off the market or be treated to meet standards of flammability. The standards are outlined in the act for different types of goods.

- The Federal Trade Commission Act requires several different types of labels, including permanent care labels (the ones that specify how to clean the garment), nutrition information for certain packaged foods (the standard box of information about calories, protein, fat, carbohydrates, and vitamin content found on almost all foods), and furniture labels (which must include woods, veneers, nonwood components, and place of origin).

In addition to these, state and local regulations now require unit pricing (the price per unit of measure, not just the price per package), and freshness dating on perishable goods. Seals of approval from Underwriters Laboratories, the American Gas Association, and other independent testing laboratories appear on appliances and some housewares.

As you can tell, labeling has become a major part of satisfying legal demands for the sale of safe and/or wholesome goods. So much of labeling is mandatory today that you might assume buyers have no say in this part of the manufacturing process. In fact, it is in the buyer's interest to negotiate for labels that will best satisfy the customer's needs—and that, of course, depends on the type of product. Think about the number of labels, their size and appearance, their placement, and the information they must contain to be as useful as possible. Consider whether the labels should provide more than the legally required "facts"—perhaps some information about performance as well—and how much can fit on a single label, with printing on both sides. Too many labels are confusing and unsightly, and in garments, they can be downright uncomfortable!

Price and Product ID Labels

Most manufacturers today willingly tag outgoing merchandise with specific information for the retailer—the suggested retail price and UPC (bar code) or SKU number, linking the item to a standard classification, vendor, style, size, color, and so forth. The SKU is printed as a sample for customer approval, then encoded by computer to create the customized tags. We've already mentioned the evolution (or perhaps "revolution" is more accurate) of pricing and product identification with the Radio Frequency Identification (RFID) systems. But no matter what the system, like packaging, product identification is usually best done at the point of manufacture. This is a point that must be discussed and agreed on with each vendor—unless, of course, you are Wal-Mart or Albertsons, and you are big enough to tell the vendors they must adapt to *your* system by a certain date in order to continue to do business with you. In 2005, this is the case with RFID and these retailers in particular.

SALES ASSISTANCE

Sales support is a big part of partnerships between manufacturers and retailers. It is not uncommon for major manufacturers to court their key accounts by assigning a dedicated sales team to a single, large customer. Think of the hundreds of sales offices that have sprung up in Bentonville, Arkansas, since the meteoric rise of the Wal-Mart empire, and you see the trend. The point for suppliers is to keep their products top-of-mind when retailers and their buyers are being bombarded with competitor information and decisions to make. And it's not all marketing hype—vendors can be valuable in terms of doing market and competitive research, advising on the use of shelf space, even paying to help redesign a store or a section. They create **plan-o-grams**, custom diagrams that show exactly how merchandise might best be arranged in a store section for maximum sales. They help train floor salespeople and/or split the costs of their salaries with the store.

The vendors complain that their retailers have focused more and more on financial concerns, like mergers and acquisitions, and less on sales and service. They say they have no choice but to step in and help see that their products are sold. What do *you* think?

Trainers and Demonstrators

Major product lines have their own sales trainers who travel to stores and conduct on-site seminars, attend department sales meetings, and so on. Buyers should make it clear that their assistance is welcome (which it truly is), but it is more helpful when there is some advance notice of their arrival and expectations of store personnel.

Often, the sales trainers arrive with a "special offer" for the sales team—a small commission for every unit sold in a certain time period. These are referred to as **PMs** (for "push money"), and their propriety must be considered on a case-by-case basis by senior management, certainly with input from the retail buyer. The question should be whether the PM serves as a fun incentive for the team, or whether the end result is that they neglect the sales of other product lines in the store. Permitting an occasional sales bonus program, that is not restricted to selling one particular line, is legally a much smarter move than a PM program, which may be considered unethical.

In a few lines (particularly cosmetics, housewares, and food products), vendors hire **demonstrators** to work in the stores. You see them passing out product samples and coupons in supermarkets, or doing cosmetic makeovers in department stores. In fact, in the cosmetics industry, sometimes the salespeople manning the counters for the various "designer" brands are actually employees of the cosmetic company, not the store.

The only caveat here for the store is to be sure that customers know when they are working with someone who is going to recommend a particular brand or line, *because that's their job*, rather than providing the impartial assistance of a store employee. If demonstrators are used on a regular basis in a store, the buyer should advocate that these people be given at least a basic orientation about store sales policies, to ensure they know and will abide by them. Some demonstrators do the selling, then hand the customer over to a store employee to finalize and ring up any resulting sales; others consummate the sale themselves. When employees' sales amounts are being tallied on a quota system, this is an important distinction and can be an area of conflict if not spelled out immediately.

The venerable Robinson-Patman Act appears once again on the topic of demonstrators. The FTC has taken the view that the cost of demonstrators' services must be in proportion to each buyer's purchases in order to be "fair." Many sellers and large buyers feel this is too stringent a definition, and that the law prompts buyers to order more than they normally would, just to order "enough" to qualify for demonstrators' services. They suggest the value to the sellers of having the in-store demonstrators should be considered as part of the equation.

Warranties and Service Plans

"Service after the sale" is a hallmark of many retailers and brand-named products. Many products, from tires to power tools to home appliances, include some type of installation, service, warranty, and/or repair program—a major attraction for busy consumers and one that they will often pay extra for. These services must be offered at the time of sale, at the retail level; but they are almost always supported by the manufacturer, often under contract to local service and repair companies. An important consideration for buyers is what type of service and warranty plans are offered, and at what cost to either the store or the end user, by the manufacturer. It may require actually reading and comparing warranty documents.

In a warranty, the manufacturer agrees in writing to assume responsibility for certain failures of their products. In the 1970s, in response to wide consumer complaints that warranties were ambiguous and hardly seemed to cover anything in practice, Congress passed the Magnuson-Moss Warranty–Federal Trade Commission Improvement Act, which went into effect in 1975. The law applies to most "consumer goods" (but not foods or drugs covered by other laws) and requires warranties to include the following:

- The terms and conditions of the warranty, in clear and simple language.
- All pertinent information to be able to use the warranty if necessary, including the name and address of the warrantor, the product or parts covered (and not covered), the time period for which the warranty applies, the procedures to follow if the product fails to perform as warranted, and any costs that the consumer must bear (such as shipping the item back to the manufacturer).
- The document cannot include any disclaimer of implied warranty. This means the wording can't contradict any logical assumptions about the product's basic safety, effectiveness, or suitability for the purpose for which it was sold.
- It can be either a *full warranty* (any defect is remedied at any time without charge to the customer, with a choice of refund or replacement) or a *limited warranty*. The latter varies greatly in terms of "limits," but these must be spelled out clearly in the document.

Although most warranties are made and honored by the manufacturer, the burden rests on the merchant to deal with the customer who shows up at the store with the blender that doesn't blend. By law, the retailer has the responsibility to make available a copy of the warranty for any item that costs more than $15 at retail if a customer asks to see it. (It is the retail buyer's job to ensure these are available and accessible, either online or in sufficient quantity on paper.)

After the sale, most retailers prefer to simply exchange or give store credit for faulty merchandise than hassle with repairing it, as they are in a better position than an individual consumer to get satisfaction from the manufacturer. For the store, it is a matter of courtesy and customer service. For the buyer, items under warranty and the way they are handled offer another means to test the long-term reliability of a vendor. Return rates in the stores and complaints about faulty merchandise should raise a red flag and prompt a reevaluation of the goods and their quality and appropriateness for your retailer.

PROTECTING YOURSELF AND YOUR STORE

It's a big and competitive world out there, and retail buyers must be ready for anything. The following section of the chapter deals with vendor practices that we have seen too frequently not to warn against them. A new buyer, or one who is uncertain about an offer, policy, or situation, should involve his or her merchandising manager or other upline staff members to make a decision jointly, perhaps by committee. Some of these topics have been touched on in this and other chapters, but we gather them here under the overall umbrella of precautions you must take in order to abide by the laws and ethical standards of the industry.

Product substitutions. Careful analysis of goods bought by sample or inspection, and careful checking of shipments against sample and specification details, are imperative in order to avoid misrepresented or substituted merchandise. Unscrupulous suppliers use substandard raw materials, then rush orders at the last minute so the store has little choice but to accept the inferior goods, because they are *needed* on the shelves and there's no time to find replacements.

Substitutions are only acceptable with advance notice, and in cases where the manufacturer has been unable to locate sufficient materials, certain colors, and so on.

Failure to follow instructions. Some retailers require the sellers to make their guarantees in writing, especially about delivery dates. Buyers can help to meet their own deadlines by ordering early enough, placing reasonable delivery dates on orders, and dealing with vendors who are well organized about their production schedules.

The other major failure on the part of vendors is not following shipping instructions. This adds greatly to the cost of transportation, especially when shipments must be rushed at the last minute. Buyers should always compare the shipping charges after delivery with the terms first negotiated—and should not be shy about charging back the difference if the additional cost was caused by the vendor.

Price and service discrimination. We've talked a lot in this textbook about small-store buyers' complaints that they just can't compete with the larger stores in terms of prices, rebates, and quantity-based allowances. The law does recognize the validity of certain price differences when items are bought in quantity or by a special method of sale. But if a small buyer has reason to suspect downright price discrimination, he or she may bring the matter to the attention of the Federal Trade Commission.

Indirect price increases. One thing to watch for in dealing with vendors over time is a tendency to gain a bit more profit for themselves—not by raising the billed price, but by lowering the established discount rates, charging the buyer an increased portion of the transportation costs, or reducing advertising allowances. It would be unreasonable for a buyer to insist that these terms never be changed, but it is definitely reasonable to note—and discuss with the vendor—a pattern of slowly but surely squeezing an extra percentage or two out of every transaction. Another way this is done is to slightly reduce the weight or volume of the product without reducing its price. This happens more often than you'd think with household products, over-the-counter drugs, candy bars, and paper products. Consumers may not notice . . . but as the buyer, it's *your job* to notice.

Refusal to sell to price-cutters. Before the so-called fair trade laws were changed, manufacturers sold under retail price agreements that required merchants to charge a minimum, set price for their goods by contract. Today, individual retailers have the right to price merchandise as they please, so the tendency for manufacturers is to set prices "indirectly" by refusing to sell to the retailers who are known for deep discounting to consumers. (Mega-merchants like Wal-Mart and Costco appear to be immune from the trend, simply because of their incredible volume.) The caveat here is that a retail buyer is never allowed to demand that a supplier refuse to sell to another retailer.

Manufacturing only "to order." Some vendors refuse to take an inventory risk, putting nothing into production until a firm order is received and never overproducing. Buyers feel that vendors *should* share the inventory risk, at least in the cases of staples and fashion goods that should have the potential to become regular reorders. It does make sense that a manufacturer has less risk overall than a retailer, because the manufacturer can supply customer demand anywhere in the world, whereas the retailer may not sell the item in all of its stores, or may be a regional instead of national chain.

In short, the retail buyer wants some assurance that goods that sell well will be available for quick reorders. It is reasonable to ask that a manufacturer have some finished goods on hand.

Agreements among vendors. Antitrust laws prohibit agreements among competing vendors that are "in restraint of trade," and price agreements fall under this category. But there are also situations (chiefly through trade organizations) in which vendors exchange information and details about prices, terms of sales, and the credit terms they offer. There's not much the buyer can do about this, except to note that when the information is used to "standardize" the rates in an area, it may be worth mentioning in negotiations.

Direct selling to consumers. Except for job lots, retail buyers do their best to avoid purchasing from vendors who make it a practice to sell also to the general public. We realize that commerce today often blurs the lines of propriety, but manufacturers and wholesalers who are serious about catering to the retail trade should not do so on one hand and compete with their retailers on the other.

Selling to competitors. Most buyers of convenience and food products recognize the necessity for their suppliers to sell to their competitors as well, but they expect manufacturers of specialty products to, at least, designate a limited number of stores as their franchise agents—and, in some instances, to set up a single, exclusive agent in a retail trading area. In higher-priced lines of apparel and accessories, the expectation is that the merchandise should not be made generally available. Mass distribution truly does change the image of a product, especially if some of the merchants who carry it are discounters.

There is no easy solution to this dilemma for the buyer. In fact, it is one of the main reasons larger stores have created their own private brands—they *know* these won't get into the hands of their competitors. The only other precaution is to demand the right to considerable advance notice if the manufacturer decides to change its policy and widen the availability of its merchandise. With information about just "how wide" the new distribution will be, the buyer can decide whether to liquidate the inventory and drop the line altogether.

Commercial bribery. This term is defined as giving something of value by a vendor to the agent of another, in order to induce purchase or special promotional attention. Three general types of bribes are recognized—gifts, subsidies, and money—but the rules about them are fuzzy in practice, as we noted in the earlier discussion about PM ("push money") programs. PMs are considered subsidies and are differentiated from cash payments by the requirement of product sales to get them. Cash payments do not—they are out-and-out bribes under the current law, made with the greatest secrecy and the greatest sense of obligation on the recipient's part.

Some buyers accept gifts as part of the common courtesies of doing business. They insist that they don't expect them, that they are offered freely, and that receiving them does not change how or what they buy. Subsidies are also often defended, on the grounds that they do not injure the store in terms of merchandise selection, and that they prompt a little extra effort on the part of the floor salespeople. Most retailers have found it is simpler to prohibit them all than to worry about being part of a federal restraint of trade or discrimination investigation.

Education and Regulation

Better trade relations may be promoted in three ways: education, self-regulation, and government regulation. Education is the surest, but undoubtedly the slowest, way, as it is earned through informed discussion of ethics and competitive practices in schools and colleges.

Trade associations are another force for education—and for change, with powerful lobbying arms to ensure that Congress keeps good business in mind in its retail-related lawmaking. There is at least one trade association for almost every aspect of the retail industry: shoe sales, electronics sales, liquor sales, grocery sales, hardware sales, you name it. At various times, groups of both retailers and manufacturers have attempted to self-regulate trade practices and make requirements of their members, but they've had to tread carefully, simply because the existing antitrust laws make it difficult to exchange price information without being accused of price-fixing. This seems to be a never-ending source of frustration.

Therefore, much of the improvement consumers have seen in trade practices over the years has been the result of pressure from trade and consumer organizations on government to regulate the retail, wholesale, and importing industries. Most of the laws, dating all the way back to the Sherman Antitrust Act of 1890, have to do with the following:

- Breaking up or preventing monopolies in certain industries
- Protecting the consumer from unethical selling practices and false or misleading advertising
- Requiring that foods and beverages be safe, sanitary, and correctly and accurately labeled with weight, nutrition, and content information
- Requiring that labels include safety warnings for potentially dangerous merchandise (i.e., choking hazards for children under a certain age), foods and drugs and/or additives
- Providing protection for trademark owners from illegal use of their products or brand names by others
- Requiring that all credit terms be disclosed to consumers if they buy on credit, and that credit be granted equally to all creditworthy individuals on the same terms
- Requiring that warranties be clear and dependable, from the consumer's point of view

The informed buyer will make it a point to keep up with the news about their industry and the business, legal, and legislative changes in it over time.

CHAPTER SUMMARY

After the "thrill of the buy," the reality of doing business with a vendor—season to season and year to year—involves ongoing negotiation and a great deal of common sense. It begins with filling out the order form, which should include enough detail to be a concise summary of every facet of the original order. It continues with follow-up on the part of the buyer, to ensure the vendor is abiding by the deadlines and shipping terms to which the parties agreed in advance.

Manufacturers offer numerous services, from custom packaging items to price tagging—but each must be carefully checked and approved at several points from factory to store. The buyer has the final say about canceling undelivered orders, or if shipping charges for orders received are excessive or inaccurately billed.

Vendors also help extensively to move their products. This is to be expected but also is not without ethical challenges. Retailers are asked to participate in sales promotions, couponing, and rebate programs; to put up tons of point-of-purchase sales materials; and to gladly schedule product demonstrators and visits from sales reps to train store personnel. The fine print and real value of manufacturers' warranty and service policies to end users should also be considered.

At times, bonuses and gifts are offered to buyers and other store employees for sales consideration. These must always be carefully considered, and any retailer should have a written policy about what types or values of gifts and favors, if any, are permissible. The federal antitrust laws are not just for retailers, but for suppliers as well. Retail buyers should keep up on these laws and should be alert for signs about how the suppliers they have chosen handle their own business ethics.

DISCUSSION QUESTIONS

1. How would you handle a manufacturer who consistently failed to meet product delivery deadlines?
2. Can you think of anything else that should be in a retailer's code of conduct that is not listed in the section of the same name in this chapter?
3. Is it necessary to include on an order form a demand statement that "All goods, labels, and prices covered by this order must conform to all current government regulations?" Do you think it would be enforceable in court?
4. Of the laws to promote competition, which do you think is the most likely to be violated because a buyer just was not aware of it? Which do you think is most likely to be violated knowingly, but without coming to the attention of federal investigators?
5. The cosmetic company Clinique has become famous for its major sample-sized product giveaways to consumers several times a year. Knowing what you now know about the retail laws, how do you think Clinique manages to do this legally?
6. What is your opinion of the practice of providing *PMs* to floor salespeople?
7. As a grocery buyer, how would you work with demonstrators to see that they are doing their part to further the goals of the store—not just the goals of the manufacturer who hired them? Would you work differently with cosmetics demonstrators in a department store setting?
8. Do you think a store should refuse shipments of any goods that arrive without an approved order form? What about goods that arrive from a vendor who failed to follow precise shipping instructions?
9. How effective do you think federal laws have been in breaking up or preventing monopolies in the retail industry?
10. Write no more than a page (double-spaced) about how you think technology has changed retailer-vendor relationships—and whether you think the changes are for the better, or not.

ENDNOTES

1. U.S. Census Bureau and U.S. Department of Commerce, Washington, D.C., August 20, 2004.
2. Carolina Services, Inc., an Inmar Company, Winston-Salem, North Carolina, 2003.
3. Carolina Services, Inc., an Inmar Company, Winston-Salem, North Carolina, 2003.
4. Steven Boal, CEO, Coupons, Incorporated, Mountain View, California, 2000.

Pricing and Selling

Price is only one of the selection factors in a consumer's decision to buy a product or pass it up. However, price plays other roles as well. From the relative worth or value of an item to the individual purchaser; to the satisfaction it gives the person for finding "just the right thing;" to the perceived utility of the item—much of the transaction is psychological, and even subconscious. More simply stated, the customer buys or rejects an item based on whether he or she perceives it is *worth what it costs*. This value/price relationship is key to the process of pricing items to sell at retail.

In this chapter, you will learn about the most common pricing formulas and how to use them. We will discuss the following:

- Profit margin controls
- Calculating initial markup and required markup
- Determining profitability of a department or store
- Pricing individual items
- Price line structures
- Markdowns and closeouts
- Calculating profits
- A retail buyer's role in the selling process

To illustrate basic customer psychology about pricing, suppose that a man decides he needs a new tie and feels (although he wouldn't put it exactly this way) that it would provide him with $28 worth of utility at the moment. (He'd more likely say, "I don't want to spend more than $28 on it.") In your store, he is pleased to find a tie for $14 that meets his requirements (pattern, color, length). The tie has a "utility value" of 14, or an **inducement quotient (IQ)** of 2 (28/14), expressed as an IQ of 200.

If he were to consider buying a second tie, also at $14, its marginal utility would probably be less, perhaps no more than 14, yielding an IQ of just 100 (14/14). The IQ is a numerical way of expressing what the customer would say as, "If I buy it, it will be because it's a good deal—but I don't really need it."

Although the second tie might be bought because its utility equals its price, the customer would not feel compelled to buy a third tie. He would tell you he "wouldn't be getting his money's worth." What he means is, a third tie would have an IQ of less than 100. Can you see why?

The sad truth for retailers is that if this customer's discretionary income is limited, he may not buy any of the ties—or he may buy another item with a utility, expressed in dollars, that he feels would be greater than $28 spent on a couple of ties. So in theory, consumers do set priorities when they decide how to spend their money. It's just that their methods are not always rational, and at best, they're hard to measure. The components of the decision are a mix of utility factors:

- The built-in selection factors of the item
- The nature, reliability, and status of the retailer (often a reflection of the customer's past experience with the store)
- The nature and credibility of the promotion
- The services offered as part of the sale
- The location of the retailer
- Availability of the product (in stock, or delivery time if it must be ordered)
- Credit terms available

Improving the performance of these individual factors results in building up the numerator (top number) of the inducement fraction, thereby increasing the value-over-cost quotient (IQ) or inducement to buy.

Lowering the price means reducing the denominator of the fraction, which is another way of increasing the IQ. From an operational viewpoint, this is simple because one of the roles that price serves for the store is a quick and easy tactic. In most cases, by the time a product is up for sale, its selection factors are set and not changeable. Price, and price-related topics like credit terms, are among the true variables on the list for a store to work with.

Of course, it's not as simple as making fractions. Creativity, thoughtful analysis, and management expertise are among the skills and knowledge necessary to make pricing decisions. Over the long run, they are the toughest kinds of competitive edges to meet or beat.

PROFIT MARGIN CONTROLS

A senior management team sets certain limits on a retail buyer's freedom of pricing in order to cover expenses and the merchandise costs, which should result in a margin of profit. The profit margin is a goal that is expressed in every department's merchandising plans, and the margin may be spot-checked and controlled at various stages of the buying-selling process. So let's look at what happens at each of these stages, in terms of price.

Initial Markup

When an item first arrives for sale at a store, the key factor is the **initial markup**—the difference between the invoice cost of the item (that is, the cost from the manufacturer or wholesaler, before any discounts were applied) and the very first ("original") price that is marked on it to sell at retail. Initial markup is not the price itself; it is the *percentage of the original retail price that represents profit.*

As an example, if the original retail price of an item is $2 and the invoice cost is $1.20, the difference is 80 cents. The initial markup is thus 80 cents, or 40 percent of the original retail of $2.

The costs and original retail prices of all articles are figures that are kept routinely, so it is easy enough to track them for an entire planning period. By adding together the figures for all the items purchased for the department during the time period, and all the articles that were already in inventory at the start of the period, you have the value (either retail or cost) of your **total merchandise handled (TMH).** You can also subtract

$$\frac{\text{The total retail prices of all the items}}{-\text{ The total costs of all the items}}$$

. . . and the resulting figure is your **cumulative markup.**

If the opening inventory was $207,000 at cost and $400,000 at retail . . . and net purchases during the period were $117,000 at cost and $200,000 at retail, let's do the math:

$$\$207,000 + \$117,000 = \$324,000 \text{ TMH at cost}$$

$$\$400,000 + \$200,000 = \$600,000 \text{ TMH at retail value}$$

$$\$600,000 - \$324,000 = \$276,000 \text{ cumulative markup}$$

Since we also need to know the markup as a percentage, we simply divide

$$\frac{\$276,000 \text{ (the cumulative markup)}}{\$600,000 \text{ (the total retail value)}} = 0.46, \text{ or } 46\%$$

Management sets seasonal goals for the markup percentages in each department, and that's how to determine if yours is meeting it.

The initial or cumulative markup is the margin that must pay for all subsequent costs of operation, including its own reductions, until it eventually yields the desired profit. Some retailers have a rule for setting initial markups: they add a fixed ratio or percentage to the cost of any item. A common rule is to make the retail price exactly double the cost, which is a 50 percent markup at retail, and 100 percent at cost. Others increase the cost by one-third, which is equivalent to a 25 percent markup at retail.

However, there is a more realistic way to consider expected expenses and price reductions in planning markups. It is a formula:

$$\frac{\text{Planned expenses + profit}}{\text{Planned sales + reductions}} = \text{Planned markup percentage}$$

Here is an example for a store that anticipates sales of $100,000, expenses of $32,000, and reductions of $3,000, and had aimed for a profit of $5,000:

$$\frac{\$32,000 + \$5,000 + \$3,000}{\$100,000 + \$3,000} = \frac{\$40,000}{\$103,000} = 38.83\% \text{ required markup}$$

The same formula may be used with percentage figures instead of dollars, for planned sales:

$$\frac{32\% + 5\% + 3\%}{100\% + 3\%} = \frac{40\%}{103\%} = 38.83\% \text{ required markup}$$

The required markup for each department of a store cannot be figured in quite this way unless *all expenses* are distributed to departments. However, by including operating expenses for the total store, the formula can reflect the store's operating philosophy. And the markup for each department is planned, to yield the required total for the company as a whole. Here's another example, for a discount store with far fewer expenses (only $20,000) than an upscale department store:

$$\frac{\$20,000 + \$5,000 + \$3,000}{\$100,000 + \$3,000} = \frac{\$28,000}{\$103,000} = 27.18\% \text{ required markup}$$

As you can see, the discount store doesn't need to mark prices up as much in order to meet its goal. Different departments within the same store operate on different markup amounts—and it is especially important to note that different products within a department may have different markup amounts. The goal is that overall, they average out to the required (or cumulative) markup figure. This is critical in determining a pricing strategy, within a department or within an entire store.

Reductions

A reduction in price can be made for a variety of reasons. A **markdown** is a purposeful reduction in price, with the intent of speeding the sale of items that have not sold at full retail price. (Later in this chapter, we discuss markdowns as a promotional tool.)

Discounts, either to consumers or to employees, are also price reductions. Almost every merchant allows some type of discounting, either in the form of coupons or for groups like senior citizens and students; and most allow their staff members to deduct a percentage from their own purchases as an "employee discount." It is important to keep track of these, to be able to estimate them for a planning period.

Shrinkage is the loss of stock caused by record keeping errors or theft. The latter category has become a serious problem for U.S. merchants, with shrinkage accounting for almost 2 percent of sales in most stores.

Maintained Markup

In the formula for computing required markup, we mentioned a $3,000 item called "reductions." This means that goods totaling $103,000 in original retail value were consumed (so to speak) in generating $100,000 of recorded sales. It is against this $103,000 that the initial markup (of 38.83 percent) is applied in order to get the markup amount in dollars, of $40,000.

This amount—shrunk by $3,000, so it is now $37,000—becomes the **maintained markup**. As a percentage, it is quoted in relation to net sales, not gross sales (and net sales in this case are $100,000). Therefore, the maintained markup is expressed as 37 percent.

A quick series of calculations should show us how the figure is deduced. It is important to remember in making calculations that we always consider the original retail price as "100 percent" of an item's value.

100 (percent) − 38.83 (initial markup percentage) = 61.17 (or 0.6117, as a decimal)

3 (percent of reduction) × 0.6117 = 1.83 percent (cost of reductions)

38.83 (initial markup percentage) − 1.83 (cost of reductions) = 37 percent (maintained markup)

As a pricing gauge, the maintained markup is more awkward to use than the initial markup—not only because the formula requires one extra step to compute but because it introduces one more item to have to estimate. The rate of reductions for a specific product or product line is not easy to "guesstimate." However, the maintained markup formula is useful for analyzing results to date, keeping track over time of how well a product line or a store department is doing.

FIGHTING SHRINKAGE

In 2001, retailers lost 1.7 percent of their total annual sales to shrinkage—a total of more than $31 billion a year. The National Retail Security Survey is an annual project of Richard Hollinger, PhD, criminology professor at the University of Florida, who analyzes theft incidents from 118 of the largest U.S. retail chains.

The reasons behind the numbers are startling:

Employee theft	48.5 percent	$15 billion
Shoplifting	31.7 percent	$9.7 billion
Paperwork errors	15.3 percent	$4.7 billion
Theft by vendors	5.4 percent	$1.7 billion

Hollinger says an average family of four will spend more than $440 in higher prices because of inventory theft, and merchants are using technology to fight it. They're equipping merchandise with tiny, computerized antitheft tags, video monitoring, and equipping point-of-sale terminals with antitheft software. Reward programs are also in place for employees who notice and report theft.

Source: ADT Security Services, Inc., Boca Raton, Florida, November 26, 2002.

Gross Margin

A store or department's **gross margin** is the amount (either in dollars or a percentage) of profit it has made during a time period; it is also called **gross profit**. Getting this figure requires that the department know two other figures: the amount of net sales and the total cost of goods, for the time period.

- The *amount of net sales* means adding together the actual retail prices that all the goods were sold for and subtracting any costs associated with making those sales. Costs would include items that were transferred into the store from another store, employee discounts, returned items, thefts, and so on—anything that would diminish the dollar value of the actual sales.
- The *total cost of goods* is what they cost to buy in the first place from the manufacturers or wholesalers, including any transportation charges paid by the store. (Many retailers don't include cash discounts from the manufacturers in this figure, but some do.)

After the maintained markup has been figured, cash discounts from the manufacturers may be added in at this point, and workroom or backroom costs (for apparel, things like alterations and price-tagging) are subtracted. A basic gross margin calculation is shown in Table 12-1, with examples of the sales and expense categories that go into it.

Net Operating Profit

When all operating expenses have been deducted from the gross margin, the result is called **net operating profit**, or **net profit from merchandising operations**. In the example used earlier in the chapter to figure required markup, this is the profit figure of $5,000. Literally, net operating profit means

- Net (when all the expenses are subtracted . . .)
- Operating (the department is doing business . . .)
- . . . (at a) Profit

This information is broken down further into two figures: net profit before taxes and net profit after taxes. But we'll let the accountants take it from there. As a retail buyer, you've got enough to do just pricing things fairly.

PRICING INDIVIDUAL ITEMS

Much pricing is done by habit, custom, and tradition. In the garment trades, for example, for many years it was the practice to manufacture with specific price lines in mind. Dresses sold by their makers at $15.75 and $28.75 were traditionally retailed at $21.95 and $35.95, respectively. Manufacturers in most other consumer product lines also produced their goods with certain traditional retail price

Table 12-1 Determination of Gross Margin Using Retail Method

	At retail	At cost	At retail	At cost	At retail	Cumulative % of markup % sales
Inventory February 1				$10,000	$19,000	
Gross Purchases		$5,500	$10,000			
Less purchase returns and allowances		450	900			
Net purchases				5,050	9,100	
Transportation in				500		
Transfers in		$240	$500			
Less transfers out		90	200			
Net transfers in				150	300	
Markups			$375			
Less markup cancellations			100			
Net markups					275	
Total merchandise handled				$15,700	$28,675	45.2
Gross sales			$7,000			
Less sales returns and allowances			430			
Net sales			$6,570			
Gross markdowns	$600					
Less markdown cancellations	250					
Net markdowns			350			
Employee and special discounts			225			
Estimated merchandise shortages			70			
Total merchandise deductions					7,215	
Book inventory (at retail)					$21,460	
Book inventory (at cost:; (100% − 45.2%) × $21,460)				11,760		
Gross cost of goods sold				$3,490		
Maintained markup (net sales less gross cost of goods sold)				$2,630		40.0
Add purchase discounts (including anticipation)				75		
				$2,705		
Less alteration and workroom costs				200		
Gross margin (net sales less total cost of goods sold)				$2,505		38.1

points in mind. This did not prevent discounters from selling at lower price points—but their methods, too, became customary among chains of those types. Eventually, the more traditional retailers retaliated, asking that manufacturers either offer exclusive lines or, at least, differentiate the products sold to lower-price competitors. And with that, the private-label explosion and retailer-manufacturer co-branding began in earnest.

As mentioned in previous chapters, it is by means of exclusivity—differentiation, innovation, and special services—that most retailers find their niche and compete successfully over the long run. But unless the retailer has a particularly unique product or a special version of a product, most buyers price at points that are commonly accepted in their "type" of retail business. This is not price collusion. Rather, it is an outgrowth of the fact that similar types of competitors have similar expense structures and similar markup requirements to meet them. They therefore end up pricing by a sort of implied competitive consent.

That said, there are a few basic methods used to price individual items.

Keystoning and Other Pricing Policies

The simplest pricing policy is to add a flat percentage of profit to each and every item. A common strategy, called **keystoning**, sets the retail price as double the cost. This is equivalent to a 50 percent markup at retail and 100 percent markup at cost. Another popular policy is to increase the cost by one-third, which is equivalent to a 25 percent markup at retail.

Often, a store has a minimum markup percentage figure below which products cannot be priced without approval of senior management. This is known as a **price floor**. And discount retailers may not have a price floor at all. Their goal is to make money by selling lots of items, each at a very small profit. This is called a **penetration policy**, and it is also used when a store wants to "penetrate" a market quickly and/or to keep similar discount competitors out of the market.

Applying the Markup Percentage

You can use the markup percentage that you figured earlier in this chapter as a pricing guide when figuring the "normal" retail price of an article, if you know its cost. Remember, the retail cost of an item always starts at "100 percent" in an equation.

Let's look over the shoulder of a buyer who is at market, considering buying an attractive wall clock in a variety of colors. He knows his required markup is 38 percent. The vendor is asking $46.50 for the clock at wholesale. What kind of retail price could be put on this clock?

$$\frac{\$46.50}{100\% - 38\%} \ = \ \frac{\$46.50}{0.62} \ = \ \$75.00 \text{ "normal" retail for the clock}$$

Now the buyer has some good information with which to make his decision. And if he knows that his store's direct competitors will surely sell (or are already selling) the same style of clock for $68, he's got some options:

1. Search for a more desirable clock (say, one with more features) to buy at $46.50 and sell for $75.
2. Search for a clock just as good as the one being sold by his competitor, but that can be sold at $68 or less without undercutting his normal 38 percent markup.
3. Go ahead and buy this clock, and retail it for the lower price, accepting the lower markup (and trying to make up for it elsewhere in the department).
4. Buy this clock and retail it for $75, but offer in your ads to pay the difference in cash to anyone who buys the clock, then sees it for less anywhere else—hoping, of course, that very few people will go to the trouble to take advantage of the offer.

Choice 2 represents a second way to apply initial markon in pricing. Having decided to meet or beat the $68 price, the buyer multiplies this price by the *costing complement* of 0.62 (100% − 38%):

$$\$68 \times 0.62 = \$42.16$$

To make the normal markup, at a retail price of $68 or less, our buyer will have to find a clock that costs $42.16 or less at wholesale. Assume that one is found at $ 41.50. Normal retail would then be

$$\frac{\$41.50}{0.62} = \$66.93$$

If $68 is a common price line, the buyer might very well retail the clock at that price, taking a markup of slightly more than 38 percent. However, the buyer has to consider the impact of his price decision on competitors. Will it prompt them to put their clocks on sale, advertising an even lower price? Will it start a price war on clocks in their market area? More than likely, both clocks will be sold at both stores at similar prices—not because they're scheming together to keep the prices high, but because they're both playing it safe and falling into line with the customary retail price range for this type of merchandise.

Using Rate of Sale

Theoretically, each item should be priced to maximize the dollar profit return. Consider a box of envelopes that costs $1.98. Priced at $3.00, it would have a markup of $1.02, or 34 percent. At a retail of $3.24, the markup would be $1.26, or 38.9 percent. However, if the $3.00 price produced a demand of 131 boxes sold per week, it would yield

$$131 \times \$1.02 = \$133.62$$

If the $3.24 unit price reduced the demand to 100 boxes per week, the markup dollars would be

$$100 \times \$1.26 = \$126.00$$

The advantage clearly lies with the $3.00 price, although on paper it shows a much lower markup percentage. The point here is that an item's rate of sale must be considered in creating its price.

Buyers must also keep in mind the budget standards for which they are responsible. If the buyer is supposed to bring in a 38 percent markup at a planned total sales volume, he or she will be cautious about putting lower markups on items without the approval of upline management, no matter how well they are expected to sell.

Loss Leaders

Selling at cost or near cost for promotional purposes is called **loss-leader pricing**. It is designed to draw traffic into the store by direct appeal, and to establish a reputation for "low prices." (As we now know, the term "low" is relative.) An item priced so low that it cannot make a contribution toward general overhead can only be justified in inventory if it helps sell more of those products that do make a contribution toward overhead and profit. And by bringing more people into the store, the lure of lower prices does just that.

The loss leader concept perfectly illustrates the "mix" concept of pricing—that if a department or store is to make its profit goals, it mixes some low markup items, some at "regular" markup and some at higher markups. This does not imply that the latter items are exorbitantly priced, just that they are in more upscale categories, or in particular demand, or offered to attract a particular type of customer.

Not every sale that occurs below average markup is a loss leader. There are also other reasons to price low, which we discuss in greater detail later in this chapter.

Deviations from Normal Markups

There are a number of reasons for which a buyer can deviate from a normal or average markup percentage. They typically fall into three categories.

Cost factors. Unusually high or low relative expenses and costs may be considered in determining prices. These could include the following:

- Handling charges (receiving, tagging, alterations, packing, delivery, and credit, to name a few)
- Carrying charges (the space occupied by the items, the shrinkage, and interest paid on the initial investment). The rate of stockturn on the item has a bearing on these costs, as the higher the stockturn, the lower the carrying charges.
- The possibility of obsolescence, as measured by how many of these items have to be marked down—because it is faddish, or seasonal, merchandise.

Contractual limitations. Except for a few states, the vendors (manufacturers) no longer have the right to set a minimum retail price for items by contract.

However, it is still possible for the retailer to have consignment arrangements with manufacturers. In these situations, the manufacturer—as owner of the product—can set the retail price.

Demand factors. These are easy to recognize but difficult to quantify. They include, but are not limited to:

- Competitors' prices for comparable goods (or identical goods)—again, not price-fixing, just keeping up with the market.
- The degree of exclusivity of the product (when you're the only one carrying it, you can charge more for it than if several stores offer it).
- The market trends that prompt consumers to think it is a must-have item: It's versatile, it's new, it's stylish, and so on.
- The acceptance by the public of certain price ranges or lines for this type of purchase.

GROUP PRICING

One of the most useful devices to simplify the merchandise assortment is to buy based on predetermined **price lines**. Rather than pricing each item on the basis of cost, markup, and demand requirements, an advance decision is made to establish specific retail price points, and stick to them as you buy the merchandise for the assortment. A "cost range" can be developed for each wholesale price, and whatever you buy in that range is automatically priced at the corresponding retail price point. Thus, flashlights may be grouped as follows:

Retail Price	Cost Range (at wholesale)
$8.00	$4.00–$4.40
$10.00	$5.00–$5.50
$12.00	$6.00–$6.60
$15.00	$7.50–$8.25
$18.00	$9.00–$9.90
$21.00	$10.50–$11.55

Stores that follow a general policy of deep and narrow assortments—with only two or three items of a given product type—will use the **price lining** strategy. Those who plan wider assortments will have more price lines, and, it stands to reason, not all stores will have items at either the least or most expensive price levels.

A formal price line structure that tends toward the highest possible prices for the items is known as **skimming** in the retail industry. Prices can be higher when new items are being introduced, or when demand must be limited because the amount of product is limited. It may also be used by an elegant store as an easy method of maintaining a prestigious, high-dollar image.

Setting Price Lines

Experience has led us to create some simple rules about how to establish price lines that will work for any type of retailer, with the six-part process as follows:

1. Set the lines at points where past sales reports (and retail intelligence about competitors) indicate the broadest public acceptance. Manufacturers have done much the same type of research to come up with their "suggested retail prices."
2. Plan three major price lines—a high, a medium, and a low, relative to the store's clientele. Carry the most complete assortments at these price points, and at each of them, be sure to include some items that are of absolutely outstanding quality, even if these are carried with a less than normal markup. (Amazingly, this theory was first proposed by retailer E.A. Filene in 1930. It is still in wide use today.)
3. This step is optional, depending on how big the retailer is and how much advance purchasing the budget permits. Plan secondary or "intermediate" price lines, "between" the three major lines. That gives you a total of seven lines; add more only if large volume permits broad and deep assortments at additional points.

   These seven price lines have been recommended as the "ideal" assortment plan, but many stores have found it too costly to stock seven price varieties of anything, and often, the market does not offer goods in sufficient quantity (or of sufficient difference) to justify the in-between price points.
4. Plan the price lines close enough to one another to make it possible for the typical customer who fails to find the desired article at one price to consider the assortments at the "next price up." The spread can also be larger between the highest and middle prices, say, than between the middle and low prices. If the mid-priced item costs $8.95, the higher-priced one in the same category might be $10.95 (a difference of $2, or 22 percent); but if the mid-priced item in another category is $39.50, the higher-priced line may be $49.50 (up a full $10) and still considered reasonable for the type of product or additional selection factors.
5. Establish a pattern of price endings. The choices here are:

   - **Odd-cent pricing**, ending a price with 98 cents or 99 cents (as in $5.99 or $11.98), a rather obvious but often-used ploy to influence the customer's perception of a bargain.

- **Even pricing** (as in $109 or $25), for stores that tend to be less "promotional" and/or upscale items like designer fragrances and jewelry.

6. Vary the fullness of assortments as well as the promotional emphasis as the season progresses. Normally, early in the season, the highest price line should be heavily stocked and the best displayed, overall. At mid-season, it is the mid-priced line that should be built up and heavily promoted. And late in a season, the emphasis should be shifted to the lowest full-line price.

Pros and Cons of Price Lining

Price lining does provide the customer with a wide assortment at a single price, which simplifies (and probably speeds up) the consumer's buying decision. They can concentrate on a particular price that's comfortable for their budget and will not have to compare similar items at a variety of prices. It also reduces the total amount of inventory required to support the business. If each assortment of selection factors was carried in each of the price ranges, the stock totals would mount.

Price lining can reduce errors in pricing, because the lines are decided on in advance and they don't often change. It greatly simplifies the assortment planning and budgeting processes, too.

In negotiations, the retail buyer may use the upper cost limit of a price line as a bargaining tool, to persuade the vendor to lower wholesale cost so that the item may fit into a more popular, slightly lower price line. The resulting increase in sales benefits both parties. However, by settling on a few categories of prices, the buyer doesn't have as much flexibility to change them—if an item really takes off, or if it's moving too slowly, a price line system does not lend itself to marking up or down unless a special sale is involved, like a closeout. Price lining also works better in department store merchandise, like clothing, than it does with supermarket wares.

Price Zones

Some merchants who do not formalize their pricing structure into price lines use a different concept—almost price lining in reverse—called **price zones**. They pick the price ranges and then develop an assortment for each range, or "zone." Thus, instead of a $5.00 price line, there may be a zone of $4.25 to $5.75.

The theory is that prices within the zone are highly substitutable, so if a person doesn't find exactly what he or she wants at one price, it will be readily accepted at another price within the zone, since the prices are not far apart. For purposes of stock and purchase control, each zone may be treated as a planning unit.

REPRICING

The original price of any item in a store represents a temporary decision; it is always subject to revision in light of customer reaction to the initial price. All too often, it is easy to think of markdowns as somebody's "mistake"—an item that was overbought, or didn't sell fast enough. But in addition to being a corrective tool, they are also a major device for sales promotion and profit building. Following are some of the most common reasons for markdowns:

- Buying the wrong item—wrong for the season, for the customers, wrong selection factors, and so forth. (You can't win 'em all!)
- Buying too much of the right item, often by reordering too late in a season.
- Buying an inadequate color or size assortment of the right item, meaning there were interested customers, but they couldn't find just what they needed.
- Slow sales because of lack of promotion and sales support for the item.
- Pricing the right goods too high in the first place.
- Underpricing the goods, such that customers question their quality.
- Shopworn merchandise—makeup smears, rips and tears, missing buttons, and so on.
- Closing out odds and ends of product lines at the end of a season—more jackets than pants are left over from a line of designer separates; canned pumpkin and cranberry sauce the week after Thanksgiving; and so on.
- Reducing prices as a promotional tool.

Careful planning of assortments, judicious item selection, correct order amounts, and careful stock handling should minimize many markdowns; some should not be immediately disregarded as losses, but rather as promotional tools at a buyer's disposal. They may, in fact, become a way to increase profits.

Markdowns as Promotional Tools

A buyer may correctly estimate, for example, that 100 units of a style of little girls' spring dresses can be sold for Easter—provided, of course, that the buyer carries a complete assortment of sizes and colors right up to Easter weekend. To do this, it may be necessary to stock 125 dresses, even though 25 pieces will have to be sold at markdown in the weeks after Easter. The total dollar margin that can be realized by selling 100 dresses at a full markup and 25 dresses at a substantial price cut may be more than would be achieved in buying only 100 dresses and selling 80 of them before Easter. Because of depleted sizes and colors, there might still be 20 dresses to mark down after Easter—and a good deal of pre-Easter volume might have been sacrificed.

The point is that, at least with fashion merchandise, it is a prudent policy to buy considerably more of a "good thing" than can be sold at initial markups. To buy just enough to tap only the "top layer" of customer demand might greatly curtail the sales and profit opportunity. Using the markdown makes it possible to tap two or three layers of customer demand, at different times in the season. This is because even the bargain hunters are important customers. They are loyal, especially if they know that hunting down a bargain in your store is a fun and often fruitful experience. And they *can* contribute to profits—as long as the margin finally realized exceeds the wholesale and handling costs of the items sold. In fact, even when the margin at final clearance is nonexistent or negative, you might say the item sold may have made its contribution to profit simply by supporting the assortment that prompted the customers to buy from it earlier in the season.

This does not mean buyers should deliberately overprice merchandise early in a season, then mark down most of the stock after the initial flurry of consumer purchases. Sooner or later, customers will catch on to that little scheme. But to illustrate the way a lower markup percentage can equate to higher dollars of profit, consider this example:

> A package of peanut butter crackers that has popular appeal as a quick, handy snack costs the retailer 45 cents per unit and regularly sells about 100 units a week at 60 cents. For "one week only," it is priced at 50 cents. Customers who already like these crackers do a considerable amount of stocking up, and a few new ones buy them too. Sales jump to 400 units for the week! At a 45-cent cost, and a 50-cent retail price, the markup is 5 cents each, or $20 for the 400. At the 60-cent "normal" price, the margin was 15 cents each—but the profit for selling the 100 units is $15.

Following are other factors to consider in markdowns:

- There will probably be some increase in direct handling, selling, and advertising costs for putting an item on sale.
- Quantity discounts may reduce the merchandise cost slightly, since you're buying in greater numbers. In the case of the crackers, even if the vendor gave the store an extra penny off per unit, that's an extra $4 of profit for the week's margin.
- The tendency for customers to stock up does steal from future sales, so that even at the sale price of 50 cents, the *rate of sale* could be slower.
- Prolonged use of one specific item or brand for this kind of markdown could lead to a competitive "no-win" price war with other stores.

Setting Markdowns

To use markdowns effectively as a promotional tool, and also to reduce losses when clearance is necessary, there are a few rules to follow from experience:

1. Take the markdown while active demand still exists for the goods, rather than waiting until sales drop so drastically that you're practically having to give them away. It is better to err in the direction of marking down too early than waiting too long to do so.
2. The only exception to Rule 1 seems to be the seasonal clearances in high-end stores that emphasize quality, leadership, and exclusivity. Often, this type

of store can create its own active demand late in the season by advertising a storewide clearance or "last chance" sale, attracting customers who don't usually buy in the store at regular prices.

3. Determine the best times in each season to make appeals to customer groups that seem to bypass your offerings at original prices. You're looking for a time when the markdown, along with advertising, display, and personal salesmanship, will tap into a responsive audience. Most stores have to experiment with this strategy, but it can be interesting and profitable.

4. The first set of markdowns should be large enough to move the major portion of the goods, but not so large as to ensure a sellout. Allowance must be made for the accumulation of odd sizes and colors, damaged and soiled merchandise, and so on. It may take a total of three markdowns—which is not too many—to dispose of an entire lot.

5. The amount of the markdown will vary with the nature of the goods. A low-priced staple (such as milk) enjoys a heavy response even if it is reduced in price only a dime per quart, but a fashion item typically must be reduced by at least 20 percent to appeal to a new level of customers. There is also a difference by price level—that is, a $4 price may move a $5 slow seller, but a $400 price is not likely to be equally effective in moving a $500 item. To tap a new layer of customer demand here, the $500 article may have to be offered at half price.

6. There is a difference of opinion among retail professionals as to whether items can "step out of" the regular price line pattern when they are marked down. That is, should you mark goods down to the "next lowest" regular price line, or establish special and distinctive markdown prices for them? A good compromise is to mark down experimental, higher-priced goods into the next, full-line regular price as soon as they fail to draw a good response as originally priced; but for mid-range price line items, mark them with "special clearance prices." The inference on the racks and shelves is something for everyone—a little better deal for the loyal shopper, and a steal for the bargain hunter.

Some stores have an automatic reduction plan for fashion merchandise. A clothing store may introduce a blouse that cost about $20 at a retail price of $39.95. Any that remain unsold in 10 days are marked down to $32. After another 10 days, the remaining items are reduced again, to $25. Ten days later, a final markdown reduces the blouse to $19.95. Whatever doesn't sell after that is offered to employees in an in-house sale, sold to a jobber for discount resale, or even donated to a local charity.

MAXIMIZING SALES AND PROFIT

At any given moment in the retail life of an item, there is a price point that will maximize profits. This is the point at which the sales volume opportunity, multiplied by the unit price, exceeds the merchandise costs and expenses by the largest margin. In economic theory, this is the point at which marginal revenue equals marginal cost. The examples in this chapter have been oversimplified of necessity, but they should work to sharpen your judgment on pricing.

Although there is a relationship between price and demand, the formula for pinpointing it is by no means precise. Economic law states that, when all else is equal, demand varies in some inverse relationship to price. That means as the price of a product goes down, the demand for it increases.

Figure 12-1 shows a fairly common type of demand curve. As price drops 20 percent (from $5 to $4), the demand increases more than 165 percent (from 0.375 to 1.0 unit). However, a 25 percent drop in price (from $4 to $3) produces only an 87.5 percent increase in demand (from 1.0 unit to 1.875 units).

Farther down the curve, at the $2 price, a 25 percent drop (to $1.50) produces an increase of somewhat less than 22 percent in demand (0.656 divided by 3). These differences in ratio—between price changes and corresponding demand changes—determine the elasticity of demand. You will note the following:

- At the top of the curve (from $5 to $2.25), the demand is most elastic. It changes much faster than the price ratio changes.
- At the bottom of the curve, the demand is not elastic (i.e., it is "inelastic"), because its rate of change is smaller than the corresponding price change ratio.
- Also note that around the price of $2.25 the rates are even. The demand here is said to have "unitary elasticity." Note that an 11 percent drop in price (from $2.25 to $2.00) produces close to an 11 percent increase in demand (from 2.695 units to 3.0 units).

The curve in Figure 12-1 is a common kind of demand curve because it illustrates the way elasticity changes at various price levels for most products. When prices are relatively high, a price reduction brings a sharp increase in sales. As the price gets lower and lower, equal rates of markdown have a gradually smaller effect on the rate of sale. The point is eventually reached at which the total dollar revenue (price multiplied by rate of sale) begins to lessen, although demand is still rising. All of this can be calculated today by computer, on sales forecasting software.

A Model Store Budget

We gain a better understanding of the principles in this chapter by examining Table 12-2, an analysis of a fictitious store's operations. Our imaginary retailer sells 1 million units at an average price of $6 each. In a closer look at the figures:

- Some expenses, identified by an asterisk (*), vary based on dollar sales volume, such as commissions to salespeople. Interest and insurance charges on inventory, and amounts for advertising, also vary with dollar sales. In the example, the dollar variables are 7 percent of sales.
- Other expenses, identified by a dagger (†), vary based on the physical volume of goods sold, and these are usually expressed as a flat cost per unit, or flat

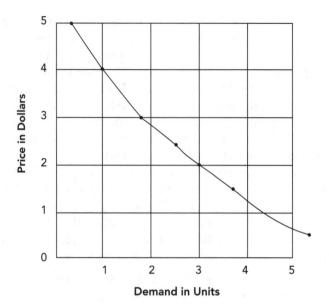

(1) PRICE	(2) DEMAND	(1) x (2) TOTAL REVENUE
5	0.375	1.875
4	1.000	4.000
3	1.875	5.625
2.25	2.695	6.064
2	3.000	6.000
1.5	3.656	5.484
1.0	4.375	4.375
0.5	5.094	2.547

Figure 12-1
Demand curve
showing inverse
relationship to price.

cost per transaction. The theory is that, within a given category, it costs no more to handle a higher-priced item than it does a lower one. These expenses include materials handling and audits of sales receipts. In the example, the average unit sold is $6; therefore, $6 million in sales result from 1 million units. The total costs for all unit variable expenses are $630,000, therefore:

$$\frac{\$630,000}{1,000,000} = 0.63, \text{ or 63 cents per unit}$$

- Fixed expenses, identified by a double dagger (‡), such as the rent or mortgage payment on the building, bear no fixed percentage relationship to the sales of any one unit. In some cases, when a portion of the rent is tied to sales volume (as is sometimes the case with commercial building leases), that part of the rental expense is handled as a dollar variable (Vd).

Single expense centers may vary in more than one way. For example, commissions on sales have been stated as a dollar variable, but the number of

Table 12-2 Analysis of Total Store Operation

	$	% of retail	Operation per average unit of sale
Original retail of goods consumed in selling	6,600,000	100	$6.60
Invoice cost of goods	3,630,000	55	3.63
Initial markup	2,970,000	45	2.97
Actual sales	6,000,000	100	6.00
Reductions (from orig. retail)	600,000	10	0.60
Maintained markup (sales less invoice cost)	2,370,000	39.5	2.37
Merchandise alterations	−30,000	0.5	0.03
	2,340,000	39.0	2.34
Cash discounts	+150,000	2.5	0.15
Gross merchandise margin	2,490,000	41.5	2.49
Dollar variable expenses*	−420,000	7.0	(Vd) 0.42
	2,070,000	34.5	2.07
Unit variable expense†	−630,000	10.5	(Vu) 0.63
Contribution net	1,440,000	24.0	1.44
Fixed Expenses‡	−1,140,000	19.0	1.14
Net operating profit	300,000	5.0	0.30

*Expenses that tend to vary with dollar sales volume.
†Expenses that tend to vary with physical volume of goods sold.
‡Fixed expenses, such as fixed rental and depreciation of fixtures, and so on.

hours of selling time tends to vary with the rate of unit sales. If the latter is the case, straight selling expense may be charged as a unit variable (Vu). However, it makes sense that a certain basic sales force is needed, even in the slowest periods, so that part of the selling cost should be charged as a fixed expense.

Most expense centers (called "cost centers" in many companies) have a fixed core of this sort. Part of their costs should be charged to fixed expenses—not per unit or per transaction, and not a dollar variable. When handled this way, a larger proportion of the retailing expenses is shown as fixed, and a smaller proportion variable, depending on sales activity. In our model, about 52 percent of the total expense is considered fixed, and 48 percent variable.

You might even say that, during slow sales periods, expenses are even more fixed. There are times when a bare-bones sales force could handle a lot more sales than they are getting—and at times like those, items that generate *any contribution net at all* are valuable. The relatively large overhead of a store can soak up all the contribution dollars it can get. However, if too great a proportion of the business is built on low contributors, the result is that the busier times will be penalized, at least on paper, when added facilities are required for relatively smaller additional amounts of business.

Analyses of this kind can become complex, since variables do not move in straight lines and fixed expenses can move up or down in graduated steps. But by studying Table 12-2, you will at least become familiar with the concept of unit profitability. It underscores, for example, why lower price lines are relatively more expensive to handle than higher price lines and, as a result, should theoretically be sold at higher markup percentages.

Few stores use unit profitability for each and every item they sell, but it is an important concept in determining how to price merchandise. Retail management is more often concerned with an adequate profit margin from a whole mix of items than from individual items bought and sold.

THE BUYER'S RESPONSIBILITY FOR SELLING

A truism of the retail profession is that "Goods well bought are half sold." We have no idea who said it, but it perfectly expresses the dual nature of the retail buyer's role in the success of his or her own career. Pricing policies fall in both "halves" of the business, and in most retail businesses, it is the responsibility of the buyer to make these recommendations and follow through on them with regular research and analysis of sales trends and competition.

Advertising, display, and publicity surely impact pricing, and it is often frustrating to the buyer that these functions are uniformly delegated to other departments in the management chain. The two factions must learn to work together on timing (of wholesale purchases, merchandise deliveries, and ad schedules); on the actual goods and which selection factors should be promoted; and on the emphasis to be placed on individual products and product categories. This becomes even more critical with online and catalog sales. Only with team effort can a retail store reach its full sales potential, no matter what prices the goods are tagged with.

Another factor the retail buyer has little control over is training of the sales force. All too often in retail, "training" means showing a person how to operate the point-of-sale terminal and clock in and out with a time card—not how to actually *sell goods to the public* and feel enthusiasm for helping them meet their needs. Again, the retail buyer who takes the time and insists on having a role in this critical function should always be able to brag about the quality and dedication of the sales staff.

In the next few paragraphs, we outline a few of the plans or systems stores have used over the years to delegate sales-related responsibilities to their buyers. It's not wholesale advocacy or dismissal of one or the other, but a short history of the various ways the tasks have been managed.

One Individual as Both Buyer and Seller

The earliest department stores—and today, some smaller stores—have a merchant-buyer or department manager who is responsible both for buying and selling of merchandise. The rationale, of course, is that the person most responsible for buying the goods at wholesale will be the most knowledgeable about his or her selling points and would, in fact, be the most eager to sell them at the maximum amount of profit.

While there is assuredly some natural follow-through inherent in this system, most stores soon discover that it is physically impossible for one person to perform this dual role. Even in a single-location store, the duties are complex and the merchant-buyer cannot be in two places at once (i.e., who sells when the buyer is at market?). Department supervision is left to subordinates. The other problem is that not all buyers want to take the leadership role of supervising a sales staff—and not all are good at it, for that matter.

The Service Superintendent

With the growth of the customer-service concept in large stores, it was decided over time that salespeople should be in a division of the store dedicated to good personal selling, instead of under the authority of executives (buyers and district merchandise managers) who are primarily responsible for merchandise selection. A new job title, the service superintendent, was established on a par with the buyer and DMM, but with the responsibility of customer service duties.

The problems we've seen with this arrangement are that no matter what the organization chart says, the floor salespeople regard the buyer as their "real" boss. The service superintendent focuses on customer questions and complaint resolution, which takes the focus away from leadership and certainly from creating strategies to increase sales. They know the store systems and regulations, and how to handle day-to-day problems, but not necessarily how to motivate the sales staff for profitable results.

The Mazur Plan

A commonly adopted system from the 1920s and 1930s was developed by economist Paul Mazur: to put the salespeople under the responsibility of the buyer, but to retain a department manager or service group to handle floor routines and provide feedback on the service given by the salespeople. And since buyers aren't physically in stores enough to provide continual floor supervision, it was assumed that they would delegate much of their authority to assistants that they, of course, trained.

This plan did not wholly resolve the shortcomings of the old one-person-buys-and-sells plan. In many instances, neither buyers nor their assistants supervised the salespeople as they should have, because they were too much involved with the more complicated responsibilities of buying, pricing, and merchandising.

The Sales Division

As the decades marched on, many organizational planners continued to suggest that buying and selling functions should be separated. It wasn't enough, they argued, to have a department manager and a customer service person (or department); there should be a division with complete responsibility for *selling*. With this viewpoint, some stores created a major sales division, broken down into two departments: publicity (advertising, display, and special features) and sales management (with division managers and department managers). The primary tasks of sales management were to supervise personal selling and to take added responsibility to ensure that their stocks were complete, cooperating closely with the retail buyers toward this end. In some instances, the entire store was organized into a "two-pyramid" plan—every function was either part of "buying," or part of "selling," except for the few groups (like accounting and human resources) that served both.

Once again, in practice, some practical problems arose. Coordination between the buying and selling divisions was difficult to achieve. Buyers argued that the two functions were, in reality, two sides of a single function. They were not happy to turn over responsibility for what they had bought to another division, giving up any further control. Special problems had to do with advertising allowances and other promotions negotiated between buyers and manufacturers. Under the new setup, all such plans were subject to the additional approval of the sales division, which buyers felt tied their hands.

The Branch Plan

An impasse was finally reached in the larger stores by a new development: expansion. As chain stores opened, the organizations had no choice but to separate buying and selling into "twin-line" functions, joined at the top of the organization chart. Opening multiple units made it impossible for one person to do both buying and selling.

In the twin-line organization, which is the most common today, the department's sales managers in each branch are not "assistants" to the central buyer. They report to the branch (store) manager and are responsible for the sales results of their departments. They do have some merchandising responsibilities—for keeping up the planned depth of assortments, reporting demand, and sometimes doing routine reorders of merchandise. But they are primarily concerned with selling and customer contact.

Learning from History

Separating buying and selling, as ideal as it may seem in theory, can also become a classic excuse for buck-passing. If each department is charged with half the responsibilities and sales are not what they should be, each is likely to blame the other for the failures of the integrated whole. And who can say who is right? Instead, it is more important to measure *what* is right. So buying and selling is a symbiotic relationship. Integration and conflict exist side by side, and this must be acknowledged while the two sides work together, to decide the following critical elements of their mutual business:

- **The selling features of the merchandise.** The buyer is not infallible here, but no one should know more about the selection factors, and how they will appeal to customers, than the buyer. The buyer must be able to communicate these clearly and enthusiastically enough to spark the creativity of the "sales side" of the team, which includes the floor sales staff, as well as those who set up the fixtures, plan the window displays, take the photographs, and write the copy for the advertising.
- **Timing.** This may be a matter of featuring something brand-new, or something at the height of its popular acceptance as a profitable fad. Either way, once again, the buyer is the specialist who determines this, and who is responsible for insisting it gets the emphasis it requires in promotional campaigns, ads, and displays.

LAYOUT POINTERS

Buyers can suggest these tips to the sales team:

- No merchandise classification should be introduced into stock until it can be presented in adequate depth and breadth.

- The arrangement must be convenient to customers, with counters and fixtures arranged so they can readily find what they're looking for—and this applies to both advertised and unadvertised merchandise.

- Think of each fixture or each display as a separate entity that must be made productive by the proper selection of items that are placed on it.

- The arrangement should have a "point" to it—whether it is the breadth of assortment, fashion rightness, or high level of taste.

- Color should be used for its attraction value, even when it means massing different styles and sizes all together.

- Goods bought especially to meet competition should be noticeably presented to the passing customer.

Fixtures should show some uniformity in design and color, not introduced for no other reason than the needs of a single product or brand.

- **Stock arrangement and presentation.** The buyer is often in a strategic position to suggest standardized plans for each of the sales departments. Today, with the emphasis on customer self-service to cut costs, it is even more important that the goods be arranged and displayed so customers can make decisions before they require the attention of a salesperson.

In all the years of attempts to organize and coordinate retail buying and selling, the industry has learned a few things very clearly. One is that *the items that should be bought are those that will sell the most readily.* However, *what has been bought must still be sold, as quickly and as profitably as possible.* Because no one can flawlessly anticipate customer demand, what *has been bought* consists only partly of the goods that *should have been bought.* And what *has not been bought* is the cause of lost sales and customer disappointment.

CHAPTER SUMMARY

You may assume from this chapter that retail buyers spend their days hunched over calculators or inserting numbers on a computer spreadsheet, trying to make one big mathematical formula balance out at the end of a week, month, or other sales period. That's not really the case, but it is important to note that in the end, the math truly does govern the outcome. (Luckily, much of it *can* be done nowadays by computer!)

This chapter covered the basics of determining how much to increase an item's wholesale price in order to sell it at retail. We explained several *markup* theories—from simply doubling the wholesale price, which is called *keystoning,* to setting *price lines* and *price zones* for groups of similar merchandise to attract different types of customers.

In addition, we explained the many reasons goods are marked down. Some are preventable, like damaged goods and employee theft, but smart buying in the first place will also minimize them. Again, there are several markdown strategies. Supermarkets are the fondest of the *loss leader,* marking a few items down significantly each week (usually staples) to encourage store traffic. The amount of markdown that will catch a customer's attention varies depending on the type of goods, and markdowns are considered "sales" when their goal is to promote items at lower prices and get shoppers into the stores.

At any point in its life, every product has a price that can be calculated to the penny to show exactly when it starts making profit instead of costing the store. While it is important to be able to perform these individual calculations, most stores look at a bigger picture. They price by estimating the potential profit they need to get from overall categories or departments, then price the items therein accordingly—some items a bit higher, some lower—with the goal of coming out ahead on the whole product mix. This is why, in places like supermarkets, some items seem to be such great deals, and others are not.

And finally, the chapter offered a brief history of the ways department stores over the decades have attempted to combine the complementary (but very different) functions of buying goods and selling them. It is seldom that a single individual or department can manage both of these important tasks, but it is critical that the team works together—because both help determine the store's pricing policies and, ultimately, its profit levels. A good retail buyer can, and should, be the driving force in this collaborative effort.

DISCUSSION QUESTIONS

1. Do buyers tend to depend too much on price-cutting to increase the *inducement quotient* of a product, and not enough on increasing its total utility?
2. In this chapter, we discussed the strategy of overbuying, at least slightly, in some types of apparel. Using the same theory, would it be smart to overbuy in these other product categories: Fresh produce? Pet food? Fine cigars? Men's razors? Briefly explain your answers.
3. The buyer is planning initial markups for the fall season in a ladies clothing department. She estimates the following:

   - Net retail sales of $300,000 for a six-month period
   - Direct expenses for the department at $75,000
   - Reductions (including shrinkage) at $25,000

   She is shooting for a profit of $30,000. What initial markup will be necessary to meet her objectives? And what other factors should she consider before the actual markup is determined?
4. Under what conditions, or for what types of products, would you plan *price zones* instead of *price lines*?
5. Which pricing method works best for these venues, in your opinion?

   a. Internet sales
   b. Catalog sales
   c. Upscale department store
   d. Specialty pet store

6. Why does a retail buyer need to know how a *demand curve* works? How would demand elasticity probably vary in connection with the following products?

   a. Meat and fish in a warm country with poor refrigeration facilities
   b. Meat and fish in areas with adequate, modern refrigeration

    c. Designer dresses, versus generic dresses

    d. Men's dress shirts, in season and after the close of a season

    e. Closeouts of odd sizes of shoes, versus promotion of a full size range

7. What could a buyer suggest to build more enthusiasm into a sales force that he or she does not have direct control over?

8. As a buyer, would you advocate using an *automatic markdown plan*? Why or why not? Is there any type of product for which it might *not* work well?

9. Of all the methods that have been tried over the years to "mix" the buying and selling functions, pick one and try to improve on it in two or three paragraphs. Would today's technology have minimized the problems the "old" system had?

10. Knowing what you now know about pricing items at retail, how would *you* do it? Do you think the current systems, some of which have been around for at least a century, fit the current economy? Why or why not?

Glossary

2005 Sunrise Compliant The term for the target date for companies to have updated their scanner and computer equipment to read not only UPC codes but EAN codes.

A

advance order A regular order, but placed for delivery at some future time, rather than for quick delivery.

advancement of seasons The tendency of apparel and accessory vendors and retailers to cut prices before a season is over, even if customer demand has been active, and start promoting next season's line early, a common but financially questionable practice.

advertising allowance An agreement for a manufacturer to pay for some portion of the retailer's advertisement of the manufacturer's products.

anticipation The term for a small discount offered to a retailer by a manufacturer if an order is paid for earlier than it is due.

anticipatory buying Placing orders well in advance so that goods will be manufactured and delivered promptly.

approved resource list A buying system based on a list or catalog of approved goods and/or vendors at predetermined prices from which individual stores can order.

assortment The range of choices available to customers in a certain line of products, in terms of selection factors like sizes, colors, and styles.

Auto-ID See *Radio Frequency Identification*.

B

back order An order, or a portion of an order, that the vendor has not filled on time but intends to fill as soon as the goods in question can be manufactured or procured.

bar code See *Universal Product Code*.

benefit segmentation   The process of grouping consumers into market segments according to the benefits they desire from their retail purchases.

blanket order   An order that covers the store's requirements for all or part of a season, but does not indicate specific shipping dates or details. The store places requisitions against blanket orders as the goods are needed.

BOGO   Acronym (and common nickname) for "buy one, get one free" promotions. Pronounced "bogo." (Also called "BOGOF.")

bottom-up   A method of merchandise planning in which the managers of each individual store (or department, in a smaller store) forecast what sales should be, then compare the actual figures to the forecast when the time period is over. Also called a *built-up* plan.

breadth   The number of product lines, or the number of items in a product classification, an indication of the variety of goods of a certain type carried by a store.

bricks-and-mortar   A physical store building, as opposed to selling goods online or by catalog.

broker   A wholesaler who is a manufacturer's agent, normally for a variety of noncompeting manufacturers and/or specialty products of smaller firms that cannot afford to hire an exclusive, full-time sales force.

buying direct   Purchasing items at wholesale directly from a manufacturer, not through an importer, wholesale distributor, or similar middleman.

buying office   A business located in a major market center that provides intermediary services to retailers and retail buyers, including product development, research and information, access to vendors, international contacts, assistance in setting up buying trips, and others. Also called a *buying group*.

buying plan   A master schedule of items to buy, with delivery dates and price ranges, in order to fulfill a model stock plan. Buyers take this plan to market with them to keep them on task.

buying system   The organized method by which a store replenishes its stocks of basic goods.

C

C&F quote   A price quote from an overseas vendor that includes "cost plus freight," but requires that insurance on the cargo must be paid by the buyer's company.

cannibalization   The tendency of new products or line extensions to steal some of the sales and market share of an existing, similar brand, which is sometimes another product of the same manufacturer.

cash-and-carry   A sale that involves no credit terms, and may include a discount for accepting the merchandise "as is" and paying for it in full.

centralized buying   Performing all (or most) buying activities from a single office, either as a cooperative or as the single buying headquarters for a chain of stores.

CIF quote   A price quote from an overseas vendor that include "cost, insurance, and freight."

classification   The name for a grouping of a particular type of product, such as dresses or shoes.

classification controls   The central ideas or primary demands that make up a product assortment.

clipping service A company that can be hired to keep track of ads or news items about particular companies or topics, in newspapers and on radio and television.

co-branding A private-label creation process in which a retailer and a brand-name manufacturer team up, often using the image of a celebrity or cartoon character to boost recognition of the product. Also called *product licensing.*

commission office A buying office paid by vendors or manufacturers whose products are represented by the office, not by retailers. Also called a *merchandise-broker office.*

commissionaire A buying office in a foreign country that is operated by citizens of that country to assist other nations' merchants in making importing deals with local manufacturers.

consignment A sales arrangement in which a retailer acts as an agent for the vendor. The retailer accepts and displays merchandise for sale, and pays for only what actually sells, when it sells.

continuous replenishment A restocking system in which merchandise is re-ordered regularly or automatically.

contract wholesaler A wholesale distributor or manufacturer that enters into buying and servicing contracts with several retailers, creating an informal or voluntary buying group.

cooperative advertising A promotional plan in which multiple vendors share the costs of major advertisements. Commonly nicknamed *"co-op" advertising.*

corporate buying office A buying office owned and managed by a large retail chain, for the use of that chain. Also called a *syndicated office.*

coupon A printed promotional offer used by shoppers to redeem a cash value or free item in retail stores.

cumulative markup The figure that represents what a group of items cost at wholesale versus what they are priced to sell at retail, expressed either as a dollar figure or a percentage.

Customer Relationship Management A popular management concept that involves retailers tracking their customers' identities and product choices in order to build loyalty and personalize the shopping experience. Abbreviated *CRM.*

customs house broker A third-party person or company that assists merchants in getting imported goods through the U.S. Customs process promptly and legally.

D

dating terms The wording on an invoice that indicates the length of time the seller will extend credit to a buyer, and whether a discount will be available for early payment.

demand elasticity A measurement (that can be graphed) of how customers' perceived need for a certain product or selection factor changes depending on its price.

demand rigidity The relative firmness of a customer's desire or need for a certain selection factor in choosing a product.

demographics Statistics that count and group people by gender, age, nationality, income, and other physical or geographic factors.

demonstrators   Contract salespeople, often hired by manufacturers, to sell products in retail stores by showing how they work or offering free samples.

distribution orders   Documents that instruct a warehouse or operations department about the goods to be delivered to the stores in a chain.

drop-shipper   A manufacturer that ships directly to a customer when an order is placed at a store (or on a Web site, in a catalog, etc.) instead of sending the merchandise to the retailer for order fulfillment.

duty   A tax levied by a government on the importation, exportation, use, or consumption of goods. Also called a *tariff*.

E

EAN code   The abbreviation for an alternative bar code system used for product identification in at least 80 countries (not the United States or Canada). The acronym stands for *European Article Numbering*.

Efficient Customer Response   Another term for *Quick Response*, usually used in the grocery industry. Abbreviated *ECR* (yes, just like "electronic cash register.")

electronic cash register   See *POS terminal*. Abbreviated *ECR*.

Electronic Data Interchange   The transmission of data by computer between businesses in a supply chain, such as invoices and purchase orders, by standardizing the electronic "language" that the computers use. Most often referred to as its abbreviation, *EDI*.

Electronic Product Code   Abbreviated EPC. See *Radio Frequency Identification*.

Electronic Shelf Labeling   A low-frequency radio technology used in electronic price tags on store shelves so that prices can be changed by computer without having to manually change the shelf tags. Abbreviated *ESL*.

endcap   An end-of-aisle product display, such as those seen in supermarkets.

EOM   Abbreviation for "end of month," as used on sales invoices.

EOM dating   See *proximo dating*.

European Article Numbering   See *EAN code*.

even pricing   The practice of pricing items in even amounts (as in $109 or $25) instead of *odd-cent pricing* ($108.98 or $24.95).

export commission house   A third-party exporting company that represents foreign manufacturers and receives a commission from them on the volume of goods they sell.

Export Control Classification Number   An identification number for a type of product being exported from the United States. This number is required on the export paperwork by the U.S. Customs Service and is obtained from a master list of classifications. Abbreviated *ECCN*.

export sales representative   A salesperson who represents certain manufacturers in their countries or regions, selling the wares on buying trips to other nations.

Extensible Markup Language   A nonproprietary computer metalanguage, which is used by programmers to create documents that can be easily transmitted between computers. More flexible than *EDI*, it is the newest trend in business communication by computer. Abbreviated *XML*.

external information   Research data gathered from outside a company.

F

facing   The portion of goods on a store shelf or display that "faces out" to be seen first by the customer. Also called *stock face*.

facing allowance   A slotting fee paid to increase the amount of shelf space a product line gets in a store.

failure fee   A payment made by a manufacturer to a retailer when its new product doesn't end up meeting predetermined volume targets.

FAS   See *free alongside*.

fixed fee   A standard amount paid monthly by a retailer to a buying office; usually a percentage based on the store or chain's sales.

flagship   The term for the first, main, largest, or headquarters store in a multistore chain.

FOB   See *free on board*.

foreign export merchant   A wholesaler in a foreign country who specializes in exporting goods from that country.

formal entry   The term for processing any shipment into the United States worth more than $2,000 in value. It requires the importer to post a bond to ensure payment of duties and compliance with Customs rules, and that specific paperwork be submitted to Customs.

free alongside   A freight term meaning the vendor pays for getting the freight "up to" a ship or aircraft, but not for actually loading it onto the vessel. Abbreviated *FAS*.

free fill   The requirement that a manufacturer or supplier provide an amount of new product to a retailer free of charge in order to promote it.

free on board   A freight term that means the vendor or manufacturer pays shipping charges to a certain point, then the retailer pays any transportation costs after that. Abbreviated *FOB*. "FOB" terms can be further specified: FOB destination, FOB origin, FOB shipping point, and so on.

freight-forwarder   A company licensed by the U.S. Maritime Commission to arrange the shipping of goods on behalf of exporters; often used by smaller exporters and manufacturers to be responsible for individual shipments.

G

geodemographics   The theory that people who live in a certain geographic area share some characteristics that determine what and how they buy.

Global Data Synchronization Network   A cooperative international effort between the organizations that administer UPC codes and EAN codes, to set up "data pools" of product information that can be exchanged between trading partners in the rush to update their systems to be able to read newer-generation bar codes. Abbreviated *GDSN*.

global tag   See *GTAG™*.

Global Trade Identification Numbers   The newest system of product identification by bar code that uses a combination of the UPC and EAN numbering system. Abbreviated *GTIN*.

GMROI   The abbreviation for "gross margin for return on investment." See *gross margin return*.

gray market (1) The term for goods manufactured in a foreign country, bearing a United States trademark and imported without the consent of the U.S. trademark's owner. (2) Goods that are manufactured in the United States, sold to overseas distributors, and reimported to the United States to sell in stores at lower prices that compete with the same items at full retail price.

green marketing Companies that advertise their adherence to environmentally sensitive buying policies, using this policy to differentiate themselves from competitors.

gross margin The amount of profit a store or department has made during a time period, expressed either in dollars or as a percentage of sales. Also called *gross profit*.

gross margin return A measurement of how profitable a store or department is; the amount it makes on every dollar it invests to cover expenses and profit. Abbreviated *GMROI*.

GTAG™ The trademarked name for a *global tag*, the microchip placed on or in products to identify them using Radio Frequency Identification.

H

Harmonized Tariff Schedule of the United States The master list of classifications of items, which is used to determine the rate of duty (importing tax) paid on the item when it goes through U.S. Customs. Abbreviated *HTSUS*.

high shades In fashion apparel, the trendy, "most fashionable" colors for a season.

I

import commission house A company that represents a variety of foreign manufacturers, handling the importation paperwork, storing the goods until they are sold, and receiving a commission for the sales.

import merchant A person or company who does business by bringing goods into a country from other nations and reselling them at a profit as a middleman. Commonly called an *importer* or *import distributor*.

import program A buying office's organized efforts to help retailers procure goods from other countries.

inducement quotient A numerical way of expressing a customer's degree of want or need for a product that "induces" him or her to buy. Abbreviated *IQ*.

initial markup The percentage of the original retail price marked on an item that represents the profit to be made on that item (if the price is not lowered for any reason).

internal information Data gathered on an ongoing basis within a company, such as sales reports, department overviews, and employee surveys.

J

job lot An assortment of styles or products (usually clothing) from unrelated lines that a vendor has been unable to sell at regular prices and is now offering at a reduced, flat price per item.

just-in-time production A plan in which a manufacturer makes just enough items on demand to fill a particular order, minimizing the manufacturer's required storage space and related costs. Abbreviated *JIT*.

K

keystoning   The common retail practice of doubling the wholesale price of an item to arrive at its retail price.

L

landed cost   The total cost of imported goods, including their wholesale price plus packing and shipping, commissions, insurance, import duties, and so on.

lifestyle marketing   Creating strategies to sell goods to people based on their expectations, behaviors, and motivations. Also called *lifestyle retailing*.

line extension   A different version of a brand-name product, like an additional flavor, diet, or caffeine-free version of a soft drink.

loss leader   An item that is priced extremely low, possibly at no profit to the store, and advertised to get customers' attention and drive increased sales by increasing foot traffic.

M

maintained markup   The figure that represents the total amount of *markup* on a group of items, after *shrinkage* or other price reductions have been deducted.

markdown   A reduction in price.

markdown money   A percentage of a total wholesale purchase that the vendor pays the buyer to reduce the net cost of having to mark down some of the merchandise for sale.

market   A business complex where large numbers of vendors rent showrooms or have facilities in close proximity. Some are specific in the types of products offered (furniture, apparel, etc.); others are general merchandise markets.

Market Development Funds   Money paid by manufacturers to retailers for end-cap displays and to fund promotions and merchandising programs for the products. Nicknamed *street money;* abbreviated *MDF.*

market minus   A price that is less than the normal market price of an item.

market plus   A price that is higher than the normal market price of an item.

market segmentation   The division of a market into identifiable groups based on the trends and needs of its members, and the targeting of products to satisfy them.

marketing concept   A focus by manufacturers and retailers on what consumers will want, and the ways they meet these needs while making a profit.

markup   The amount added to the wholesale price of an item to allow the store to make a profit and offset expenses. Also known as *markon.*

maximum amount   The greatest number of a particular item that must be in stock at a store at any given time. Also called its *provision.*

merchandise manager   A person who is in charge of managing the buying functions in a retail environment; the supervisor of a buyer or group of buyers. Also called a *merchandising manager;* sometimes a *district merchandise manager* or *DMM.*

merchandise mix   The variety of types of products available in a retail store for consumers to choose from when they shop. Also called a *product mix.*

merchandising   In retailing, the process of anticipating customer demand and procuring goods to meet that demand.

minimum amount   The smallest number of a particular item that must be in stock at a store at any given time. Also called a *unit OTB*.

Model Assortment Plan   A summary, usually in chart form, of multiple buying plans for the buyer to use at market to ensure that the model stock plan for each assortment is met. Abbreviated *MAP*.

model stock plan   A written overview of the optimum assortment of goods in stock that will best satisfy the customer demand a store expects during a specific time period.

multichannel shopper   A person who shops at the same business using more than one outlet—at a retail location, online, by catalog, and so on.

multinational corporation   A company that is headquartered in one nation but is owned by another company in a different nation.

N

net marginal productivity   The amount of complementary sales and pulling power of each additional item in a product line that benefits the entire line.

net operating profit   The result when all operating expenses have been deducted from the *gross margin* of a business and a profit remains. (Otherwise, it is a *net operating loss*.)

never-out list   A list of items in very active demand in a store, sometimes over-ordered to ensure they are always in stock.

O

odd-cent pricing   The common practice of ending a retail price in 98 cents or 99 cents to give the customer the perception of lower price—$3.99 instead of $4, and so on.

off-price   (1) Merchandise that is being offered at a discount from its normal, regular price. (2) Retailers who specialize in selling this type of merchandise.

on memorandum   The term for a sale with return privileges, allowing the retailer to return items that do not sell within a certain time period for a credit or refund, less a small percentage restocking fee.

open order   An order placed through a buying office; the office chooses the vendor best suited to fill the specifications of a retail buyer.

open POS system   A computer network for recording retail sales that can be used with different types of hardware or software; an alternative to buying a proprietary, name-brand system that may include licensing fees.

opening stock distribution   A buying plan typical of clothing and department stores, in which department managers decide on beginning ("opening") stocks for staples and reorders, and central buyers introduce new items as needed.

open-to-buy   (1) The dollar amount that a retail buyer has left in the budget to spend for a certain time period. (2) A buying system that allots dollar amounts for the retail buyer to spend for a department or product category. Abbreviated *OTB*.

P

paper distributors   The workers in a retail chain who generate the paperwork to get incoming items sorted and shipped to each store within a district.

parallel imports   Gray market goods. See *gray market*.

penetration policy   A common practice of discount retailers to flood the market by selling large quantities of items at a very low markup (profit).

physical distributors   The workers in a retail chain's warehouse or operations division who handle the goods when they arrive from the manufacturers to prepare them for shipment to the individual store locations. Usually simply called *distributors* or the *distribution center.*

plan-o-gram   A custom diagram of a store, section, or shelf layout that shows how the merchandise might best be arranged for maximum sales.

PM   The abbreviation for *push money.*

point-of-sale   (1) The cash register area where people go to exchange cash or credit cards for their goods; the actual point at which the goods are sold in the store. (2) Jargon for sales materials designed for use in this area. Abbreviated *POS.*

point-of-sale terminal   An electronic or computerized cash register or its display screen. Commonly known as a *POS terminal.*

POS system   The network of computer terminals and master computer that make up the system for ringing up sales in a retail store.

price agreement plan   See *approved resource list.*

price floor   A minimum markup percentage figure below which products cannot be priced at retail without approval of senior management.

price line   A specific retail price point in a *price lining* system. See *price lining.*

price lining   The establishment of specific retail price points, so a buyer can search for items at wholesale that can be sold at those prices at retail.

price look-up   An item for sale that doesn't lend itself to labeling with SKU numbers or bar codes, requiring that its identification code be punched into the system manually. Abbreviated *PLU.*

price zones   Similar to *price lines*, these are set price ranges used to mark all goods in a product category within the range.

primary information   Data collected by a retailer (or on a retailer's behalf) for a specific purpose, such as a survey or report.

primary motivation   The physical or survival-related instincts of consumers, like hunger and sleep.

private buying office   A buying office that works a single store or chain.

private label   Merchandise developed and manufactured for a specific retailer that allows the retailer to build customer loyalty for the store as well as the brand. Also known as *private brand*, *house brand*, and *store brand.*

promotion   An effort or program designed to increase sales for a certain time period by calling special attention to items. Promotions may have "themes"—a holiday, a new movie, a special event, and so on. They may involve a category of goods (lawn equipment, linens, etc.) or specific name brands or private-label items.

provision   See *maximum amount.*

proximo dating   Another term for *EOM dating*, in which the length of time for payment of an invoice is calculated from the end of the month in which the goods are received.

psychographics   Statistics about lifestyle details of consumers, such as their priorities, personality traits, and values.

pulling power   The ability of a product (or line of products) to increase sales without taking sales away from the established assortment.

purchasing agent   A buying office in a foreign country operated by American citizens living in that nation to assist U.S. retailers in making importing deals with local manufacturers.

push money   Commissions paid to salespeople for each item they sell in a particular merchandise line. Commonly known by its abbreviation, *PM* or *PMs*.

Q

Quick Response   An expansion of the EDI concept to include more technology and more inter-business functions in order to ensure the fastest possible times for ordering, deliveries, inventory management, sales results, and so on. Abbreviated *QR*. Also see *Electronic Data Interchange*.

quota   A strict limit on the quantities of certain items that can be imported into a country, either for political or economic reasons.

R

rack jobber   A retail service company that takes responsibility for certain, specialized sections of stores. Their employee visits individual stores to stock and price, clean, put up new displays, check inventories, and so on.

Radio Frequency Identification   A system in which products for sale are tagged with a microchip that contains identification data about the product (amount, price, and so on). The tag emits a low-frequency radio signal that is read by a computerized reader and can be transmitted instantly to an online database. Abbreviated *RFID*.

rate of flow   The expected demand for (outflow) and anticipated delivery of (inflow) merchandise in a store department or product classification.

rate of sale   The relative speed at which an item is expected to sell in a store, usually tracked on a weekly basis.

rebate offer   A promotion that requires the consumer to fill out and send in a coupon or document with a specified proof of purchase, to the manufacturer of a product in order to receive a small payment or free item.

renewal fee   A slotting allowance paid by a manufacturer to keep its products on a retailer's shelf. Nicknamed a *pay to stay fee*.

replenishment buying   The repeat purchase of items to replace the ones that have sold, to keep a store fully stocked.

reserve   The amount of merchandise in a store's inventory, awaiting sale.

resident sales agent   A person who represents a group of foreign manufacturers, selling their wares, placing orders, and handling the importing paperwork.

retail buyer   The person with responsibility for selecting and purchasing goods for a retail store or chain of stores.

retail intelligence   A term for collecting *secondary information* about the retail industry.

Robinson-Patman Act   A federal law enacted in the 1930s that prohibits price discrimination and requires sellers of products to offer any of their ancillary services fairly to all customers, no matter how large or small.

ROG   Abbreviation for "receipt of goods," as used on sales invoices.

S

sanction   A type of boycott, typically used to put political pressure on a nation by forbidding imports and/or exports of merchandise between countries.

secondary information   Existing research from another source that a retailer may use to find out more about customers, market trends, or a particular market area.

secondary label   Merchandise that is similar in quality to a manufacturer's regular goods but made specifically to sell at lower price points.

secondary motivation   A learned instinct for social interaction (like greed or sympathy) that prompts a person to feel good or improve his or her own self-perception when exercised.

selection factor   An attribute of a product that prompts a consumer to select or reject it in a retail setting—its size, price, color, style, and so on.

shrinkage   The loss of merchandise caused by record keeping errors or theft.

skimming   A price line structure that prices items higher when they are new, exclusive, or in high demand.

SKU number   (1) The abbreviation for stock keeping unit. (2) An individual identification number of a product assigned for inventory purposes. It is a term in such common usage that few people realize what it stands for, and the number is simply referred to as a product's *SKU* (pronounced "skyoo").

slotting allowance   A common but controversial practice (mostly in the grocery industry) in which manufacturers pay a variety of fees to buy shelf space or better visibility for their products in retail stores. Sometimes called *new item fees* or *shelf fees*.

special order   An order placed at the store level, for a single unit to satisfy the demands of individual store customers.

specification   A *selection factor* that is a requirement for a product, as determined by the buyer.

specification sheet   A written list of every requirement for a product, created by a buyer to give to prospective vendors for their price bids. Commonly called a *spec sheet*.

staple assortment   See *staple stock system*.

staple stock system   The master list of items and quantities a store or department carries to meet basic customer needs.

stock order   An order placed by a buyer directly with a vendor for replenishment of items already in stock. Also called a *regular order*.

stock turnover rate   The number of times in a certain period that the average amount of stock in a store department is sold. Commonly known as *stockturn*.

stock keeping   The process of handling, checking, and protecting the goods between the time they are received and the time they are sold; or the ordering and sales-expediting tasks necessary to maintain inventory assortments.

stock keeping unit   An individual product (which could be a single item, a case, a multipack, etc.) as measured in inventory. Abbreviated, and more commonly known, as "SKU." See *SKU number.*

stock-to-sales ratio   A calculation of sales by dividing the value of the total stock (at retail) at the first of each month, by the sales of that month. A store's goal is to decrease its stock-to-sales ratio.

subsidy   A government payment to businesses in a particular domestic industry, which allows the business to export its products more cheaply to other nations.

syndicated office   See *corporate buying office.*

T

tariff   See *duty.*

tear sheet   A copy of a newspaper advertisement, given to a vendor as proof that the ad was placed.

tie-in   A sale in which a supplier requires that a retailer buy one item in order to get another, which may be unlawful.

top-down   A method of merchandise planning that begins with sales and cost estimates from senior executives that are divided into plans and budgets for individual departments and their buyers to carry out.

Total Merchandise Handled   The number of items, both in existing inventory and new orders, that come into a store or department during a specified time period, used to figure average costs and *cumulative markup.* Abbreviated *TMH.*

trade deficit   The economic term for unbalanced trading between countries; a country that imports more goods from other nations than it exports to them in return has a *trade deficit.*

trade terms   Terms of sale, usually for an imported shipment of goods.

trend extension   The practice of using past sales trends to help predict the future.

U

umbrella branding   A product line that includes items from many different product categories, sold exclusively at a particular store.

unit OTB   See *minimum amount.*

Universal Product Code   An identifying pattern of lines and spaces of varying widths on product packaging. It represents a code of numbers and letters that identify the product and manufacturer to a computerized scanner that reads the code. Abbreviated *UPC,* and commonly known as a *bar code.*

UPC code   The abbreviation for *Universal Product Code.*

upselling   The practice of prompting a customer to consider purchasing an item in a slightly higher price range, either in person or by pricing policy.

V

Vendor-Managed Inventory   An agreement between retailer and manufacturer to have the manufacturer's sales representative keep a section of the store or a particular product line in stock and sufficiently promoted. Abbreviated *VMI.*

W

want slip   A daily form, filled out in a retail store department, that lists every request for merchandise not in stock, and whether a substitute item was sold in its place.

warehouse requisition plan   A centralized buying system, often used by grocery and drug stores, in which the store manager selects inventory from a checklist of necessary stock and can reorder as needed from a central warehouse location.

Index